"K-pop Dictionary is a fun mix of common slang and adages frequently found in K-pop and Korean Dramas which will help provide a base for understanding that goes far beyond subtitles. As a YouTube personality who focuses on the ever-changing world of Korean entertainment, I see this book being an extremely useful resource to anyone interested in improving their comprehension of Korean Dramas and K-pop."

\- Stephanie Ishler, Hallyu Back -

K-Pop Dictionary 케이팝 딕셔너리
Over 700 Essential Words and Phrases to Fully Understand
K-Pop, K-Drama and Korean Movies!
By Woosung Kang

For permission requests, contact us at:

marketing@newampersand.com

Printed in the Republic of Korea

ISBN-13: 979-11-88195-94-7

newampersand.com

Daebak! Hello, K-Pop fan! Congratulations on your bold decision to embark on a journey to the fantastic world of K-Pop! Let's take a moment to share the joy. You have chosen your favorite, and you can tell who is the *maknae* of the group, right? Oh, and you must know who is in charge of the *visual* and has the best *aegyo* that melts your heart!

Well, it's okay if you don't have a clue about what I just said because that is probably the reason you chose to read this book. It is designed so you can learn the most up-to-date vocabulary used in K-pop lyrics, TV shows, K-Dramas, and the like.

As the title of this book suggests, this is not an ordinary dictionary. It is specifically designed to explain what these words mean in a K-Pop and K-Drama context. These are like encrypted codes that can only be understood if you know the background information, such as where they originated and when and how they are used. Without this knowledge, you are missing out on all the news and updates other fans are talking about!

For that reason, this book also includes real-life examples of the words in action. You will gain a thorough understanding of the words and their background information. You can use this book as a quick reference guide any time you run into K-Pop and K-Drama lingo or as a study reference by utilizing the conversation examples included on every page. Whatever your goal, this will be a great way to expand your K-Pop and K-Drama knowledge and to give yourself a window into the fascinating world of Korean culture!

You will notice that sometimes there is more than one spelling variation. Despite the fact that there is a standard method of Romanizing Korean words using Latin letters, K-Pop fans and translators have chosen haphazardly to use whatever they think is appropriate. Those Romanizations have then spread across the Internet, eventually becoming the new standards used by everyone. So, this book includes the versions that are popularly used among K-Pop fans, but spellings in Hangul (Korean alphabet) are also provided. You can always cross-check in case you want clarification and further detail.

Hwaiting!

- **Over 700** essential Korean slang words and phrases every K-pop fan must know.
- **Pronunciation guide** to help you say the words accurately.
- **Definitions** as well as their origin and cultural background.
- **Real life** conversations and examples.

HOW TO USE THIS BOOK

1 애교 **Ae Gyo** **2** **3** (ae-gyo)

4 **"Acting Cutesy"**

6

A compound word made up of two Chinese characters, where 애 "*ae*" means "love" and 교 "*gyo*" means "beautiful". It is a display of affection through various expressions, such as making cute gestures or speaking in baby talk. While strongly associated with feminine traits, male K-pop idols often display these affections, and it is not frowned upon.

5
Yuna: Dad~! Can I pweease use your car? (Baby voice)
Dad: Only if you do the cutie dance!
Yuna starts dancing like a 5-year-old girl
Dad: I'm such a sucker for your ***aegyo***!

1   This is how the word is written in *hangul*, the Korean alphabet !

2   This is the romanization of the word. Notice that while there may be no spaces between syllables when written in Korean, I put spaces between syllables to help you easily understand the pronunciation. (애교 *Aegyo* vs *Ae Gyo*)

(Note: More often than not, there are multiple versions of how the same word is spelled (Romanized), but I'm introducing the version most commonly used by K-Pop fans around the world.

3   This is what it sounds like:

(Note: This is the closest approximation possible because it is difficult to replicate the Korean pronunciation using the alphabet.

4   Definition of the term, including the etymology, hidden nuances, and cultural context.

5   Learn how K-pop fans are using it!

6   Intuitive illustrations for better understanding.

How to read and pronounce the Korean alphabet

	Name	Pronunciation Initial / Final	English Approximation	Korean Example
ㄱ	기역 gi-yŏk	g / k	good	가수 gasu
ㄲ	쌍기역 ssang gi-yŏk	kk / k	skin	꿈 kkum
ㄴ	니은 ni-ŭn	n / n	nano	노루 noru
ㄷ	디귿 di-gŭt	d / t	dog	다리 dari
ㄸ	쌍디귿 ssang di-gŭt	dd	stall	땀 ddam
ㄹ	리을 li-ŭl	r / r	roman	라면 ramyŏn
ㅁ	미음 mi-ŭm	m / m	man	마법 mabŏp
ㅂ	비읍 bi-ŭp	b / p	bean	보배 bobae
ㅃ	쌍비읍 ssang bi-ŭp	bb	spit	빨리 bbali
ㅅ	시옷 si-ot	s / t	sing	소리 sori
ㅆ	쌍시옷 ssang si-ot	ss	see	싸움 ssaum
ㅇ	이응 i-ŭng	silent / ng	**vowel sound**	아기 agi
ㅈ	지읒 ji-ŭt	j / t	jam	자유 jayu
ㅉ	쌍지읒 ssang ji-ŭt	jj	hats	짬뽕 jjamppong
ㅊ	치읓 chi-ŭt	ch / t	change	최고 choego
ㅋ	키읔 ki-ŭk	k / k	king	커피 kŏpi
ㅌ	티읕 ti-ŭt	t / t	time	타자 taja
ㅍ	피읖 pi-ŭp	p / p	prize	피로 piro
ㅎ	히읗 hi-ŭt	h / t	home	해변 haebyŏn

The Korean alphabet consists of 14 consonants and 10 vowels. The ones in gray are special; they are "tense consonants" because they are pronounced with a harder, stiffer sound. Keep in mind that there are no English or Roman letters that perfectly describe the sounds, so these are the closest approximations! But don't worry—the more you listen to K-pop songs and watch K-dramas, the clearer the differences should become!

	Pronunciation	English Approximation	Korean Example
ㅏ	a	grandpa	자두 jadu
ㅑ	ya	see-ya	야구 yagu
ㅓ	ŏ	up	접시 jŏpsi
ㅕ	yŏ	young	명화 myŏnghwa
ㅗ	o	go	고무 gomu
ㅛ	yo	yogurt	교사 gyosa
ㅜ	u	root	우주 uju
ㅠ	yu	you	소유 soyu
―	ŭ	good	그림 gŭrim
ㅣ	i	hit	소리 sori
ㅔ	e	energy	세기 segi
ㅐ	ae	tablet	대박 daebak
ㅒ	yae	yes	얘기 yaegi
ㅖ	ye	yes	예복 yebok
ㅙ	oae	where	안돼 andwae
ㅞ	ue	quest	췌손 hweson
ㅚ	oe	wet	최고 choego
While ㅚ is ㅗ + ㅣ so "oi" seems right when followed the rules, but it's pronounced as "oe", and it's not considered a "double vowel", either.			
ㅘ	wa	what	과일 gwail
ㅟ	wi	wisconsin	귀 gwi
ㅢ	ŭi	we	의자 ŭija
ㅝ	wŏ	wonder	권투 gwontu

And the vowels in gray are called diphthongs, or complex vowels, meaning "double vowels". They are made up of two vowels to create one sound. One thing you might have noticed is how ㅐ and ㅔ practically sound the same and ㅚ / ㅙ / ㅞ the same! It might look like a waste of ink, but their meanings differ when written. Until the late 20th century, people used to distinguish the minute differences coming from the tongue and mouth position, but the differences in technique are seldom observed nowadays, and most Koreans can't tell one apart from another.

5-Year Curse

Jinx Whereby Popular Groups Will Face Hardships or Disbandment in Their Fifth Year

Many Fans of K-pop superstitiously believe there's a reason popular groups like H.O.T., Big Bang, TVXQ, Shinhwa, and Super Junior have experienced bad luck over the past five years. Others have shrugged it off as pure coincidence. They believe people have a habit of taking ordinary events and turning them into curses!

Tomi : Breaking news, guys! Cutie 5 just broke up!
Yena: Oh no, the **5-year curse** is true… they debuted exactly 5 years ago!

애교살 AeGyoSal *(ae-gyo-sal)*

Lower Part of the Eyelid

It's a compound word made up of 애교 *aegyo* ("acting cutesy") + 살 *sal* "flesh", which refers to the lower eyelid, (not to be confused with eye bags that sit below "*aegyo sal*" and give you a hung-over zombie look). It's termed so because fuller "*aegyo sal*" makes eyes look bigger and more youthful. It's commonly achieved through plastic surgery and is usually performed by injecting one's own abdominal fat or a commercial filler.

Jenny: Hey girl, your eyes look different. What happened?
Tina: Can you tell? I just got my **aegyo sal** injected at Dr. Kim's office.
Jenny: Oh, that's sweet! You do look younger. Will I get the same result if I drink 5 glasses of wine and have an all-nighter tonight?
Tina: You can try, but I'm sure it will only get you puffy eyes!

애교 AeGyo *(ae-gyo)*

Acting Cutesy

A compound word made up of two Chinese characters, where "*ae*" means "love" and "*gyo*" means "beautiful". It is a display of affection through various expressions, such as making cute gestures or speaking in baby talk. While strongly associated with feminine traits, male K-pop idols often display these affections, and it is not frowned upon.

Yuna: Dad~! Can I pweease use your car? (Baby voice)
Dad: Only if you do the cutie dance!
Yuna starts dancing like a 5-year-old girl
Dad: I'm such a sucker for your **aegyo**!

아점 AJeom *(a-jŏm)*

Brunch

A compound word made up of "**아침**"*achim* ("breakfast") + "**점심**" *jeom shim* ("lunch") = "brunch". Some people have an interesting way of distinguishing one from another. If a meal is average, it is "**아점**", but if a meal is worthy of Instagram, then it's brunch. This is largely due to some Korean people's tendency to associate imported English words with a more stylish lifestyle.

Taeho: Hey baby, let's go get achim!
Minji: Wha… achim? It's already 11:30AM!
Taeho: Well, then, jeom shim it is!
Minji: More like **ajeom**, right?
Taeho: Maybe, depends on what we are having.
Minji: I don't know… maybe eggs benedict with mimosa?
Taeho: It is brunch then!

애교 Aegyo

아템 A Tem (a-tem)

Item

The way kids and teens speak, especially during Internet game play.

Mingoo: Attack! Attack! Destroy this hideous monster!
Mingoo's game character defeats the monster.
Jiwon: Dang! You did it! Did you get any *atem*?
Mingoo: Hells yeah! I got this holy shield as a reward!

아놔 A Nwa (a-nwa)

"What the…"

Something that automatically comes out of your mouth when you are irritated or angry. It is actually the first part of the exclamation (e.g., "**아놔**" *a nwa* "**정말**" *jeong mal* ("really") "**화난다**" *hwa nan da* ("I am angry")) while leaving out the rest of the phrase. This will send a much clearer message.

Sohee: Hon, you should come see this…!
Kai: What's up?
Sohee: I accidentally unplugged your computer…
Kai: *A Nwa*…

아이구 Aigoo (Aigo) (a-i-gu/go)

"Oops"

An expression used to show frustration, embarrassment, and surprise. English equivalents are "aw man" and "oops". It is also used when scolding somebody.

Aigo! I forgot to do my homework!
Aigoo, I have no money in my wallet.
Did you break this vase? *Aigoo*, you clumsy little bastard!

애빼시 Ae Bbae Si (ae-ppae-shi)

Full of Aegyo

An abbreviation for "**애교**" *ae*gyo ("acting cutesy") + "**빼면**" *bbae* myeon ("if wihout") + "**시체**" *shi* che ("corpse")". Meaning, "Without aegyo, a person is a corpse" = "A person is nothing but aegyo".

Wonmi: Darling~ my love~ <3 <3 <3
Hojoon: LOL! Why are you so full of *aegyo* today?
Wonmi: Not just today~ every day *^ _^*
Hojoon: Yup, that's why people call you *ae bbae si*!

Age Line

Group of People Born in the Same Year

The term "line" can be translated as "grouping" or "belonging", and when combined with the term "age", it means a group of people who were born in the same year. It is always grouped by the last two digits of the year, rather than their age.

Tammy, Yo, and Juno are from the *93-line* (o)
Tammy, Yo, and Juno are from the *23-year-old-line* (x)
Ara: Nice to meet you all! My name is Ara, and I was born in 1994. Oh, my blood type is AB.
Yumi, Jihun, and Tony: Welcome to the *94-line*!

97 Age Line

아놔 A Nwa…

아이구 Aigoo…

아재 Ajae (a-jae)

Someone (Male) Outdated

A Gangwon province dialect for "아저씨" *ajuhssi* ("uncle"), "middle-aged man" or "married man", but can be used to address an unfamiliar adult male. It is often translated as "mister" in English. Recently, this word has been associated with someone who is archaic or old-fashioned.

> Goyoung: What did one plate say to the other? Lunch is on me! LOL!
> Bo: *Ajae* please…

아재 개그 Ajae Gag (a-jae-gae-gŭ)

Dad Jokes

A compound word made up of "아재" *ajae* ("outdated") + "개그" *gag* ("jokes"). When used, it does not bring about laughter but an awkward moment of silence. It is not only *ajaes* that make lame jokes, though. Regardless of age, if someone is not up on the latest trends and tells old, tired jokes, they are an *ajae*.

> Making an *ajae gag* adds at least 20 years to your actual age.

아줌마 Ajumma (a-jum-ma)

Married or Middle-aged Woman

A word for a "married or middle-aged woman" often translated as "madam" in English, but when used in certain situations, its nuance is subtly different. For example, if a young woman behaves badly, calling her "*ajumma*" serves as a slap on the wrist because there are negative connotations associated with the word, such as being pushy, loud, and sometimes selfish. The most distinctive characteristic of this word is a woman with permed hair, similar to that of a grandmother. Some people believe "*ajumma*" is the third gender in Korea.

> Wow, that *ajumma* literally stole that old man's seat!
> Did you hear that? Jenny became so *ajumma* after having 2 kids!

아저씨 Ajusshi (a-jŏ-ssi)

Married or Middle-aged Man

The male counterpart of "*ajumma*", this is a word for a "middle-aged man" or "married man" but can be used to address an unfamiliar adult male. It is often translated as "mister" in English. While similar to "ajumma", there are fewer negative connotations associated with it. The biggest insult would be calling a young man "*ajusshi*" because that means he is old-fashioned or outdated.

Ashley: *Ajusshi*! Can you tell me the directions to Seoul?"
Kyuwon: Um… Okay… But FYI, I am not *ajusshi*… I'm only 13…

악플 Ak Peul (ak-pŭl)

Malicious Comments

A compound word made up of "악" *ak* ("evi"l) "플" *peul* ("reply/comment"). This has been a huge problem in Korea because of cases where celebrities have committed suicide after being cyberbullied on the Internet. This is also a tactic used by certain fan clubs during "fan wars".

Mira: Wow! I have over 200 comments on the selfie I posted last night.
Hailey: Um… did you read any of them?
Mira: Yeah… They are all *ak peuls*… But I got over 200 comments! Yes, I am popular!
Hailey: Not sure if you are too dumb or just too optimistic…

알바 Alba/Arba (al-ba)

Part Time Job

A shortened phrase for "arbeit", which is a German word for "to labor", but has been used to mean "part-time job" in Korea.

Sangmi: What are you doing this Friday night?
Taeho: I have to do *arba* until 11 PM.
Sangmi: Oh no, how many *arbas* are you doing?
Taeho: Four, 'cause I need money to buy my idol *Oppa's* album!

올킬 All-kill

Winning All Major Music Download Sites

A word used to describe an artist or a group topping all major music download sites (i.e., Melon, Soribada, Dosirak, etc.). It is termed so because it is "killing all the charts". It is relatively easy to achieve an *all-kill* in the daily charts, but weekly or monthly charts are more difficult.

Yay! Our Oppa's new single *all-killed* the charts!

안무 An Moo
(an-mu)

Choreography

One of many essential elements (i.e., good "visual", friendly fan service, etc.) that an idol group must have to make an album successful. It is designed to complement the "concept" of their album (e.g., "sexy", "innocent", or "strong"). Some of the notable examples are "Tell Me Dance" by Wonder Girls and "In-line 5-Cylinder Engine Dance" by Crayon Pop. An Moo is an extremely important factor that determines the success of an album because well-designed dance moves alone can make a song go viral.

Mina: OMG! Did you see Biggie Biggie's new *an moo*? The dance moves are so sexy!
Yesol: I can't wait to see!

안물안궁 An Mool An Goong
(an-mul-an-gung)

"I Did Not Ask and I Am Not Curious."

An abbreviation for "안 물어봄" *an mool eo bom* ("I didn't ask"), "안 궁금함" *an goong geum ham* ("I am not curious"). This is what you say to stop someone who frequently pours out unsolicited information.

Jinsoo: So I woke up today at 7AM, had 2 cups of coffee, and hit the gym at 9AM, right? After that, I took a shower for 20 minutes, got dressed up, and went to work. Oh, and I had Chinese for lunch!
Yoosun: *An mool an goong*… you can stop now.

안습 An Seup
(an-sŭp)

Pathetic Situation

An abbreviation for "안구에" *an* goo e ("in the eyes") + "습기" *seup* gi ("moisture") = "moist eyes". It is your body's natural reaction to strong, emotional events, such as your "bias" going into the army or failing to top the music charts.

Hyomin: Oh no! LOL!
Wonkyu: What's up?
Hyomin: Alex was performing on the stage at this girls' high school, and he just tripped, his shoe came off, and the best part is, his sock had a huge hole in it. All the girls there must have seen it.
Wonkyu: LOL! That is really *an seup*…

안드로메다 Andromeda

Out of One's Mind

Literally meaning "sending someone's common sense to the Andromeda Galaxy", it refers to someone who does not have the ability to make good judgment calls or who is not able to behave in a practical and sensible way. It is a popular phrase among the younger generation.

Caleb: LOL! I just farted in my girlfriend's face!
Miha: OMG. Did you send your brain to *Andromeda* or something?

Antis

Anti-someone

A shortened phrase for "anti-someone".
A person or a group of people who show hatred toward a certain artist or a group, mainly because of an ongoing rivalry between the artists or a group they like. Some would go as far as sabotaging their rival's concerts or sending threatening packages, like knives, blood-covered dolls, etc.

JAJA has so many *antis*, especially from the ABAB fan club. I am pretty sure it's because JAJA crushed them by all-killing the chart when their new song came out at the same time theirs did. ABAB's sales were just lackluster.

아싸 Assa (a-ssa)

"Oh Yes!"

An expression that automatically comes out of your mouth when something is in your favor, such as your favorite idol group winning the Dae Sang at the Golden Disk Awards.

(Marcus and Taeho playing poker)
Marcus: *Assa*! I got a full house! Gimme your money!
Taeho: Not so fast! I got a royal straight flush! *Assa*! I win!

안돼 Andwae (an-dwae)

"You Can't", "Can't Be Done"

Literally meaning "No, you can't", or "It can't be done", it is often used to express disbelief, amazement, fear, shock, or defiance, having the same effect as saying "no way!"

Tina: Oh my god! News broke out that your favorite Idol group XOXO's member has been secretly dating that back dancer girl.
Minyoung: *Andwae*!

(a-mu-mal dae-jan-chi)

아무 말 대잔치

A Mu Mal Dae Jan Chi

Verbal Diarrhea

"아무" (*a mu*) means "anything/whatever," "말" (*mal*) means "saying/utterance," and "대잔치" (*dae jan chi*) means "big party/fiesta." Put together, it means "Saying Whatever Party" = "Verbal Diarrhea." It's used to refer to a situation where someone simply doesn't shut up and keeps spewing meaningless stuff.

> Tony: Yo! I know what I want for my birthday! I want a Ferrari!
> Ki Yong: That's awesome! Why not a Porsche?
> Tony: That should work too! Actually, I want a unicorn with air conditioning + GPS navigation.
> Ki Yong: Hey, what about a souped-up ostrich? I heard they can run pretty fast!
> Megan: OMG... I thought you guys were throwing a birthday party, not an *amu mal dae jan chi*...

A.R.M.Y

BTS Fan Club

An abbreviation of "**A**dorable **R**epresentative **M**.**C**. for **Y**outh," which is the BTS fan club. The fan color is silver-gray.

> Nicole: I decided to join the *A.R.M.Y*!
> Wanda: Damn, for real? You are going to be shooting people and stuff?
> Nicole: Come on, girl! Get with the program! I am joining the BTS fan club *A.R.M.Y*!
> Wanda: My apologies.

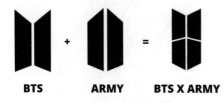

BTS   **ARMY**   **BTS X ARMY**

(a-pŭ-ri-ka TV)

아프리카TV

afreecaTV

Korean Online Broadcasting Platform

It's a Peer-to-Peer (P2P) video streaming service platform that started in 2005 as "W." This gave birth to BJs (Broadcasting Jockeys), or the independent broadcasters who run live channels with varying themes.

> Jeremy: Did you hear the news? Seho's been making tons of money on *afreecaTV*!
> Tim: What? Where in Africa? Kenya? Jamaica?
> Jeremy: No, dawg... It's a web-based personal TV station thingy... and Jamaica is not even in Africa...

After School Club
애프터스쿨클럽

Internet-Based Live-Music Request TV Talk Show

Often shortened to ASC, its Arirang TV's Internet-based live music request television talk show with three hosts: Kevin Woo, Jae, and Park Jimin. It's a popular show among international K-pop fans because the show is in English with Korean subtitles.

Dan: Yay! Done with school! Time to watch *After School Club*!
Nina: You're such a nerd going to a school club. Just go home and do some fun stuff!
Dan: I was referring to the K-pop TV Show!
Nina: Oh, I take back what I said. I'm definitely watching tonights episode too.

Ah Ah
아아

Iced Americano

Abbreviation for "**아이스**" (*a-i-seu*, "ice") + "**아메리카노**" ("Americano"). Originally, it was used widely by teenagers as a chatting/texting abbreviation to save time typing, but its gaining popularity in real-life settings as well.

Cashier: What can I get you?
Customer: *Ah-Ah!*
Cashier: Excuse me? Are you hurt?
Customer: *Ah-Ah!* Man, Iced Americano! You need to keep up with the latest trends!
Cashier: YASBT!
Customer: Excuse me?
Cashier: Your Abbreviations Suck Big Time!

(a-ssa / in-ssa)
아싸 / 인싸
Ah Ssa / In Ssa

Outsider / Insider

Short for "**아웃싸**(사)**이더**" (outsider) / "**인싸**(사)**이더**" (insider). It's used to categorize/label people on the basis of whether one belongs to a group. As for outsiders, one could become an outsider as a result of bullying, but one could also choose to become an outsider if one does not wish to belong to/hang out with a certain group.

Dong Ho: Hey guys, can I join you guys?
Mark: No way, Jose! You are like the biggest *ah ssa* at school.
Dong Ho: But I have a pair of tickets to KCON.
Mark: Welcome to the club. You are officially an *in ssa* now.
Dong Ho: But its from last year's KCON event.
Mark: What the… back to *ah ssa* status, now!

에어컨
Aircon

Air Conditioner

A Konglish term, short for "**air con**ditioner." In Korea, summers are really hot and humid (especially around the monsoon season), and "**에어컨**" usage skyrockets during that time. Many households, however, are afraid of keeping it on all the time because of whats known as the "progressive electricity rate," which is a six-stage rate system. When you reach a certain level (stage) of usage, the rate will increase progressively. The workaround? People go out to local banks or supermarkets (they always have "**에어컨**" on to the max) to beat the heat.

Jeong Kyu, a cash-strapped student in Korea, couldn't dare to turn on the *aircon*, despite the scorching heat, because he was hit with a $1,000 electricity bill last month.

아이씨
Aish

"Damn It!" "Crap!"

An interjection used to express frustration or surprise.

Melinda: *Aish*! I forgot to bring my wallet!
Tony: *Aish*! That means I have to pick up the tab!

악녀 Ak Nyeo (ak-nyŏ)

Evil Female Character

"악" (*ak*, 惡, "devil/evil") + "녀" (*nyeo*, 女, "female/woman"). It refers to the evil female character in K-dramas and K-movies. There are two types. 1) Femme fatale - she plays innocent but is evil at heart. Her goal is seducing the main male character, destroying any girls around him, and conquering him. 2) Downright evil - she manipulates people and creates conflicts among them, so she can lord it over everyone.

Juan thought Grace was a real angel until he found out that she was three-timing, not even two-timing, him from the beginning. It was too late when he realized she was a pure *ak nyeo*.

(ak-ma-eui pyŏn-jip)
악마의 편집
Ak Ma Eui Pyeon Jip

Manipulative Editing / Out of Context

"악마" (*ak ma*) means "devil/evil" and "편집" (*pyeon jip*) means "editing", so its literal meaning is "editing of devil" or "editing by devil." It refers to the act of quoting, editing, putting parts together, and removing parts from their entirety and the surrounding matter to distort their intended meaning. In the K-pop world, reporters and journalists are often criticized for engaging in such activities to make them look sensational and stimulating to the viewers and readers. For example, they will pick a very provocative headline (i.e., "Hani of EXID can't get married!") for an interview article with a celebrity, but guess what? It's bait! Reading the actual article would soon show the reader they have been completely fooled (i.e., "Hani can't get married because she is too busy!"). But in Korean variety TV shows, its often used to create a funny situation, just for a laugh.

Nancy: Ooh! My interview with the news reporter on health & fitness is on TV now!
Victor: Damn… Is that you with the face blurred out? And why does it say "overweight patient…?"
Nancy: God damn it! That's what I call an *ak ma eui pyeon jip*! They made me look like an obese fool!

알쓰 Al Sseu (al-ssŭ)

Lightweight

Literal meaning is "**al**cohol trash" because its a combination of "**알**" (*al* of "**al**cohol") + "**쓰레기**" (*sseu rae gi*, "trash"), but it refers to someone who has a low tolerance for alcohol.

Everyone knows Amy is an *al sseu*. That's why they gave her milk.

Angels

Teen Top Fan Club

The name of the fan club for Teen Top. It's an abbreviation for "**A** Teen Top is **N**othing divided like a simple fraction. **G**lory is **E**ndless until the **L**ast time." It also means Teen Top will protect their fans like an angel, and the fans will do the same for Teen Top. Fan color is pearl light lavender.

Angela knew that joining *Angels* was her destiny because her name has Angel in it, and she lives in Los Angeles!

악플러 Akpler (ak-pŭl-lŏ)

Troll / Cyber Bully

A compound word made up of a Chinese word "**악**" (*ak*, "evil") + "**플**" (*peul* "reply/comment") + "~er" = Someone who leaves malicious comments. This has been a huge problem in Korea because of cases where celebrities have committed suicide after being cyberbullied on the Internet. In extreme cases, they are sued for defamation and end up behind bars for the offense.

Tommy applied to 20 different companies but didn't get a single interview offer. Upon researching, he realized that he put *akpler* as work experience.

American Hustle Life

Reality Show Featuring BTS

It's an eight-episode reality show by Mnet featuring the BTS members in Los Angeles. The plot is as follows: BTS members believe they are going to the USA for their new album but find out they have to spend 24 hours in Los Angeles with a hip-hop tutor while carrying out various missions in order to experience and understand true hip-hop culture.

American Hustle Life is what made BTS who they are today.

AOA

AOA stands for **A**ce **o**f **A**ngels, and is a six-member girl group (Jimin, Yuna, Hyejeong, Mina, Seolhyun, Chanmi) formed by FNC Entertainment. They debuted in 2012 with the song titled "Elvis." They performed at KCON 2015 in Los Angeles. In 2016, AOA hosted their own reality show titled "On Style Live - Channel AOA." Notable songs include "Short Hair," "Heart Attack," and "Good Luck."

Xihao: What do you call a group of 6 celestial beings who can sing and dance?
Wendy: I dunno.
Xiaho: *AOA!*

AOE

AOA Fan Club

It's an abbreviation for "**Ace of** Elvis," which is the name of the fan club for AOA (Ace of Angels). The name "Elvis" is also the title of the groups debut song and the name of a very special person in music whom they admire.

Many people mistakenly joined **AOE**, thinking its a fan club for Elvis Presley.

(ap-do-jŏk)

압도적
Ap Do Jeok

Overwhelming / Dominating

Something enormous, immense, inordinate, and massive, and is often used to praise someone/something very highly. More specifically, when someone/something is so great, especially in a competitive setting like sports, and no other competitor stands a chance, this word sums up the whole situation.

Poll results are in. BTS won the "Album of The Year Award!", and it was not just a victory; it was an **ap do jeok** victory! They won by a landslide.

(a-pa-tŭ)

아파트 Apart

Condominium

A Konglish term meaning "condominium," the most prevalent form of housing in Korea due to the limited amount of land and high population density. While it comes from the English word "apartment," there is a fundamental difference: "apartment" in English refers to a housing unit available for rent, but in Korea, they are more similar to condominiums because they are owned, not rented.

Many celebs buy their parents an **apateu** when they make a lot of money as a token of appreciation for their support.

APINK

Apink stands for a company name: "**A** Cube (entertainment) + **Pink** (women)," a six-member girl group (Park Cho-rong, Yoon Bo-mi, Jung Eun-ji, Son Na-eun, Kim Nam-joo, Oh Ha-young) that debuted in 2011 with the song titled "I Don't Know." They have won more than 30 music awards since their debut.

In 2016, they performed alongside OneRepublic, Bebe Rexha, and Far East Movement for MTV Music Evolution in Manila. Notable songs include "NoNoNo," "Mr. Chu," and "Five."

James: Yo, did you know there are different kinds of pink?
Damien: Nope, never heard about it.
James: That's what I thought. **APINK** is the best pink of them all.
Damien: You dork…

애플힙
Apple Hip
Apple Bottoms

A Konglish term referring to round, healthy, plump buttocks achieved through arduous exercise, especially squatting. It's termed thus because they are shaped like an apple, and they are more of a symbol of fitness than a sexual object, as it inspires women to work out hard and eat right.

Maya: Hey! Check out my **apple hips**! I've been doing squats every day!
Chuck: **Apple hips**? They are more like rotten apples, girl!

(a-ri-rang)
아리랑 Arirang
Traditional Korean Folk Song

A Korean folk song estimated to have been around for more than 600 years, with some 3,600 variations of 60 different versions of the song. For this reason, its considered the unofficial national anthem of Korea, as evidenced by the fact it was sung when South and North Korea formed a unified team in the Olympic Games.

If you want to live in Korea and really blend in, you should learn to sing and understand **arirang**, as well as their official national anthem.

AROHA
ASTRO Fan Club

The name of the ASTRO fan club. "**ARO**" comes from "**ASTRO**", and "**Ha**" from the Korean word "**Hana**", which means "one" or "only". Combined, they mean "ASTRO is the one and only." Fan color is vivid plum and space violet.

Hawaiians say "ALOHA", and we ASTRO fans say "**AROHA**"!

(a-ri-rang TV)
아리랑TV
Arirang TV
Korea's All-English TV Station

An all-English TV station broadcast globally, a useful resource for those wanting to know whats going on in Korea on a real-time basis because you can watch news, documentaries, and dramas that are either dubbed in English or broadcast with English subtitles. They have popular K-pop shows, such as Simply K-pop, Pops in Seoul, and Showbiz Korea.

To an English speaker like myself, **Arirang TV** is a freaking godsend.

ARS

Automated Phone Answering System

Short for **A**utomated **R**esponse **S**ystem, it refers to the pre-recorded set of menus/protocols that works in place of a human operator. In Korea, it is used widely by TV shows for the purpose of receiving donations/contributions real-time by charging a certain amount of money per call made or as a voting tool for competitive audition-type TV shows.

Dad: Jenny! Come here at once!
Jenny: Whats going on, Dad?
Dad: Look at the phone bill! 300,000 WON, **ARS** Music Show Vote Now? What the heck is this?
Jenny: Oh, Dad! It's how much I love my *oppa*! ;)
Dad: Goodness gracious… you never spend a dime on your dad…

B.A.P

B.A.P stands for **b**est, **a**bsolute, **p**erfect and is a six-member (Yongguk, Himchan, Daehyun, Youngjae, Jongup, Zelo) boy group formed by TS Entertainment in 2012. They debuted with the song "Warrior" and had eight episodes of a show titled B.A.ps One Fine Day that aired on MBC Music. Notable songs include "Warrior," "Put 'Em Up," and "Rose."

The newly debuted group **B.A.P** is as awesome as their name Best, Absolute, Perfect!

B1A4

B1A4 stands for "**B**e the **one**, **all for** one" and is a five-member (CNU, Jinyoung, Sandeul, Baro, Gongchan) boy group formed by WM Entertainment in 2011. They debuted with a song titled "O.K.," which was first introduced to the public through a webtoon titled "다섯개의 수다 (*da seot gae eui su da*), "The Five Talks". In 2013, they won "New Artist of The Year " at Japan's Gold Disc Awards. Notable songs include "Beautiful Target", "Baby Good Night", and "Rollin."

The members of **B1A4** really get along with each other. No wonder their group name stands for "Be The One, All For One".

ASTRO

ASTRO stands for "Star" and is a six-member (MJ, JinJin, Cha Eunwoo, Moon bin, Rocky, Yoon Sanha) boy group formed by Fantagio in 2016. They debuted with a song titled "Hide and Seek" and were named one of The best new K-pop groups of 2016 by Billboard. Before their debut, they had their own reality TV show "ASTRO Ok! Ready," which aired on MBC Every1. They performed at Staples Center in Los Angeles at KCON 2016. Notable songs include "Crazy Sexy Cool" and "Breathless."

Serena: Dad, I'm into **ASTRO** these days!
Dad: Oh, I'm so proud of you, Serena! You are going to be a NASA girl!
Serena: What are you talking about? I meant **ASTRO**, the K-pop *oppas*!

(ba-bo)
바보 Babo

Idiot, Silly

Not an extremely derogatory term compared to possible alternatives. It is often used in friendly settings as well.

Mihyun: Oppa! Do you know what tomorrow is?
Ohwi: I dunno, Monday?
Mihyun: You are such a **babo**! It's our one-year anniversary!
Ohwi: Aigoo.

B2uties

BEAST Fan Club

Name of the BEAST fan club and stands for the loving relationship between the group and the fans (i.e., Beauty and the Beast). The group is now known as HIGHLIGHT, and their fan club name is LIGHT. Fan color is Gray.

Amanda: I just joined the **B2uties** ^^ I'm officially a **B2uty** now.
Zoe: You sure? You should have joined BEAST 'cause you look more like it than a **B2uty**…

바가지 BaGaJi (ba-ga-ji)

Rip-off

Literal meaning is "gourd" or "large bowl." It's used in the form of "바가지 쓰다 (*ba ga ji sseu da*, "to put on a gourd"). As you might have guessed, when you put a gourd over your head, you can't really see whats going on around you, hence you can be easily tricked or get taken for a ride. "Pull the wool over one's eyes" is the English equivalent.

Kyoko: I bought this USB for $30! It was on sale! Lucky!
Tod: Damn, you can easily get it for $5 on Amazon! You got **bag a ji**'d!
Kyoko: Baggage? I didn't buy any baggage. I bought this nice USB stick!
Tod: It means you got ripped off…

BEAST (Highlight)

Highlight, formerly known as BEAST (a.k.a B2ST, stands for "Boys of East Standing Tall"), is a five member (Yoon Doo-joon, Yong Jun-hyung, Yang Yo-seob, Lee Gi-kwang, Son Dong-woon, Jang Hyun-seung (left the group in 2016)) boy group formed by Cube Entertainment. They debuted in 2009 with a song titled "Bad Girl." They received numerous awards at the Golden Disk Awards, the Seoul Music Awards, and the Melon Music Awards. Notable songs include "Shock," "Midnight," and "Ribbon."

The only beast I'm not afraid of is **BEAST** oppas.

바라기 BaRaGi (ba-ra-gi)

Loyal Admirer

Stemming from the word "해바라기" ("sunflower," literal meaning in Korean = "해" (*hae*) means "The Sun" + "바라기" (*ba ra gi*, "admirer"), when you substitute "해" ("Sun") with a different subject, it means you are an admirer of that someone. For example, "태연 (Taeyeon) 바라기" means "Taeyeon Admirer".

Ever since Sheena saw G-Dragon on TV, she fell in love and became a G-Dragon **ba ra gi**.

배고파 Bae Go Pa
(bae-go-pa)

"I'm Hungry"

The term "배" *bae* means "stomach", and "고파" *gopa* means "hungry". Hence, if you insert a different term in place of "배", it means "something hungry = hungry for something (i.e., 사랑 *sarang* 고파 *gopa* = "love hungry"

Girlfriend: **Bae Go Pa!**
Boyfriend: What do you want to eat?
Girlfriend: I dunno… maybe Mexican food?
Boyfriend: Ok, then let's go get some Burritos.
Girlfriend: I dunno… maybe Chinese?
Boyfriend: Okay, let's go to that Dim Sum place.
Girlfriend: I dunno… maybe I am not hungry.
Boyfriend: WTH? What do you really want?
Girlfriend: Now, I am upset.

바바리맨 Ba Ba Ri Man

Flasher

"바바리" (*ba ba ri*) means "trench coat", and it comes from the word "Burberry", a brand famous for their trench coat. Hence, a "바바리맨" (*ba ba ri man*) means "trench coat man" and is used to refer to a flasher.

When Jenny first came to Korea, she thought **Ba Ba Ri Man** was the name of a Korean superhero.

배우 Baewoo
(bae-u)

Actor

For a female actress, it is "여 (*yeo*) *baewoo*", as "*yeo*" means "female".

Teddy is a great singer, but he would have made a good **baewoo** if he chose that path.

베이글 녀/남 Bagel Nyeo/Nam
(be-i-gŭl nyŏ/nam)

Someone Who Has a Baby Face With An Amazing Body

For female idols, "bagel" is a compound word made up of "(**ba**)by face" and "(**gl**)amorous", thus pronounced as "bagel". This is a term exclusively used for female idols who have younger-looking faces and voluptuous bodies. For male idols, "glamorous" is changed to "gladiator".

*In Konglish, "glamorous" means "voluptuous".

Hyuni's such a **bagel neyo** – she has the face of a high school girl and the body of a pin-up girl.
I never knew Wonki had such a great body because of his baby face. He is a great example of a **bagel nam**.

발연기 Bal Yeon Gi (bal-yŏn-gi)

Sloppy Acting

Literally means "acting with foot" because the word "**발**" *bal* ("foot") is used as a prefix to refer to something of low quality. In the Korean entertainment industry, many idols want to break into acting because it exposes them to greater opportunities, like getting a CF. While many idols have made the transition successfully, many have delivered lackluster performances. A good example is Jang Soo-won, a former Sechs Kes idol, who earned the nickname "Robot Actor" for his unpolished acting abilities.

Ura: Did you see the new drama last night? Ugh… I couldn't stand a moment watching our oppa doing **bal yeon gi**…

발라드 Ballad (bal-la-dŭ)

Sentimental and Emotional Song About Love

One of the most popular K-pop genres. Ballad singers are thought to have better singing skills than "dance groups". This is why the members of idol groups, who have great singing skills, choose this genre when they go solo and need an "image makeover".

When Semin sings a **ballad** song, his fangirls drown themselves in tears.

반대 Ban Dae (ban-dae)

Objection

A term you should familiarize yourself with if you are an avid fan of K-Drama. In Korea, a couple wanting to marry must first seek approval from the parents of both families. However, (in order to make it more dramatic) there's always someone who doesn't like the idea. Some of the reasons are 1) He/she does not come from a wealthy family or 2) The couple is actually brother and sister, separated at birth.

Minki: Mom, Dad, please allow us to get married!
Mom: I don't know. What do you think, honey?
Dad: **Ban Dae!**
Minki: But Dad, why?
Dad: Her personality is so similar to your mom's, and I don't want to see you suffer like I did.

(ba-ram-dung-i)

바람둥이
Ba Ram Doong I

Playboy

"바람" (*baram*, "affair," "cheating") + "둥이" (*doong i*, "someone who does something") - someone who loves to flirt with other girls, especially when he is already in a relationship.

William has been dating five girls at the same time but didn't like to be called a *ba ram dung i* because he firmly believed he was just spreading love, making the world a better place.

BABY

B.A.P Fan Club

It's the name of the B.A.P. fan club, formed in 2012 at the official inauguration event titled "1st **BABY** Day", where more than 4,000 fans from all over the world showed up to celebrate the beginning. Fan color is spring green.

Maggie: I'm officially a *BABY* now!
Won Ho: Woot? You're 15! You're a grown-ass woman!
Maggie: I mean I joined the B.A.P Fan Club! Bam!

(bae-chŏk)

배척 Bae Cheok

Hating And Leaving Out Certain Member

Literal meaning is "to exclude" or "to boycott". When used in a K-pop fandom context, it refers to the act of ruling out a specific member of a group out of hatred.

Rule #1: Do not EVER *bae cheok* any of the members. Love them ALL!

(bae-gyŏng-ŭm-ak)

배경음악
Bae Gyeong Eum Ak

Background Music

"배경" (*bae gyeong*, "background", "backdrop") + "음악" (*eum ak*, "music"). It is one of the most important elements of a movie, drama, and variety TV show as it sets the mood, emotion, and adds a dramatic effect. Not to be confused with Original Sound Track (OST), which is the compilation of all individual songs (instrumental, karaoke, ED, BGM) used in the work. BGM is music used as a background piece.

I wish I had my own *bae gyeong eum ak* that automatically plays whenever I make an appearance.

백일 Baek Il

100th Day

We all know Koreans, especially couples, are obsessed with counting days, and every monumental achievement is celebrated with romantic events. Aside from being a symbol of perfection (100%), the number 100 has carried a significant meaning throughout history, as evidenced by the fact that they throw a birthday bash for their newborn baby, which was considered miraculous, considering how difficult it was for newborn babies to make it past the first 100 days in poverty-stricken 20th century Korea (especially around the Korean War). Gifts, such as a "couple ring", are usually exchanged.

Today is such a special day because its our *baek il* anniversary! But of course, I'm celebrating it by myself because she doesn't know we are going out…

박치 Bak Chi

(bak-chi)

Someone Who Has No Sense of Rhythm

"박" (*bak*) comes from the word "박자" (*bak ja*, "rhythm") + "치" (*chi*, "stupid/ridiculous"). Put together, it refers to someone who has no sense of rhythm, making it difficult for a person to dance or sing to music.

When Sammy was a trainee, he struggled because he was a *bak chi*.

백퍼 Baek Peo

(baek-peo)

100%

"백" (*baek*, "100") + "퍼" (*peo*, short for "퍼센트 (**per** cent))," hence the meaning "one hundred percent."

Mira: I have a feeling that Jake and Michelle have been secretly dating…
Ivan: Really? Are you sure?
Mira: *Baek peo*… I saw them walking out of a hotel together.

발컨 Bal Con

(bal-con)

Slow and Unskilled

"발" (*bal*, "foot") + 컨트롤 (**con**trol). It literally means "controlling with foot" and is a derogatory term referring to someone who's slow and unskilled, especially when playing video games, because the word "발" is used as a prefix to refer to something of low quality.

When Tony had a 30 game losing streak playing Starcraft, people started suspecting he was playing with his foot and gave him the nickname "*bal con* Tony".

반도 Ban Do
(ban-do)

Korea

"한반도" *han ban do* means "The Korean Peninsula" and "*ban do*" alone means "Peninsula". Since there aren't many countries that are peninsulas, netizens simply use it to refer to Korea. It is most frequently used in the form of "반도의" *ban do eui* ~sth = "sth of Korea". For example, "반도의 패션 (fashion)" is "Fashion of Korea".

> Wayne: Dude, what is that thing you're eating? Brian: It's Kimchi! *Bando*'s staple food!

바나나우유
(ba-na-na-u-yu)
Banana Milk (Woo Yoo)

Banana Flavored Milk

A delicious Korean banana-flavored milk that became famous overseas thanks to a popular commercial featuring Lee Min Ho.

> Mmm, this *banana milk* is so delicious! It's amazing that it contains no real banana!

반말 Banmal
(ban-mal)

Informal Way of Speaking

Literally meaning "half-words", it is an informal (talking down) way of speaking. It should only be used by those close to you or younger than you. It is extremely rude when used toward someone older than you or before a close friendship has been established. Foreigners who are unfamiliar with the Korean language are mostly forgiven for making such mistakes.

> Wow, before I got better at Korean, I talked to my professor in *banmal*. Now, I feel so embarrassed! Ignorance is bliss.

반모 Ban Mo
(ban-mo)

Talking/Speaking in an Informal Way

An abbreviation for "반말 모드" *ban mal* ("informal way of speaking") *mode*. This occurs either through an implicit mutual agreement (because participants are of a similar age or they have developed a certain level of closeness) or by permission (usually the older participant initiates this and lets the younger follow suit).

> Doori: Hello, Mr. Kim, how is your day going?
> Hoon: What's with all the formality, man? We are both in the 5th grade! Let's go *ban mo*, buddy!
> Doori: Aight dude!

밥 Bap
(bap)

"Meal" or "Punching Bag"

Literal meaning is a "meal" or a "bowl of rice", but it is figuratively used to refer to someone who is looked down on as easy prey ("easy meal").

Min: Hey, you wanna play Starcraft? 1:1?
Tony: Again? I can beat you with my eyes closed. You are my **bap**!

뻥 Bbeong
(ppŏng)

"Bull" "Lie" "Fib" "Hot Air"

An adjective to describe the popping sound of an object (e.g., a balloon), but it is colloquially used to refer to something that is not true or overly exaggerated.

Alexander: Dude! You just got a letter from the FBI!
Victor: WTF? What does it say?
Alexander: OMG… What did you do, man…
Victor: Why? Just tell me already!
Alexander: It says… "**Bbeong**!"
Victor: I will kill you one day…

뻘글 Bbeol Geul
(ppŏl-gŭl)

Useless/Meaningless Post

"뻘" *bbeol* means "useless" and "meaningless" in Korean dialect and "글" *geul* means "a writing/post". Newly registered users on Internet forums often write these to reach a certain level/membership (e.g., rookie, junior, senior, contributor, etc.), which is granted after meeting a certain threshold (e.g., 20 posts).

Joann: What are you doing?
Max: I'm busy writing a bunch of meaningless **bbeol geul**'s.
Joann: For what?
Max: This stupid forum says I have to make 20 posts to be able to read others' posts.

뽀대 Bbo Dae
(ppo-dae)

"Swag"

Synonymous with "간지" *ganji* ("fashionable/cool") and can be used interchangeably. It is used to express admiration or awe.

Dongyu: Look at my new ride!
Nathan: Is that a Ferrari?
Dongyu: Hell yeah!
Nathan: It's full of **bbo dae**.

뽐뿌 Bbom Bbu (ppom-ppu)

Encourage, Incite, Egg On

Originated from the English word "pump", when someone becomes overly excited and becomes "all pumped up" often as a result of a compliment. This tactic is especially effective when the person is incapable of making clear judgments (e.g., intoxicated).

Bongmin: Ok, which one should I get? Red or Blue?
Tina: They both look great on you! Get them both! Oh, this white one also looks terrific on you. Hm, you should also get this pair of shoes!
Bongmin: Stop… **Bbom bbuing** me…

뿌잉뿌잉 Bbuing Bbuing (ppu-ing ppu-ing)

Something You Say to Look Cute

A word describing the act of someone (usually girls) employing a cute (*aegyo*) behavior in an attempt to display their charm. The behavior involves putting two fists next to their cheeks and making a circular motion while saying the term "*bbuing bbuing*" in a baby voice.

Sonya: Oppa are you mad? **Bbuing bbuing**~
Tony: Oh, not anymore.

베프 Be Peu (be-pŭ)

Best Friend

An abbreviation for "**be**st **p**riend" (because there is no F sound in Korean). It describes someone who is willing to go the extra mile and gladly make sacrifices for another, but sometimes, by a quirk of fate, it makes your 베프 into an arch-nemesis.

Jayna: Hey, it's official. We are not friends anymore.
Song: What do you mean? Did I do something wrong?
Jayna: No, we are **be peus** from now on!
Song: Oh my! Best Friends Forever!

베플 Be Peul (be-pŭl)

Best Reply (Comment)

An abbreviation for "**베스트**" best "**리플**" ri**peul** (reply/comment). It refers to the top-rated comment on a certain (e.g., Facebook) post. On Facebook, for example, it is the comment with the greatest number of likes received. For some, it means a lot and can serve as a self-esteem booster.

Adam: Wow! I left a funny comment on K-Dragon's photo, and it became **be peul**! I have over 500 likes so far.
Ignacio: What did you write?
Adam: I said that, if I get over 100 likes, I would post a photo of me in a bikini.
Ignacio: You should keep your word.

(bŏ-ka-chung)
버카충
Beo Ca Choong

Reloading Bus Card's Balance

An abbreviation popularly used by teenagers for "**버스 카드 충전**" bus card *choong jeon* ("reload/recharge"). In Korea, public transportation has a dedicated terminal that accepts prepaid cards (T-Money). Its balance requires constant reloading to avoid uninterrupted use.

Min: Damn, I need to get *beo ca choong* before getting on the bus.
Glen: It's used up already?
Min: Yeah, I shouldn't have let my little brother use it

(bi-chu)
비추 Bi Choo
"Not Recommended"

The opposite of "**강추**" *gang choo*. The word "**비**" *bi* is a Chinese word for "no(n)".

Joe: What do you think about this hat?
Yong: *Bi choo*… Snapbacks are so yesterday…

(bŭ-gŭm)
브금 Beu Geum

Back Ground Music (BGM)

BGM, spelled the way it sounds, it is one of the most important elements of a movie, drama, and variety TV show as it sets the mood, emotion, and adds a dramatic effect. Not to be confused with Original Sound Track (OST), which is the compilation of all individual songs (instrumental, karaoke, ED, BGM) used in the work. BGM is music used as a background piece.

Julie: Oh I can't believe my favorite drama is over.
Ashley: Me neither *crying*. It was part of my life. The *beu geum* is still stuck in my head!

(bŏ-jŏng)
버정 Beo Jeong
Bus Stop

An abbreviation for "**버스 정거장**" bus *jeong geo jang* ("station"). In K-dramas, this is where the main character falls in love with a total stranger while waiting for a bus, but it is also the place where they say goodbye to each other.

Jackie: I'm getting off at this *beo jeong*.
Wendy: Okay girl, hit me up when you get home! I'm getting off at the next beo jeong.

(bi-dam)
비담 Bi Dam

The Best Looking Member of a Group

A compound word made up of "**비쥬얼**" visual (pronounced as "**bi**sual") "**담당**" *dam dang* ("someone in charge of something") = someone in charge of "visual".

Annie: Ok girls, welcome to the first meeting of the book club. We have 6 members total… and you! What is your name?
Jenny: Jenny.
Annie: Ok, since you are pretty, you will be the *bi dam*!
Jenny: Do we really need that for a book club?

Big 3

The Three Major Entertainment Companies in the K-pop Industry

The nickname for the three major entertainment companies in the K-popindustry in Korea. They are JYP Entertainment, SM Entertainment, and YG Entertainment.

Kisoo just signed a contract with YG Entertainment. He started his career as a trainee at JYP Entertainment and debuted through SM Entertainment, and now he is with YG Entertainment! He has gone through all *Big 3*!

Bias

Your Favorite Idol

Your absolute favorite singer or group, whom you will support no matter what, hence the term.

Infinion is my *bias*! I love my oppas so much!

Bias Ruiner

Someone Who Has the Potential of Becoming Your New Favorite

An idol singer, an actor, or a group who threatens to take over the place in your heart currently occupied by your current bias.

Tiffany: OMG, who is that cute boy full of swag?
Minhee: Oh, that is Taemin, the leader of a new idol group named GOGO.
Tiffany: Holy moly Guacamole! I thought Seho *Oppa* was my one and only love, but he's so hot that he has the potential to be a *bias ruiner*.

블랙데이
Black Day

Singles' Day

Unofficial, more of a tongue-in-cheek day of consolation, observed each year on April 14th by singles in Korea. It is related to Valentine's Day and White Day. On these days, people who have not received gifts gather together wearing black and eat black-colored food, such as "짜장면" *jjajangmyeon* (a Korean-Chinese noodle dish made with a thick black bean sauce), as a means of sympathizing with each other.

Hong: Yo~ what you doing tomorrow?
Mogi: Um… It's **black day**… So, I guess I'll eat *jjajangmyeon* with you?
Hong: Singles rule!!! (cries)

Body Rolls

Sexy Dance Move

A seductive dance move by either male or female K-pop idols. The most popular example is doing the "body wave dance". The slower it is performed, the sexier it is perceived!

Wanso is so flexible that her **body rolls** remind me of the great tsunami! I bet I can go surfing on them.

블랙오션
Black Ocean

Fans Boycotting a Performance

A form of protest where fans in the audience dress in all black and do not use light sticks, thereby creating complete darkness.

After the incident, the idol group ILLO decided to kick out their member Yoon. Fans who are against the decision protested by creating a **black ocean** at ILLO's live performance on TV.

(bo-go-shi-pŏ)
보고싶어
Bogoshipo

"I Miss You"

An informal way of saying "I miss you". It can be said between two people who are close to each other, such as parents and kids or a couple. Adding "yo" at the end makes it formal (i.e., "*bogoshipoyo*").

Myung Soo: Mina, I haven't seen you in a long while. **Bogoshipo**!
Mina: Oppa, **bogoshipo** so much too!
Teacher: Hey, guys, great to hear your voice over the phone!
Kids: Teacher, **bogoshipoyo**!

(bok-bul-bok)
복불복
Bok Bool Bok

Take (Pot) Luck, Crapshoot

A compound word made up of three Chinese words: "복" *bok* ("luck") "불" *bool* ("not") "복" *bok* ("luck") = "lucky or unlucky", referring to a situation where someone has no option but to take their chances and let fate decide.

Hyori: Oh god, I wish I could know in advance which of the mystery boxes have our oppa's belongings!
Sua: You can't. It's all **bok bool bok**, you know?

(bol-mae)
볼매 Bol Mae

"The More I Look, the More Charming Someone Is"

An abbreviation for "볼수록 매력" *bol soo rok* (the more I look) *mae ryeok* (charm). It refers to someone whose charms are revealed or discovered through continued encounters. It can also refer to someone who might not be the love-at-first-sight type but over time grows on someone or becomes magnetic.

Youngmi: Hey, I heard you are still seeing that guy.
Tina: Right… I told you he wasn't exactly my style, but the more I get to know him, the more attractive he is.
Youngmi: Can you elaborate? What makes him such a **bol mae**?
Tina: He accidentally dropped a wallet one time, and it was full of $100 bills. The second time that happened, it had even more!
Youngmi: **B O L M A E**!

DAY 1   **DAY 2**   **DAY 3**

(bon-bang-sa-su)
본방사수 Bon Bang Sa Soo

"Making Sure to Watch the Original Airing of a Show"

A compound word made up of 본방 " *bon bang* ("original airing") + "사수" *sa soo* ("defending, securing something to the death"). It is a strong resolution to watch the original airing of a TV show, instead of reruns. It is extremely important because viewership ratings are based on 본방's, and idols often request their fans to do this, so they can get a good viewership rating (= they will get more TV appearance opportunities!)

Fan Club Leader: What are we going to do to back up our oppas tonight?
Everybody: WE WILL **BON BANG SA SOO** OUR OPPA'S SHOW TONIGHT!

(bon-jwa)
본좌 Bon Jwa

The Dominant One

It is most widely used in online game leagues (e.g., League of Legends and Starcraft) to refer to the champion.

Junho: Move aside! Yohan coming through!
Wang: WTH? Who is he?
Junho: How dare you! This is the **Bon Jwa** of StarCraft!
Wang: Oh, your Majesty! I beg you to forgive my rudeness. Your gold-plated keyboard and mouse are set up here.

(bu-bi-bu-bi)
부비부비
Boo Bi Boo Bi
Grinding

A type of dirty dancing where a girl stands in front of a guy, placing her hips close to his crotch, and then she starts rubbing while he places his hands on her pelvis and holds her. It can be used to refer to any kind of sexy or suggestive dancing that involves close body contact.

Wonhee: Gross! This drunk dude was doing *boo bi boo bi* on me!
Nancy: Was he good looking?
Wonhee: No!
Nancy: Oh gross!

(bul-peom)
불펌 Bool Peom
Sharing a Post Without Permission

An abbreviation for "불법" *bool beop* ("illegal") "펌" *peom* ("sharing"). This happens when the original poster explicitly prohibits the act of sharing a post, but someone finds a way to do just that.

Hyun: Mira, did you see the secret photo they posted in the private forum? I just uploaded it to my Facebook page!
Mira: Yeah, but how… isn't that invasion of privacy or something?
Hyun: Duh, everything on the Internet is copyright free!
Mira: Oh no… you should check the forum rules to make sure it's not a *bool peom*.
Hyun: I read it and deleted it.

(bul-geum)
불금 Bool Geum
"riday Night Fever

An abbreviation for "불타는" *bool ta neun* ("burning") "금요일" *geum yo il* ("Friday"). It is the most cherished day by students and workers who are on a five-day work/business platform. It is an independence/liberation day for those who have been forever longing for the moment. It is called "burning" because their passion and energy are so hot.

Julio: Bro, do you know what day it is?
Brian: Uh… Friday?
Julio: Dude you are no fun. It's not just Friday; it is *bool guem*!
Brian: I have to work tonight.
Julio: Oh.

버로우 Burrow

Hide, Disappear, Vanish

Originated from a fictional Starcraft (computer game) species, Zerg, whose characters hide underneath the surface to attack their enemies. It is used to describe someone who suddenly disappears. This skill is used most often when someone realizes they are losing an online debate.

Kyuho: There is this one dude who keeps saying the 9.11 terrorist attack was committed by aliens.
Joy: That can't be true…
Kyuho: Yup, after a bunch of guys posted links debunking his claim, he just *burrowed*.

버퍼링 Buffering

Delay / Stuttering

Originally, it refers to a situation where a multimedia element on a web page is not loading/streaming fast enough for a pleasant viewing experience. In Korea, however, it is also used to describe someone whose talking is unclear (e.g., stuttering or being equivocal/evasive), so it takes a long time to get to the point.

Tommy: Ho…ho…ho…ho…ho…I…y…
Semi: Stop *buffering* and say it already!
Tommy: Shit.

b...b...b...

(byŏl-da-bang)

별다방 Byeol Da Bang

Starbucks

"별" *byeol* means "star", and "다방" *dabang* means "coffee shop" or "tea house". This is where people buy coffee that's more expensive than their lunch!

Barry: Come meet me at *byeol da bang* at six, cool?
Tony: You mean Starbucks, right?
Barry: Welcome to 2016, man.

(byŏn-tae)

변태 Byuntae

Pervert

A character that often appears in K-dramas and Movies, they scare female protagonists by displaying their sexual desires in an unhealthy way. Usually, the male protagonist shows up and saves her (by covering her eyes with his hands).

Layla: Hey, what are you doing?
Mason: I am taking a nap in the arms of Sora.
Layla: Is that a blow-up doll with her picture printed on it?
Mason: Yeah, isn't she so lovely?
Layla: You are the biggest *byuntae* I've ever seen…

(ban-jön)
반전 BanJeon

Plot Twist

Literal meaning is "reversal", and it refers to the plot twist of a story or simply something That's completely the opposite of what everyone thought it was, such as someone who looks like a teenager and is found out to be in his 50's.

The biggest *ban jeon* in K-pop must be how Psy rose to international stardom with "*Gangnam Style*" when some people thought he was over the hill.

(ban-tchak-ga-su)
반짝가수
BanJjakGaSu

One-Hit Wonder / Flash In The Pan

"반짝" (*ban jjak*) means "shining/sparkling," but also means "short-lived,or ephemeral" and "가수" (*ga su*) means "singer." Put together, it means "one-hit wonder" or "flash in the pan".

When everyone thought Secret Five was a *ban jjak ga su*, they came out with a smash hit single, proving everyone wrong.

BANA

B1A4 Fan Club

The name of the B1A4 fan club and means 1) "**BA**" = B1A4 + "**NA**" (means "me" in Korean = the fans) 2) short for "Banada" (반하다, *ban ha da*, "to fall in love with"). Fan color is pastel apple lime.

As a *BANA*, I started eating 1 banana a day as a symbol of support for our B1A4 *oppas*.

(bang-bu-je mi-mo)
방부제 미모
Bang BuJe Mi Mo

Beautiful Person Who Doesn't Age

"방부제" (*bang bu je*, "preservative") + "미모" (*mi mo*, "beauty"). It refers to someone (not just women) who is still as beautiful as they were when they were younger.

Catherine, wanting to keep her beautiful face forever, started eating foods covered with preservatives so she can have *bang bu je mi mo*.

방송 Bang Song

(bang-song)

Airing/Broadcast

Refers to the airing/broadcasting of a TV/radio/Internet channel show/program. There are different types of *bang song* - "녹화방송" (*nok hwa bang song*, "airing of pre-recorded show") and "생방송" (*saeng bang song*, "live airing") .

The group was struggling until they had their first TV *bang song*, which was a true turning point in their career.

밥도둑 Bap Do Duk

(bap-du-duk)

Something Extremely Yummy

"밥" (*bap*, "meal/rice") + "도둑" (*do duk*, "thief"). The staple of Korean cuisine is a hot steamy bowl of rice in the middle, along with a spread of side dishes and main dishes around it. For this reason, the tasty food will make you finish your rice in an instant and want more!

There is one kind of thief that doesn't go to jail if caught, and that is *bap do duk*… They just make us fat.

방송사고 Bang Song Sa Go

(bang-song-sa-go)

(TV/Radio) Blooper

"방송" (*bang song*) means "airing/broadcast" and ""사고" (*sa go*) means "accident". It's those crazy/funny moments that happen on TV when things go off-script. Some common types are forgetting one's lines, not sticking to the script, falling off a chair, laughing when not supposed to be laughing, and singing off-key. Although it's embarrassing, it could actually work in your favor because there have been incidents where people became very famous and popular after their blooper went viral.

The biggest *bang song sa go* in K-pop is when Judy of Fantasy Girls started crying on stage because she was too nervous.

빵셔틀
Bbang Shuttle

The Bullied

"빵" (*bbang*) means "bread" and "셔틀" means "shuttle," together meaning "bread delivery boy" and refers to someone who is being bullied to serve an "일진" (*il jin*, "school gang") by doing all kinds of errands/requests, such as buying bread (pastry snacks) and delivering it to the school gang, as well as running back and forth like a shuttle bus.

Bbang shuttle is a humiliating and painful thing to do but has an unexpected benefit Dylan lost 20 pounds doing it because he had to run back and forth so much!

(ppal-li-ppal-li)
빨리빨리
Bbal Li Bbal Li

"Hurry Up, Hurry Up!" / "Quickly, Quickly!"

It's probably one of the expressions, if not THE expression that best describes the characteristics of the Korean people because they want things done quickly. Although it has many aspects, such as doing a shoddy construction job, many think the "빨리빨리" spirit is why Korea has the fastest Internet connection speed, fastest recovery from complete war devastation, speedy logistics/delivery system, and serves as the test-bed for the world's most advanced technology.

Mark: Slow down, bro! You are going 100 miles in a 60 mile zone! You are going to get us both killed!
Victor: You fool! TWICE will be on TV in five minutes, and we are going to miss it!
Mark: What!!! Put the pedal to the metal already!!! *Bbal li bbal li*!!!

BBC

Block B Fan Club

The name of the Block B fan club and an abbreviation for "**B**lock **B** **C**lub." The fans also go by the name of "Honey Bees." Fan color is black and yellow stripes that symbolize a honey bee.

Yolanda: Mom! I've got into *BBC!*
Mom: Wow congrats! That's a TV station in the UK, right?
Yolanda: Duh, Mom! It's an abbreviation for Block B Club!
Mom: Oh...
Yolanda: It's better than the TV station, Mom!

삐침 Bbi Chim (ppi-chim)

To Mope Around / To Be Salty

The state of being silent and unpleasant because you are angry or annoyed. It's the most critical thing to watch out for when in a relationship, because its like a ticking time bomb - you fail to appease your boyfriend/girlfriend immediately, and it could lead to a prolonged stalemate, with the final destination - breaking up.

When your girlfriend is in a state of *bbi chim*, she's more difficult to solve than a differential and integral calculus problem.

삑사리 Bbik Sa Ri (ppik-sa-ri)

Vocal Cracks/Fails

A slang word for a singer going out of tune, making vocal cracks/fails while singing.
It usually happens when a singer tries to hit the high notes, and it can happen to the most skilled singer as well! It's the singer's worst nightmare, and it leaves us in stitches (hilarious!).

The whole classroom burst out laughing when the professor made a funny *bbik sa ri* while giving a lecture.

뽕 Bbyong (ppyong)

Bye!

An onomatopoeia or a word that imitates the sound of someone disappearing/vanishing or appearing instantly (e.g., a magician going "poof!"). Mostly teenage girls say this because it just sounds too cute.

Xenia: Hey! Did you eat my last macaron???
Daniel: Oh, gotta go! *Bbyong!*

베댓 Be Daet (be-daet)

Best Reply (Comment)

An abbreviation for "베스트" ("**best**") "댓글" (*daet geul*, "reply/comment"). It refers to the top-rated comment on a certain (e.g., Facebook) post. On Facebook, for example, its the comment with the most likes received.
For some, it means a lot and can serve as a self-esteem booster.

Don: Wow! My comment on Suzy's new photo is a *be daet!*!!
Jody: Well, its at the top because you have so many dislikes… you should call it "worst *daet*".

비글미 Beagle Mi
(bi-gŭl-mi)

Energetic / Goofy In Adorable Way

"비글" (*bi geul*, "beagle (dog)") + "미" (*mi*, "beauty," "charm"), termed so because beagles are notorious for being overly energetic and goofy, but we all love them because they are adorable. For this reason, the term is used to refer to someone who keeps causing trouble but is still adorable.

My 3-year-old nephew is a naughty little rascal full of energy! He's got more *beagle mi* than Max the Beagle, our pet dog.

법카 Beop Ca
(bŏp-ka)

Company Card / Corporate Card

"법" (*beop*) comes from the word "법인" (*beop in*, "corporation") and "카" comes from the word "카드" (*card*). Put together, it means a corporate/company-issued credit card given to employees for business use. The cardholders often use it to treat their friends, family members, etc. because they can write it off as a business expense.

Wendy: I have a Visa card with a credit line of $2,000!
Max: I have a Master Card with a credit line of $3,000!
Tony: I have a *beop ca*!
Wendy & Max: Whoaaa

비하인드 스토리 Behind Story

Stories Behind The Scenes

A Konglish term referring to the untold stories of a certain event. Some examples in the K-pop realm could be a power struggle among group members and funny incidents that were not made known to the fans.

The *behind story* about how they decided to disband will be aired tonight.

브마 Beu Ma
(bŭ-ma)

Poster

Short for "브로마이드" (*beu ro ma i deu*, "bromide = Konglish for "poster"). For K-pop fans, a poster of their bias serves as a talisman!

Chao printed out a life-sized *beu ma* of MAMAMOO and is really enjoying waking up to it every morning.

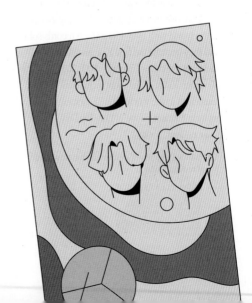

블리 Beul Li (bŭl-li)

"Lovely"

It's the "vely" part of "lovely", and is commonly used by substituting the last syllable of a girl's first name (e.g., a first name "주현" Joohyeon becomes "주블리" Joo*beuly* and "소미" Somi becomes "소블리" So*beuli*) " to mean something similar to "Ms. Lovely" or "Lovely OO."

Sohyeon always thought everyone was calling her "*So beul li*" but was shocked to find out that, in fact, they were calling her "so bully".

비혼 Bi Hon (bi-hon)

To Remain Single

"비" (*bi*, Chinese word 非, "non") + "혼" (*hon*, Chinese word "婚," "to marry"). It refers to the act of choosing not to get married.

Tony: I've decided to go *bi hon.*
Wanda: Decided? You are forced to because no one would want to date you!
Tony: Touche…

BIG BANG

Big Bang is a five-member (T.O.P, Taeyang, G-Dragon (a.k.a GD), Daesung, Seungri) boy group formed by YG Entertainment.
They debuted in 2006 with a song titled "La La La." Their song "Lies" (2007) topped major Korean music charts for six consecutive weeks and lingered in the Melon chart for 54 weeks. They are one of the biggest selling boy groups in the world with over 150 million records sold, and they became the first Korean artists to be included in Forbes Celebrity 100 (2016) and the 30 under 30 list of the most influential musicians in the world (2017). Notable songs include "Sunset Glow," "Day By Day," "Last Dance," and "Fxxk It."

BIG BANG is a symbol of evolution, both in the world of K-pop and astronomy.

빅픽쳐 Big Picture

Big Plan

An expression for a situation where something goes better than expected, especially when everyone was giving up hope. One who would have been responsible for the imminent failure would braggingly say this as if everything was part of the big plan from the get-go.

Drew humiliated himself when he tripped and fell on the street but found a $100 bill. Maybe the whole thing was his *big picture*?

Black Pink

Black Pink, which stands for "pretty isn't everything," is a four-member (Jisoo, Jennie, Rosé, Lisa) girl group formed by YG Entertainment. They debuted in 2016 with a song titled "Whistle." Their M/V for "Boombayah" was viewed more than 100 million times on YouTube in just 177 days after its release. They were the first K-pop girl group to have three #1 hits on Billboard's World Digital Song Sales chart. Notable songs include "Playing with Fire," "Stay," and "As If Its Your Last."

I have no idea what kind of color **BLACK PINK** is, but I have a feeling its a beautiful one.

BlackJack

2NE1 Fan Club

The name of the 2NE1 fan club because 21 is the highest number you can get in the card game **Black Jack**. Fan color is hot pink.

You have to be over 21 to play Black Jack at the casino, but you can be part of **Black Jack** regardless of your age!

Blink

Black Pink Fan Club

The name for the Black Pink fan club. It's a combination of the words "**bl**ack" and "**p**ink." It's been said that the members themselves came up with the name.

Jenny: Do not **BLINK** your eyes because you don't want to miss a moment of Black Pink girls!
Min: Cringeworthy.

Block B

Block B, which stands for "Block Buster", is currently a seven-member (Taeil, B-Bomb, Jaehyo, U-Kwon, Park Kyung, Zico, P.O) boy group created by Cho PD in 2011 (currently under KQ Entertainment), with the goal of making "Korea's Eminem." They debuted with a song titled "Freeze!" Notable songs include "Wanna B," "Nali Na," and "Shall We Dance."

Chiara: Get off the block! It belongs to **Block B**!
Min: Cringeworthy.

보살 Bo Sal

(bo-sal)

Saint

"보살" (*bosal*) means "Buddhist Saint" and is used to refer to someone with extreme patience and generosity along with the ability to persevere through pain, suffering, and humiliation. Mun Hee-Jun of H.O.T was known as "문 보살" Mun *bosal* (Saint Mun) because, back in the old days, many Internet trolls bashed him so badly for some statements he had made in a half-joking manner, but he didn't bat an eye, serving in the army as a model soldier, and making a successful comeback. Then, people realized they were being too harsh on him and started praising him as "보살".

Natasha caught her boyfriend cheating five times but forgave him every single time. People call her *bo sal*, but I think she's just stupid!

Boice

C.N. Blue Fan Club

The name of the C.N. Blue fan club, a compound word composed of "**b**lue" + "**v**oice." Fan color is, of course, blue.

Feeling blue? Then join *Boice*, and you will be feeling C.N. Blue 24/7.

복귀 Bok Gwi

(bok-gwi)

Comeback

Refers to the return of an idol singer or a group after a hiatus, which often entails a new single/album release, as well as TV appearances to showcase their new work. It can also mean returning to the group to which one originally belonged.

When the rumor about 2NE1's *bok gwi* plans to K-pop circulated, everyone got excited.

복붙 Bok But

(bok-but)

Copy and Paste

"복사" (*bok sa*, "copy") + "붙이기" (*but i gi*, but pronounced as *bu chi gi*, "paste"). Put together, it means "copy and paste," which is the most efficient/time-saving, tried-and-true method of completing your homework assignment. Disclaimer: use at your own risk.

Toby got kicked out of school after he got caught doing *bok but* for his essay.

CTRL+C
CTRL+V

본부 Bon Bu (bon-bu)

Broadcasting Station

Literal meaning is "headquarter," but in Korean TV shows, people use it as a way to refer indirectly to other broadcasting stations (specifically, three major public stations - MBC, KBS, SBS) because its an unspoken rule not to mention them in a conspicuous manner because they are essentially rivals competing for viewership (ratings). Therefore, they are referred to as M *bon bu* = MBC, S *bon bu* = SBS, K *bon bu* = KBS.

During the interview, Henry said M *bon bu*'s Music Today is his favorite program.

Broadcast Jockey

Independent broadcasters on afreecaTV, a P2P video streaming service in Korea. They are similar to YouTube celebs in concept, but their main source of income comes from the viewers who give them "별풍선 (*byeol poong seon*, "Star Balloons"), which they can convert to real currency. There are many types of BJs and shows. One of the most popular shows is "먹방" (*mukbang*, "Eating Show). Idol groups often appear on afreecaTV to interact with their fans through a chat window.

BJ is a legitimate, high-paying job not only in Korea but in many other countries thanks to YouTube and afreecaTV.

본상 Bon Sang (bon-sang)

Main Prize

An award given to outstanding entertainers. Unlike *daesang* ("grand prize"), there can be more than one recipient.

Power Boys was at the peak of their career when they won *bonsang* a few years ago.

B-Side

Less Known Song of an Album

The songs recorded on the flip side of a vinyl record, mainly because the company who created the album didn't think they would be as popular as the songs on the main "A-side' of the album. For this reason, *B-side* songs are usually remixes and more experimental music that are significantly different from the ones on the A-side and are rarely promoted, if at all, but for this reason, many consider the B-side songs to reflect the true color of a group.

If you are a true K-pop fan, you should pay more attention to the *B-Side* works of artists because there are lots of hidden gems.

BtoB

BtoB stands for "**B**orn **to B**eat, a seven-member (Eunkwang. Minhyuk. Changsub. Hyunsik. Peniel, Ilhoon. Sungjae) boy group formed by Cube Entertainment. They debuted in 2012 with a song titled "Insane" on M Countdown (Mnet). They won the "Singer of The Year" at the 2015 KBS Music Festival and "Best Vocal Group Award" at the 30th Golden Disc Awards. In 2016, they created a project subunit named BtoB Blue, which consists only of the groups vocalists (Eunkwang, Changsub, Hyunsik, and Sungjae). Notable songs include "2nd Confession," "Way Back Home," and "Missing You."

> **BtoB** oppas are born to beat, and we are born to love them!

(bu-jang-nim gae-gŭ)
부장님 개그
BuJang Nim Gag

Pun Jokes

"부장님" (*bu jang nim* "manager", "department head") + "개그" (*gae geu*, "gag = jokes"). Basically, they are lame, outdated jokes (mostly pun jokes) your boss makes, which you have to force yourself to laugh at in order to survive office politics.

> Boss: I know a funny joke. Here it is. "Lets talk about rights and lefts. You're right, so I left." Is this a **bu jang nim gag**? Everyone: Hahahahahahahahahahahahahahahahaha LOL OMG ROFL soooooooo funny! That sure is NOT a **bu jang nim gag**! It's so hilarious!

BTS

BTS stands for "방탄소년단" (**B**ang **T**an Sonyeondan "Bulletproof Boy Scouts," "**B**eyond **T**he **S**cene" (from 2018), also known as Bangtan Boys). It's a seven-member boy group (Jin, Suga, J-Hope, Rap Monster (RM), Jimin, V, Jungkook) put together by Big Hit Entertainment. They debuted on June 12, 2013 with a song titled "No More Dream," and since then, they have been an international sensation. In 2016, they were listed by Forbes as the most retweeted artists on Twitter and won the Top Social Artist Award at the Billboard Music Awards. They debuted on the Billboard Hot 100 with the song "DNA," which peaked at #67. Another title, "Mic Drop", was remixed by Steve Aoki and peaked at number 28. Since their debut, they have sold an estimated 5 million albums worldwide, as of 2017. Notable songs include "I Need You," "Fire," "Spring Day," and "Blood Sweat & Tears."

> English Teacher: What are your favorite alphabet letters? Me: **BTS**.

(bu-kae)
부캐 Boo Kae

Alter Ego/Gimmick

Abbreviation for *boo* 부 副 ('secondary') + **cha**racter 캐릭터. It's used when someone adopts a gimmick/theme That's different from their original character. For example, a famous actor would come up with a different name and a vastly different fashion style to perform as a rapper.

> Jenny is originally a ballad singer, but her **boo kae**, Ms. Kim, who is a rapper, is way more popular, so I think its best that she keeps that character as her main character.

HAHAHA

(bun-wi-gi)
분위기
Bun Wi Gi

Atmosphere / Ambiance / Vibe

The unique tone or mood of a place, person, or situation, or an object that is sensed intuitively. In a high context society like Korea, being able to assess the vibe/air of a situation (= being perceptive) quickly is especially important because of the social hierarchy and unspoken rules.

Michael: Hey guys, whats up with the **bun wi gi** here? Did someone die?
Joey: Our *oppas* are disbanding… and we are all just shocked…

(bung-ŏ-bbang)
붕어빵
Bung Eo Bbang

Chip Off The Old Block

A very popular Korean street food/pastry that comes in a fish-shaped bread filled with sweetened red bean paste. It's idiomatically used to refer to a parent and child who look similar to each other because they come off a fish-shaped mold, like a waffle iron, thereby producing an exactly identical batch every time.

Everyone says I'm Daddy's **bung eo bbang**, but I think I'm very different from my dad. He doesn't understand why K-pop is so awesome! Boring!

(byŏl-pung-sŏn)
별풍선
Byeol Pung Seon

Cyber Currency Used In Afreeca TV

Literal meaning is "star balloons" (a balloon with a star on it). It's a cyber currency used exclusively in AfreecaTV where viewers can gift them to their favorite BJs (**B**roadcasting **J**ockeys). They need to be purchased with real money, and they can be redeemed as real money. There have been negative effects as a result of the system, as some BJs engaged in prohibited activities, such as running a live channel that contains nudity in order to attract more viewers.

Ugh! Twice is just so hot! I wish I could send her 1,000 **byeol pung seon** ;)

C.N. Blue

C.N. BLUE stands for "**C**ode **N**ame" + "**B**urning, **L**ovely, **U**ntouchable, **E**motional". It is a four-member (Jung Yong-hwa, Lee Jong-hyun, Kang Min-hyuk, Lee Jung-shin) pop rock band formed by FNC Entertainment. They debuted in 2009 with a song titled "I'm a Loner," which set the record for reaching number one on Korea's music programs in the shortest time since its debut (15 days). They have been active philanthropists by donating money and rice to the needy, as well as founding schools in Burkina Faso and in The Philippines. Notable songs include "Intuition," "Hey You," and "Cinderella".

Mark: What color is this? Am I **C.N Blue**?
Tina: Hey! Don't play with our *oppas'* band name like that!

카레 Ca Re
(ka-re)

Curry

A Konglish term for "curry." There is no word "curry" in the Indian language. However, its said that the Dravidian word "cali", means vegetables , meat, meals, side dishes, etc., and it became known as "curry" in English. It went to Japan and became known as "care" and was later imported into Korea.

When I was in India, I tried their traditional curry, and it was quite different from the Korean *ca re*. Well, I like them both, though!

까메오 Cameo

Surprise Appearance

A brief, unexpected, surprise appearance of a well-known figure in movies, dramas, M/Vs, CFs, TV shows, and the like. Examples are Gongchan in Mamamoo's "Piano Man," Irene in Kyuhyun's "At Gwanghwamun", MV and Henry's "1-4-3," as well as Dasom and Seo In Guk in K.Will's "Please Don't."

Wow! F.T. Island *oppa* made a *cameo* appearance in my dream last night!

Cable
Cable TV Network

Unlike 공중파 (*gong jung pa*, "Over The Air (OTA) Channels"), cable TV channels are only available to paying subscribers. The biggest difference between the two is that cable TV channels are under less strict censorship regulations than OTA. This gives them more flexibility in creating TV content, and they tend to be more experimental and sometimes more provocative than OTA programs. Another difference is that many channels specialize in one specific topic, such as news, movies, K-pop, or K-drama channels.

Their new TV series was too violent and had to be shown only on *cable* channels.

CCTV
Surveillance Camera

An abbreviation for the English word "closed-circuit television," which means "surveillance camera." It's more popularly used in Korea (as well as the U.K.) than where it was originally coined (a US company introduced the first commercial CCTV television system in 1949. In that year, a government contractor named Vericon started to promote the system).

The *CCTV* footage showed exactly who was at fault, and it was me. I carefully unplugged it and smashed it completely.

콜 Call

"Accept"

A term derived from poker, where a player "accepts" another player's intention to raise the bet. It is widely used as an everyday term among the younger population.

Hoon: Yo, I'm going to hit the bar tonight. You want to join?
Mike: *Call*!

CF

Commercial

An abbreviation for "commercial film". *CF*s are enormously influential in Korea. Many nameless entertainers can become famous overnight if a *CF* goes viral.

Damn, who's that girl in that *soju CF*? She is smoking hot! My bias, Johan's got a *CF* for a new ice cream bar! Oh dear, I am going to get so fat…

CARTEL

The Union of Three Most Powerful Fan Clubs

Reference to the alliance of the three most powerful fan clubs formed at the 2008 Dream Concert that created *black ocean* against Girls Generation. It is a form of protest where fans in the audience dress in all black and do not use any light sticks, thereby creating complete darkness. **Cassiopeia + Triple S + ELF = CARTEL.**

Qiang: Did you see the black ocean created by *CARTEL* yesterday?
Tony: Yeah, it was awesome… They are like the United Nations of K-pop.

(cha-do-nam/nyŏ)
차도남//차도녀
Cha Do Nam/Nyeo

Chic City Guy/Lady

An abbreviation for "**차**가운" *cha ga un* ("cold, offish"), "**도**시의" *do shi eui* ("urban, city"), "**남자/여자**" *nam ja/yeo ja* ("guy/lady"). In K-dramas, they are often portrayed as super offish/cold colleagues or superiors at work, who (slowly) open their hearts, embrace the main character, and eventually fall in love.

Noah: What's up with that new dude? He's acting like there is no one above him.
Jordan: Yeah, she is one *cha do nam*. He's playing hard to get… He's like a New Yorker!
Tanya: New York, my ass! Didn't you guys know? He's actually a hick from the countryside, and that's why he's acting all cold to cover that up.

재벌 Chaebol
(jae-bŏl)

Conglomerate, Mr./Ms. Super-Rich

It refers to large Korean conglomerates, but can also mean someone who's super-ich. A young son or a daughter of a *chaebol* is called *chaebol 2 (i)-se*, which literally means "the second generation of the chaebol family". In K-dramas with a Cinderella-type storyline, they are often portrayed as cocky and arrogant characters who believe money can buy anything, including love.

> The new drama featuring Koyo looks like another Cinderella story! I am pretty sure I can predict how the story will unfold… That *chaebol* guy will fall in love with a poor girl from the countryside, and she will reform him into a humble man with the power of true love.

철벽녀 Cheol Byeok Nyeo
(chŏl-byŏk-nyŏ)

Woman Who Plays Hard-to-Get

"철" *cheol* means "iron", "벽" *byeok* means "wall", and "녀" *nyeo* means "woman". It refers to an impregnable woman who does not open her heart easily or accept other people's love. In K-dramas, such female characters are extremely offish at the beginning and then slowly and gradually open their hearts for that one true love of their lives. Of course, they keep hiding their emotions, just to tantalize the viewers.

> May: Man, I am calling it quits! I've been asking her out since high school, and she keeps saying no!
> Jorge: Yeah man, she is such a *cheol byeok nyeo*! Oh wait, maybe she only likes handsome men? Hahaha!

천조국 Cheon Jo Guk
(chŏn-jo-guk)

United States of America

Internet slang that literally means "1,000 Trillion Nation". Originated from the fact the amount of military spending by the U.S.A. is close to 1,000 trillion dollars, which is greater than the sum of many advanced nations' budgets.

> Victor: I am going to *cheon jo guk* tomorrow.
> Wendy: Huh? Where?
> Victor: U.S.A., stupid!

1,000,000,000,000,000

철새팬 Cheol Sae Fan
(chŏl-sae-paen)

Multifans

"철새" *cheol sae* means "migratory bird", so when used in conjunction with "**fan**", it refers to someone who is a fan of multiple groups at the same time. "다팬" *da fan*, also meaning "multi-fan", can be used interchangeably.

> Urias: I love Sensation Trio, but I also love Medium Bang.
> Toby: Um, didn't you say you love AAA?
> Urias: I know… I am such a *cheol sae fan*.

BTS

SUPER JUNIOR

(jŏng-mal)
정말
Cheongmal (Jeongmal)

"Really"

Used to express surprise or to ask about the validity of a certain situation or statement.

Hyoju: *Cheongmal cheongmal* I!
Gibeom: *Cheongmal*?
Hyoju: *Cheongmal*!

(chŏt-kon/mak-kon)
첫콘/막콘
Cheot Con/ Mak Con

First Concert/Last Concert

"첫" *cheot* and "막" *mak* are adjectives meaning "first" and "last", respectively, so it is used when more than one concert date is available.

Henry: Angelita's *cheot con* is tomorrow!
Min: Nah… I will just go to their *mak con*…
Henry: Dude! *Cheot con*s are always the best!

(chŏt-sa-rang)
첫사랑
Cheot Sarang

First Love

"첫" *cheot* ("first") and "사랑" *sarang* ("love"). It's a commonly used theme for many K-dramas, often breaking onto the scene to complicate a "love line" (a map of relationships) of a protagonist, who agonizes over his choice of women.

Bruce: It's been 3 years since Hyomin retired, but I just can't let her go.
Myong: I understand. *Cheot sa rang*s are difficult to forget.

(chi-maek)
치맥 Chi Maek

Chicken and Beer

An abbreviation for "치킨" (*chicken*) and "맥주" (*maekju*, "beer"), it is a favorite adult Korean snack/meal, especially when watching a sporting event. It can be likened to chicken wings and beer in the West. It gained massive popularity in China, thanks to the mega-hit K-drama "My Love from the Star", where Cheon Song-I, the heroine of the drama, says "Chi Maek is perfect for a snowy day". This line triggered Chinese viewers to flock to specialty fried chicken shops, and uploading selfies with a piece of fried chicken and beer became a trend on social media.

Joe: Oh! The soccer match is on!
Walter: Shoot! Forgot to order *chi maek*!

친추 Chin Choo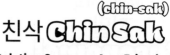

(chin-chu)

Adding Someone As a Friend on Social Media

An abbreviation for "**친구**" *chin goo* ("friend") "**추가**" *choo ga* ("addition"). This is the 21st-century Facebook-era version of exchanging contact information and is considered a less aggressive and indirect way of asking for someone's contact info, such as a phone number.

Miyako: Hi, thanks for the ***chin choo***!
Tomo: My pleasure!

친삭 Chin Sak

(chin-sak)

Deleting Someone As a Friend on Social Media

An abbreviation for "**친구**" *chin goo* ("friend") and "**삭제**" *sak je* ("deletion"). While it is a convenient way to end a relationship, it could be considered rude or offensive, especially when done without notice.

Miyako: Remember that Tomo kid who added me on Facebook? He seems like a stalker!
Jackie: Go ahead and ***chin sak*** him!

(jin-tcha)
진짜 Chincha (Jinjja)

"Really"

Used to express surprise or to ask about the validity of a certain situation/statement.

Paulina: Did you hear the news? Mimi and Changyo are dating!
Kathryn: ***Chincha***?

초보 Chobo

Newbie

A compound word made up of two Chinese words: "**초**" *cho* ("first") "**보**" *bo* ("step"), which became a popular term among online gamers around the world, thanks to ubiquitous Korean gamers, who contributed to the burgeoning of the world's largest e-sports (Starcraft, LOL, Counter Strike, and etc.) league.

Nick: I just started playing StarCraft yesterday.
Tim: Dude, you must be such a ***chobo***.

초딩 Choding

(cho-ding)

Someone Who Acts Like a Kid

A fun way of calling an elementary school student (초등학생 *chodeunghaksaeng*) . This term is also used to make fun of someone who acts like a kid.

Jihoon's favorite dishes are pizza, hamburgers, and French fries. He has such a **choding** appetite.
Kay passed out after playing a video game for 10 hours non-stop. He is still a **choding** at heart!

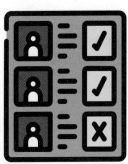

Chocolate Abs

Six Pack Abs

So called because chiseled abs look similar to blocks of chocolate.

Dongjoon's been working out so hard for the past 6 months. Look at his **chocolate abs**! Oh, I bet I can use that as a washboard.

출첵 Chool Chek

(chul-chek)

Roll Call

An abbreviation for "출석" *chool seok* ("attendance") + **check**. It is the first activity at the beginning of a school day in Korea. Some teachers opt for a visual check, and some kids take advantage of this by removing and hiding their desks and chairs to fool the teachers into thinking there is no one absent.

Student A: (Typing a text message) Dude, hurry the hell up! Teacher's about to do a **chool check**!
Student B: What! I overslept! On my way!

춤 Choom
(chum)

Dance

Considered to be one of the essential virtues or skills an idol should possess.

Tiny Baby's signature move is the propeller **choom**. She looks like a little helicopter about to take off!

취중진담 Chwi Joong Jin Dam
(chwi-jung-jin-dam)

Drunk Confession, In Wine There is Truth

A compound word made up of "취중" *chwi joong* ("while drunk") + "진담" *jin dam* ("telling the truth"). It is the act of admitting one's true feelings toward somebody, with the help of alcohol, because they find it difficult to do so when sober. While many use it as an opportunity to ask someone out, others use it to raise hell with someone. It is a useful tactic because, if it doesn't go the way you expected, you can always put the blame on alcohol (e.g., "Wow, I don't remember saying that!"). It is also the name of a popular song by Kim Dong-ryul.

Mimi: I can't believe he asked me out last night. I guess he was too drunk and just being goofy.
Yolanda: Hm, you never know. Maybe he was making a **chwi joong jin dam**.

추석 Chuseok
(chu-sŏk)

Traditional Korean Holiday in the Autumn

A major harvest festival in Korea that lasts for three days. It is celebrated on the 15th day of the 8th month of the lunar calendar. It is also called 한가위 *Hangawi*, which comes from archaic Korean. People often dress up in traditional 한복 *hanbok* and engage in traditional activities.

Michelle is wearing *hanbok* to celebrate **Chuseok** with her family.

취켓팅 Chwicketing
(chwi-ket-ting)

Ticketing for Cancelled Tickets

If you happen to lose out during the initial bloodbath of ticketing, there's always a second chance through "취켓팅", or "canceled ticketing". "취" *chwi* comes from the word "취소" *chwi so*, meaning "cancellation," which Korean fans have combined with the word "tic**keting**." Fans use this term to refer to ticketing for canceled tickets. Often fans will stay up until 4 AM to catch canceled tickets on ticketing websites.

Inbi: Ugh! All tickets are sold out!
Bonnie: Don't give up just yet! There is always a chance for **chwicketing**!

(cha-ae)
차애 Cha Ae

Second Favorite Bias

"차" (*cha*, means "next", "second") + 애 (*ae*, 愛, "love"). Your second favorite bias of a group.

> I like Suga the most, and Jimin is my *cha ae*.

(chŏn-sa)
1004 Cheon Sa

Angel

"1004" is read "천사 (*cheon sa*)", which means "one-thousand four," but it is also pronounced the same as "Angel"; hence, its used as a chat abbreviation for "Angel."

> I was born on October 4, and its *1004*. It means I'm an angel!

(chŏt-bang)
첫방 Cheot Bang

First Episode of a Show/Program

"첫" (*cheot*, "first") + "방" (*bang song*, "show/broadcast"). The very first episode of a show/program. Lots of "흑역사" (*heuk yeok sa*, "shameful/humiliating memories") are made in the first episode of a show because it captures the style/trend of the time, and after a lot of time has passed, they wish they hadn't had that hairstyle.

> Our *oppas* made a historical *cheot bang* last night, and it was incredible!

(chi-nŭ-nim)
치느님 Chi Neu Nim

"You Can't Go Wrong With Fried Chicken"

"치킨" (*chi*cken) + "하느님" (*ha neu nim*, "god"). Put together, it means "chicken is god" = "you can't go wrong with fried chicken," an example that shows how much Korean people love fried chicken.

> I don't believe in god, but I do believe in *chi neu nim*… so yummy…!

(chwi-hyang-jŏ-gyŏk)
취향저격
Chwi Hyang Jeo Gyeok

Exactly One's Type

"취향" (*chwi hyang*, "preference") + "저격" (*jeo gyeok*, "to snipe"), used to describe something/someone that suits one's taste perfectly.

Wow! Leather jacket, pants, and shoes… That's my style! *Chwi hyang jeo gyeok!*

(cho-dae-son-nim)
초대손님
Cho Dae Son Nim

Featured Guest/Special Guest

A guest invited to appear on a TV/Radio show program. Some celebs are infamously known for not appearing on TV/Radio shows in order to maintain their mysterious/lofty image.

Tony invited himself to Seho's birthday party and argued that he is a *cho dae son nim*. Yes, he got kicked out.

(cho-nŭng-lyŏk)
초능력
Cho Neung Ryeok

Super Natural Powers / ESP

"초" (*cho*, "super") + "능력" (*neung ryeok*, "ability"), referring to supernatural powers one possesses. Many K-pop fans believe their biases have a supernatural power of making their fans fall in love with no effort!

Is being able to eat more than others a type of *cho neung ryeok?*

(choe-ae)
최애 Choe Ae

Ultimate Bias

"최고" (*choe go*, "the best", "the most") + "애" (*ae*, 愛, "love"). Your favorite bias of a group.

My *choe ae* is Jung Kook, and it will never change!

(cho-gi-wa)
촉이와 Chogiwa

"I Got a Feeling" / "I Can Feel It"

"촉" (*chok*, "gut feeling"/"hunch") + "~이와" (*~iwa*, "~is coming"). A feeling or conjecture based on one's intuition rather than known facts. It's also the name of Super Junior D&E's song "촉이와 (2015)."

Dude… I can't quite remember because I totally blacked out, but I think I did stupid stuff last night… **Chogiwa**… I can definitely sense it…

(chu-ri-ning)
츄리닝 Churining

Track Suit / Sweat Suit

A Konglish term originated from the English word "training". It refers to a track/sweat suit you wear when exercising, but it is also a popular fashion style, especially among hip hop fans.

With his **churining** fashion, he thought he'd look like a cool hip hop kid, but everyone thought he looked like a couch potato.

(chung)
충 Choong

Freak

Literal meaning is "vermin/worm/insect," and when used as a suffix, it serves as a derogatory term for someone who is overly obsessed or addicted to something. For example, "control freak" = "control 충 *choong*," "someone addicted to video game" = "video game 충 *choong*." Also used to label a type of person you hate by using it as an insult/scorn. For example, 맘충 (mom 충) refers to an incredibly selfish mother who only cares about their kid, and 급식충 (*geup sik*, "school lunch (meals))" = "kids who eat school lunch (meals)" = "school children/teenagers") is a scornful term hurled at school children who behave badly.

People call me party **choog** 'cause all I do is party!

(chwal-yŏng)
촬영 Chwal Yeong

Shooting / Filming

The act of shooting/filming an object. In the K-pop world, its frequently used for "화보 촬영" (*hwa bo chwal yeong*, "promotional photoshoot") and "영화 촬영" (*yeong hwa chwal yeong*, "movie filming").

If you are a true fan, you must stay on top of your oppa's chwal yeong schedule!

(chwi-jun-saeng)
취준생
Chwi Jun Saeng

Job Seeker

Short for "**취업**" (*chwi eop*, "getting/finding a job") + "**준비**" (*jun bi*, "preparation") + "**생**" (*saeng*, "person"). Put together, it means "someone who's looking for a job." With the increasing level of youth unemployment rate in Korea, there are a lot of "취준생" who are get locked in a vicious cycle of looking for a full-time job but having to settle for an internship position that is often without compensation.

In a sense, trainees are a type of *chwi jun saeng* who work and try hard for their big day!

(coin no-rae-bang)
코인노래방
Coin No Rae Bang

Mini Singing Room (Karaoke)

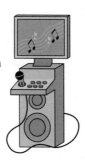

A coin (and paper bills, too) - operated compact booth-type singing room (karaoke) designed to accommodate a smaller number of patrons (usually 1~6 max). It's named so because you put money into a machine to sing a song, just like a vending machine. Compared to traditional karaoke, it makes more sense, as you don't have to book a room, which usually requires payment for at least an hour. You can just pay-as-you-go.

Whenever I need to vent, I hit *coin no rae bang* and sing all the stress away.

쿡방
Cook Bang

Cooking Show

Similar to "먹방" (*muk/meokbang*, "eating show"), "쿡방" (*cook bang*) is a show/broadcast in which cooking is the main theme. One of the most famous "쿡방" is Please Take Care of My Refrigerator by JTBC, where chefs are on a competitive mission to prepare a special meal in a given time only using the ingredients found in the guests refrigerator. Two chefs compete at a time, and the special invited guest has to pick one over the other.

When you are hungry, you definitely have to avoid watching a *cook bang*.

(con-sen-tŭ)
콘센트
Consent

Power Outlet

A Konglish term referring to "power outlet," believed to have originated from Japan. Sometime around the 1920s, employees at Tokyo Electric Power Company Holdings, Inc. invented a device that consisted of a plug and a power outlet they named "concentric plug," and outlets without the plugs are now referred to as "*consent*."

When Jiho traveled to Europe, he had a hard time figuring out where the power outlet was because no one understood his question "Where is the *consent*?"

콜라보 Colabo

Collaboration

The practice through which artists join forces to create a unique piece of work that incorporates the distinctive characters of each contributing artist.

Penny: Wow! Hyunie Honey and Timber are making a *colabo* album!
Mark: Can't wait to see that!

컴백 Comeback

Returning of an Idol After Hiatus

The return of an idol singer or a group that entails a new single/album release. It is often followed by appearing on TV music shows to showcase their new work.

Did you hear? JooJoo is making a *comeback* with their new digital single! She will be in Inkigayo this Saturday!

Concept

Image or Character One Chooses to Pursue

An image or a character that an idol singer or a group assumes. It can be either career-long or as short as a single TV show. It can change frequently, depending on the overall theme of their goal. For example, one can have "sexy" as their theme for their new album but can choose to have "comical" as their theme for the next album.

Wow, Hyunhwa really came back with the sexy *concept* she promised… She no longer embraces that cute girl *concept* that wasn't so successful.

커플링 Couple Ring

A Korean couple's public display of affection. They put a matching pair of rings on the fourth finger of their left hands, the same place they would put their wedding rings. There is no specific rule as to when couples should exchange "couple rings." Some couples go entirely without "couple rings."

Tony: All right! So we are officially going out!
Mia: Yeah! Lets go get a *couple ring*!

커플티 Couple Tee

Similar to "couple ring," Korean couples wear a matching set of T-shirts. Recently, novelty T-shirts that complete a message/pattern printed on them only when couples wearing them stand next to each other are becoming popular.

Tony: We got our couple ring taken care of… Whats next?
Mia: Oh! *Couple tees* to make everyone cringe!

(cun-ning)
컨닝 Cunning

Cheating on a Test

A Konglish word for "cheating (on a test)," it is believed to have originated from the English word "cunning," which is "clever" in a bad way, such as tricking others to get what they want.

If someone could make it to Harvard solely by *cunning* his way through, is he a genius?

(da-dan-gye)
다단계 Da Dan Gye

Pyramid Scheme/Scam

Literal meaning is "multiple steps/phases" and refers to a business model that recruits members with a promise of payments/commission sharing for enrolling others into the scheme, instead of actual investments or sale of products or services. While it might sound like a solid business model, it is actually unsustainable and even illegal in many countries because only the people at the higher level profit from membership fees from the new recruits. In Korea, there are many horror stories about going to one of the seminars, finding themselves locked up, and only being released after giving them a hefty "membership fee."

Being part of K-pop fandom is like *dad an gye* but in a good way they all want to spread the goodness, voluntarily.

D Line

Body with Protruding Belly

A term describing the shape of a body where the belly is protruding either due to pregnancy or drinking too much beer, thereby resembling the letter "*D*". Unlike "S Line", this is the type of body idols wouldn't want.

Look at Mingyo's beer belly! He used to have chocolate abs, but now he is a total *D Line*.

(dae-bon)
대본 Dae Bon
Script

The written text or words used in production of a film, movie, drama, TV show, or broadcast. Not adhering to it or forgetting one's assigned line leads to an NG (blooper). In reality TV shows, such as 2 Days & 1 Night, the whole cast is believed to be filming without a script. Improvising one's line That's not in the script is called "애드립" (ad lib).

Sam is such a perfectionist that he even drafted up a **dae bon** for his first date with Sharon.

(dae-se)
대세 Dae Se
Top Trend / All The Rage

"대" (dae) means "big" and "세" (se) means "state/situation". Put together, it means "top trend," which is an important word to keep in mind if you are into K-culture because Korean people are extremely sensitive about the latest trends and being part of them.

Mark: Yo, whats with the polka dot suit?
Peter: Haven't you heard? It's the new trend! **Dae se!**

(daeng-daeng-i)
댕댕이
Daeng Daeng I
Puppy/Dog

It's actually a result of playing with the Korean alphabet fonts that are similar in shape. That is, the correct word for "puppy/dog" is "멍멍이" (meong meong i), but just for fun's sake, people substitute the fonts with similar ones, which happen to be "댕댕이." The English counterpart is Leetspeak, which is a mixture of words spelled incorrectly with numbers for fun (e.g., c3n50red = censored).

Wong: Are you a cat person or a dog person?
Truong: I'm a **daeng daeng i** person! I love dogs!

(dan-ho-bak)
단호박
Dan Ho Bak
To Say No Firmly

"단호" (dan ho) means "firmly/strongly", and "단호박" (dan ho bak) means "sweet pumpkin." It's just a wordplay people use for fun (like "no way, Jose!"), meaning "to say no firmly"

Andrew: Hey Sera, what are you doing this Fri…
Sera: No.
Andrew: Wow, what a **dan ho bak**…

다음 Da Eum

"Next", "Later"

Also the name of Korea's second-largest Internet portal (spelled Daum).

Hoon: Hey Sohee, I've got a whole collection of WAWA's pictures you might like. Do you like this? This? What about this?
Sohee: Hm... **Da Eum! Da Eum!** Oh, stop, I like this one.

다나까 Da Na Kka

(da-na-kka)

Military Style Talking

Military-style talking where every sentence has to end in either **Da**, **Na**, or **Kka**, which are the formal/official tones of the Korean language. It became extremely popular thanks to the mega-hit K-drama Descendants of the Sun, a romantic story with a military battlefield as the backdrop.

Girl: Doc, my boyfriend has been acting weird lately.
Doc: What's the matter?
Girl: His sentences all end in ~*da*, ~*na*, ~*kka*.
Doc: Oh, is he in the army?
Girl: Impossible. He was too obese to go to the army.

답정너 Dab Jeong Neo

(dap-jŏng-nŏ)

"Askhole"

Short for **답은** *dab eun* "answer (is)" **정해져있다** *jeonghaejyeo itda* ("already decided") **너는** *neo neun* ("you") **대답만해라** *daedapman haera* ("just answer"). It refers to someone who constantly asks for your advice but always does whatever they want. (Why ask then?)

Girlfriend: Honey, should I wear the pink dress or the blue dress?
Boyfriend: I think the blue one looks good on you.
Girlfriend: Hm, I will just wear the pink one.
Boyfriend: You are a **dab jeong neo**, aren't you?

대륙 Dae Ryuk

(dae-ryuk)

China

The literal meaning is "continent" or "land mass". The term, mostly used among the younger generation on the Internet, became a nickname for China due to the fact that the country boasts a massive amount of land and population. It is most frequently used in the form of "**대륙의**" *dae ryuk eui* ~sth = "sth of China". For example, "**대륙의 기상** (*gi sang* "spirit")" is 'The Spirit of China'.

Xiao: Look at me! I just ate 30 dumplings for lunch!
Tomo: Man, that's what I call **dae ryuk** style!

대박 Daebak (dae-bak)

Jackpot, "Incredible"

A term that can be used to express amazement and excitement. Can be translated as "jackpot", "big win", "awesome", or "incredible". It is said to be one of the most common expressions used by teenage girls in Korea. As for the origin, one theory suggests that it's a combination of the Chinese word 대 大 *dae* "big" and 박 *bak* 舶 "full ship" = "big fortune." Another theory traces its roots back to the story of 흥부놀부 *heungbu nolbu*, a Korean traditional folk tale, where a poor couple treats a swallow with a broken leg which visits them with a bunch of gourd seeds to pay back the favor. When the couple split the gourds that grew so large, they found jewels and gemstones inside them. Here, 박 *bak* also means "gourd," so 대박 means "big gourd" = "big fortune."

KOKO's new digital single all-killed the charts! It is a *daebak* album! I just saw Alisha in Myeongdong! *D-A-E-B-A-K*!

닥살 Dak Sal (dak-sal)

Goosebumps, Disgusting

Literal meaning is "chicken skin". In Korean, it has a dual meaning – 1) Disgusting (negative) - when seeing a couple performing PDA (public display of affection) and 2) Goosebumps (positive) - when watching your favorite bias perform on the stage.

(At a K-pop idol concert)

Fan Girl 1: OMG!!!!!!!!!!! OMG!!!!!!!
Fan Girl 2: *OPPA*! I LOVE YOU!!!!!!!
Fan Girl 3: MARRY ME!!!!!!!!!!!!!!!
Fan Girl 1: LOL I feel like a chicken. Look at all these *dak sal*.
Fan Girl 2 & 3: Buc Buc Buc Buc? Buc Buc Buc Buc!

대상 Daesang (dae-sang)

Grand Prize, Top Award

대 *dae* "big" + 상 *sang* "prize/award" Most prestigious award one can receive.

Wow! Soye won the *daesang* at KBC's Diamond Disk Awards!

단톡 Dan Tok (dan-tok)

Group Chat

One of the many functions provided by chat apps such as Kakao Talk, where one can invite other users to talk in a group setting.
While the intentions are good, in most cases, many employees feel like falling into a hell hole when it is created by their workplace boss, who uses it to monitor and control subordinates.

Sumi: Hey, can you please invite me to the *dan tok* room?
Lola: Are you sure? Our boss will send texts non-stop!

당근 Dang Geun

(dang-gŭn)

"Fo' Sho"

Literally means "carrot", but it is also a mutated/fun version of the phrase "당연" *dang yeon* ("of course/absolutely").

Mom: Did you have carrots today?
Son: **Dang geun**!
Mom: Yes, carrots.
Son: Oh, I mean, of course!

대시 Dash

To Make a Move/
Ask Someone Out

"To make a move/ask someone out". Valentine's Day and Christmas Day are among the most popular days for this.

Minho: I really like her, but I am not sure if she will say yes if I asked her out…
Samantha: Duh, there is only one way to find out! **Dash**!

DBSK
Dong Bang Shin K

Korean abbreviation of **D**ong **B**ang **S**hin **K**i, which is the second most commonly used acronym after the Chinese version TVXQ.

Chin: Do you know what **DBSK** means?
Ursula: Yes. Dong Bang Shin Ki!

다크호스 Dark Horse

A Little Known Candidate or Competitor Who Emerges to Prominence

19th-century horse racing slang that is more popularly used in Korea than in other English-speaking countries. You can hear the word in "variety" TV shows that involve competition, such as Our Neighborhood Arts and Physical Education (Cool Kiz On The Block).

Michael: Ha! You didn't know I've been practicing StarCraft every day for the tournament, did you?
Sam: Damn, man! You da real **dark horse** now!

(tdŭn-gŭm-po)

뜬금포 Ddeun Geum Po

Something Totally
Unexpected/Random

"뜬금" *ddeun geum* means "random" or "unexpected" and "포" (*po*) means "firing (a weapon)". It originally means an unexpected home run in baseball but has recently made its way into everyday conversation. If someone says something out of the blue, you say this.

Kyle: Um, I think I want to thank you for being my friend.
Donnie: Huh? Why? That was a **ddeun geum po**.

(tdal-ba-bo)
딸바보
Ddal Babo

Daughter's Daddy

딸 *ddal* "daugther" + 바보 *babo* "fool". The literal meaning is "daughter-fool", which can be roughly translated as "daughter-crazy". It refers to a daddy who adores, is crazy about, and willing to do anything for his daughter. This is to the point that it makes him love-blind, thereby looking like a **babo** (fool). The term became popular because of a popular reality TV show *The Return of Superman* that featured awe-provoking episodes of Choo Seong-hoon and his adorable daughter Sarang-i.

Tina: Damn, John is with his daughter 24/7.
Thomas: Yeah, he is such a **ddal babo**.

(tda-bong)
따봉 Dda Bong

"Thumbs Up"

An expression used to display amazement or satisfaction with your thumb(s) up. It is actually a Portuguese word "Está bom", which means "It is good". It became extremely popular thanks to a Korean orange juice TV commercial in the 1980s that shows a group of Korean buyers visiting an orange farm in Brazil. Upon inspection, the Korean buyer says the word with his thumb up, and the farmers go crazy in excitement, all dancing the Samba. Since then, it has been synonymous with "The Best".

Mom: Son, what do you say I raise your allowance?
Son: **Dda bong**!

(tdong-cha)
똥차 Ddong Cha

Ex-boyfriend

A compound word made up of "똥" *ddong* ("poop") + "차" *cha* ("car"), meaning "honey wagon". The word 똥 is used as a prefix to emphasize that something is of low quality. It is a figurative expression referring to an ex-boyfriend who had disappointed and hurt you and is often used as "forget the **ddong cha** and wait for a brand new Mercedes (new relationship)."

Fei: Ha! That **ddong cha** keeps calling me! I wonder what he's up to now.
Judy: Huh? Are you trying to buy a used car?
Fei: No, I meant my ex-boyfriend.

득템 Deuk Tem (dük-tem)

Getting a Good Deal on Something

A term that originated from MMORPG (Massively Multiplayer Online Role-playing Games), where a player gains the abandoned item of another character or receives something unexpected as a reward for a battle won.

Toby: Oh, yes! **Deuk Tem**!
John: What did you get?
Toby: I bought an iPhone 6S for $35!
John: Let me see? Hm, it says iPhome, not iPhone.
Toby: Hot dang it… Thought it was too good to be true…

Who? 듣보잡 Deut BoJab (düt-bo-jap)

Someone/Something of No Importance

An abbreviation for "듣도" *deut do* ("ever heard") + "보도" *bo do* ("ever seen") + "못한" *mot han* ("never") + "잡것" *jab geot* ("ragtag") = "someone you have never heard or seen". It is used to hurt someone's self-esteem and is most effective when used in the most condescending way possible.

Heena: Hm… This dude on Craigslist is selling Louicici Fendini Vuittonius clutch bag for $5. It sounds like a designer brand but for just $5? Have you heard of this brand?
Uma: Nah, never heard of it. It must be a **deut bo jab** .

Digital Single

Music Track Only Available Through Online Channels

Music track only available through online channels (i.e., download and streaming).

It's official! Tin Tin just released their **digital single**! Available for download at Soribada now.

디스패치 Dispatch

The CIA of the Korean Showbiz Industry

Established in 2010, it is an Internet-based news agency that focuses on celebrity gossip and breaking news. It is currently the most dominant agency in the industry. It is said that many of the reporters are former entertainment reporters. It is most famous for delivering exclusive stories on celebrity dating scenes by what some consider paparazzi-style yellow journalism, but fans love it.

Tony: Dang! Jaeho's on **Dispatch**!
Micky: Huh? **Dispatch**? It better be something good! Otherwise, they are done.

도촬 Do Chwal *(do-chwal)*

Taking Pictures Without Permission

It is an abbreviation for 도둑 *do dook* ("thief") + 촬영 *chwal yeong* ("filming"). It is a behavior associated with someone who is a "peeping tom" and gains sexual gratification through secretly watching people undressing or engaging in sexual activities. Many K-pop idols are victimized by extreme *sasaeng fans*, who engage in extreme measures to capture their private lives.

Mina: Hey mister! Did you just **do chwal** me?
Man: Um, I was just sending a text message with my phone. Here, mine doesn't even have a camera.
Mina: But you would have if you had a camera, right?
Man: *A nwa…*

Dol

Idol

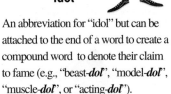

An abbreviation for "idol" but can be attached to the end of a word to create a compound word to denote their claim to fame (e.g., "beast-*dol*", "model-*dol*", "muscle-*dol*", or "acting-*dol*").

Taekyo has such an awesome body. He is my favorite muscle-**dol**.
Hyomin sure can act! She's done an awesome job as a supporting actor in the movie. She probably is the best acting-**dol** available today.

돌직구 Dol Jik Goo *(dol-jik-hu)*

Very Straight Forward Comment (Question)

"돌" *dol* means "rock" and "직구" *jik goo* means "fast ball". Literal meaning is "a powerful (rock-solid) fastball" but is used to describe a "very straightforward comment (question)". It is most effective if used when the listener is least expecting it.

Baby: Grandma, why does mom look so different without makeup?
Mother-in-Law: I guess babies really can't lie.
Dad: That is the most destructive **dol jik goo** I've ever heard…
Mom: …...

Why are you so stupid?

돌싱 Dol Sing *(dol-sing)*

Recently Divorced Person

An abbreviation for "돌아온" *dol ah on* ("returned") "싱글" *sin*gle, to mean "returned to being single". It is also used for idols who come back as a solo artist after a period of being part of a group.

Julian: Wow, who's that lady?
Yona: Oh, that's Miriam from Mexico.
Julian: Does she have a boyfriend?
Yona: All I know is that she is a **dol sing**.
Juna: Doesn't matter if she was once married or not!

(dong-an)
동안 Dong An

Face That Looks Younger Than Actual Age

동 *dong* "baby/youthful" + 안 *an* "face". This is a huge compliment, especially for someone well up in years.

> Wonjun is in his 30's, but he looks like a teenager. Such a *dong an* he has!

Dream Concert

Biggest Annual K-pop Concert

The biggest annual K-pop concert where as many as 32 high-profile singers/groups participate. Each yearly renewal has a theme, such as "Viva Korea" or "Cheer up, Korea".

> Are you going to this year's *Dream Concert*? I heard that all top 10 idol groups will perform!

(dong-saeng)
동생 Dong Saeng

Younger Sibling

A term for a younger sibling, but it can be used for anyone younger, regardless of gender. It can be used in place of someone's name, as an appellation.

> Hyoju is my favorite *dong saeng*.
> Although Bohye is my *dong saeng*, she is so mature that I often feel like I am her *dong saeng*.

(dŭ-rip)
드립 Drib

Joke Attempt

A term derived from the broadcast lingo "ad lib", which is saying something spontaneously or improvising, most frequently used in sitcoms and variety shows. It often catches other actors off-guard and causes a series of laughter, leading to an NG ("blooper").

> Yena: Oh no! Jennie's got so wasted.
> Robert: So wasted that she belongs in a trash can!
> Yena: Oh man, that was a horrible *drib*.
> Robert: Yeah, I agree.

K-POP

HAVE A MICE DAY!

덕후 Dukhoo
(dŏ-ku)

Someone Who is Overly Obsessed With Something (Culture/Object)

Originated from the Japanese term *otaku*, which is often translated as "geek" or "mania", but if it's severe in its level of obsession, it can become an object of mockery.

Kong: What are you doing, buddy?
Neal: I'm having a romantic time with my girlfriend Yumi. Can't you see?
Kong: Dude… That is just a cardboard cutout of her…
Yumi: How dare you! She is my true love!
Kong: You are such a *dukhoo*…

동공지진 Dong Gong Ji Jin
(dong-gong-ji-jin)

Flustered

Literal meaning is "pupil earthquake" because "**동공**" (*dong gong*) means "pupil" and "**지진**" (*ji jin*) means "earthquake." Put together, it describes eyes darting, something that happens when you are flustered/appalled.

My nephew looks like he's going to be a huge TWICE fan when he grows up… I saw *dong gong ji jin* in his eyes when I showed him them performing on TV.

뒷북 Dwit Book
(dwit-buk)

Fuss Around After The Event, or One Step Behind

It refers to the act of making a late response and being slow in understanding.

Kiho: Hey! Do you know *Gangnam Style*? I heard it is the hottest K-pop now.
Youngsoo: That's a *dwit book*… That was in 2012, and we are in 2016. Get with the program, man!

더치페이 Dutch Pay

Going Dutch

A Konglish term for "going Dutch" and is used interchangeable with "n빵 *en-bbang*".

She slapped me in the face when I suggested having a *Dutch pay* at her birthday dinner.

(dok-gŏ-no-in)

독거노인
Dok Geo No In

Old People Who Live Alone

"**독거**" (*dok geo*) means "living alone" + "**노인**" (*no in*) means "old person." Put together, it refers to "old person who live alone," but young people who live alone jokingly call themselves this for fun.

If Taeyang ever becomes a *dok geo no in*, I'd take care of him 24/7.

(dok-su-ri)

독수리 Dok Su Ri

U.S. Citizen

Its literal meaning is "eagle" but is used as a slang term to refer to a U.S. citizen because the (bald) eagle is the symbol of the U.S.

Wayne: Oh! Here comes a *dok su ri*!
Kim: I don't see any eagles around here.
Wayne: LOL, I'm talking about Mr. Smith, our English teacher from San Diego.

(dok-sŏl)

독설 Dok Seol

Spiteful Remark / Vitriol

"**독**" (*dok*, "poison," "venom") + "**설**" (*seol*, "tongue," "saying"). It refers to a spiteful, violent remark full of bitterness and hate that causes distress and pain to the recipient. Some people like Kim Goo-ra 김구라 and Park Myung-soo 박명수 have successfully incorporated it (more of a tongue-in-cheek style, though) into their character gimmick and gained popularity.

He called me fat! It was a *dok seol* that hurt my feelings, but it served as a good inspiration that got me started working out.

(dol-pa-ri)

돌팔이 Dol Pal I

Charlatan

"**돌**" (*dol*) comes from the word "**돌아다니다**" (*dol a da ni da*, "to roam/wander around") + "**팔이**" (*pal i* "seller" (pronounced as "*pa ri*"). Put together, it means "someone who roams around selling (rubbish, fake) things" = "a snake oil salesman and is used to refer to a charlatan.

WTF… my doctor prescribed Tiger Balm for my indigestion… I think he's a *dol pal i*…

단짠 DanJjan
(dan-tchan)

Sweet & Salty

A newly-coined slang word, short for "단 (*dan*, "sweet") + 짠 (*jjan*, "salty"), which describes the physiology of taste in which eating something salty makes you crave sweets, and eating something sweet makes you want to eat something salty again... and the cycle goes on and on. It's a term often used in "먹방" (*muk/meokbang*, "eating show").

I just finished a whole tub of ice cream and now I'm craving Doritos! It's the *dan jjan* cycle!

단콘 Dan Con
(dan-con)

Solo Concert

Short for "단독" (*dan dok*, "solo", "single") + "콘서트" ("concert"). It's usually the result of the management company's decision to promote a specific member who has good vocal skills as a solo singer.

Daesung from Big Bang is having a *dan con* because, as we all know, his voice is just out of this world.

똥배 Ddong Bae
(tdong-bae)

Beer Belly / Pot Belly

It's a compound word made of "뚱뚱한" (*ddong ddong han*, "fat/plump/chubby") + "배" (*bae*, "belly/stomach/abdomen"). It's something you will find cute if you are still in the honeymoon phase with your significant other.

It's not a *ddong bae*; its my six-pack abs I combined into one.

덕질 DeokJil
(dŏk-jil)

Geeking Out / Being A Fanboy/Fangirl

Short for "덕후" (*deok hu*, "otaku", "geek") + "질" (*jil*, "doing"). It refers to the act of geeking out or simply being yourself as a fanboy/fangirl!

BTS shoes, BTS wallpaper, BTS phone case, and BTS everything... It's a BTS *deok jil*, and I love doing it!

덕밍아웃
Deok Ming Out

To Openly Announce Oneself As A Fanboy/Fangirl

"덕후" (*deok hu*,"otaku","Geek/Buff' or "someone who is overly obsessed with something (culture/object)") + "커밍아웃" (co**ming out**) = its the act of officially coming out as a fan.

> You know that dude who kept making fun of us for K-popping? Guess what? I caught him dancing to AOA's song on YouTube, and he reluctantly made a ***deok ming out!*** He was actually one of us!

디카
Di Ca

Digital Camera

Abbreviation for "**di**gital **ca**mera," the usage of the term has been rapidly decreasing due to the widespread use of smartphones that feature their own built-in cameras.

> ***Di ca**'s* are not allowed at fan signing events, but smartphones are allowed!

등골 브레이커
Deung Gol Breaker

Someone/Something That Burns a Hole in One's Pocket

"등골" (*deung gol*) means "spine/back bone." Put with "**breaker**", it means something that breaks your spine, and its idiomatically used to refer to something/someone that costs you an arm and a leg because it comes from a Korean expression "등골이 부러지다 (*deung gol i bu reo ji da*) = "breaks my back" = working hard to make money to the point where it breaks your back.

> ZE:A is a real ***deung gol breaker*** for me because I spend everything I have buying their merchandise.

도깨비 Do Kkae Bi

Korean Goblin

Also known as Korean goblins, they are legendary creatures from Korean mythology and folklore that are believed to possess extraordinary powers and abilities. They like to play tricks on humans but also like to help them. It was also the name of a hit K-drama featuring Gong Yoo (English title = Goblin: The Lonely and Great God).

> What? You were in Los Angeles last night and now you are in Seoul? Are you a ***do kkae bi***?

어그로 Eo Geu Ro
(ŏ-gŭ-ro)

Fishing for Attention

Derived from the words "aggravation" and "aggression" it's a term used in massively multiplayer online role-playing game (MMORPG) such as WoW (World of Warcraft). In the game, when a group of players go on a monster hunt, a monster would go after the player who damaged it the most. Because of this, Internet users started using it to refer to someone who purposely engages in radical/stupid behavior in order to draw attention.

Tony, an infamous Internet troll, posted a comment saying K-pop actually originated in North Korea, and it was a big successful *eo geu ro* – over 3,000 people bombarded it.

에바 E Ba
(e-ba)

Over Reaction

Kids' and teenagers' way of saying "over reaction", but a theory claims it is actually a compound word made up of "**er**ror + o**ver** = e**va** = **e ba**". Regardless of its origin, it is used to describe the act of going too far or exaggerating too much.

Reina: Oh my god! I think BTB oppa likes me!
Joey: Why do you say that?
Reina: I got his autograph today, and he drew a little heart! I think that's a secret message he's sending to me!
Joey: That's a little *e ba*… He always does that to his fans.

E.L.F

Super Junior Fan Club

The name of the Super Junior fan club, short for "EverLasting Friends". Fan color is pearl sapphire blue.

Super Junior *oppas*! We will always be your Everlasting Friends! *E. L. F*!

엑박 Ek Bak
(ek-bak)

"Image Not Found"

An abbreviation for "엑스" *eks* ("x") + "박스" *bakseu* ("box") = "X-Box". It is not the name of the video game console by Microsoft. It refers to an error message caused by a broken image in a web browser, due to the file being not present or other possible issues. The error message is graphically represented by an empty box with an "x" symbol inside, hence the term.

Woody: What? Why am I getting all these *ek bak*s? I want to see AOB's new photos!
Ming: Sorry, man, our Internet has been disconnected. We haven't paid the bill for the past 6 months.

어부바 Eo Boo Ba
(ŏ-bu-ba)

Piggy Back

One carrying another on their back. In K-dramas, this is when "drunk love confessions" are made because it is often a guy carrying a drunk girl on his back, while the girl often blurts out her affection unconsciously.

Eunice drank so much *soju* last night I had to give her an **eo boo ba**, and guess what? She unconsciously confessed that she likes me!

어장관리 Eo Jang Gwan Ri
(ŏ-jang-gwan-li)

"To keep someone on the hook/to lead someone on"

Literally means "management of fishing ground" and is used to describe the act of pretending to be interested in the opposite sex, without a genuine intention to advance the relationship. The "fish" gets confused to the point where they wonder if they are in a relationship or not.

Shina: Hm, Jimmy keeps texting me every day but never asks me out. I wonder if he really likes me
Wondo: Sounds fishy to me… My bet is that he is just doing **eo jang gwan ri** on you. Stay away from him!

어머니 Eomeoni (Omoni)
(ŏ-mŏ-ni)

Mother

Formal way of saying "엄마" *eomma* ("mom") and for that reason, it is the polite way to address someone else's mother, like a mother-in-law.

Jenny: I am so nervous because **eomeoni** will be here for the weekend.
Soya: Your mother?
Jenny: No, my mother-in-law!

언플 Eon Peul
(ŏn-pŭl)

Promoting Through the Media

A Korean term that can be translated as "playing around with the media" to gain an (unfair) advantage. It is termed so because entertainment companies use the media to promote their singers/groups. Common tactics include writing/disseminating press releases, news articles, and gossip creation.

Man, just today, I read 5 articles about Miryo! Her company does so much **eon peul**!

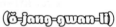

DAILY NEWS
World · Buisness · Finance · Lifestyle · Travel · Sport · Weather

(ŏ-sŏo-se-yo)
어서 오세요
Eoseo Oseyo

"Welcome" "Please Come in"

"어서" *eoseo* means "quickly", "promptly" and "오세요" *ose*yo means "please come". It is what a host says to greet guests.

(At Hong Kong International Airport)
Mingyu: Damn! Look at all these people! They think I am a K-pop Idol! Everyone is holding a sign that says *eoso oseyo*! I feel super welcome!
Hyeon: Um… maybe not? Our schedule just coincided with a real K-pop group.

(ŭi-ri)
의리 Eui Ri
Loyalty

A wild card term that became extremely popular in 2015 because of a *shikye* (a traditional sweet Korean rice beverage) CF featuring Kim Bo-seong, a middle-aged action movie star famous for saying the word *"eui ri"* every time he has a chance (he believes *"eui ri"* is the most important and the manliest thing in the world. He uses it as an excuse/answer for everything he does). The CF comically incorporated the word into product descriptions (e.g., saying "Americano" as "Ame *"eu ri"* cano"), and it became a hit. Aside from its actual meaning, people utter it simply for fun.

Bo: Yes! I finished my homework! *Eui ri*!
James: Good job, buddy! Want to go grab a beer or something?
Bo: *Eui ri*! Let's go! *Eui ri*!
James: Oh well, you don't have to say that in every sentence, but whatever makes you sleep at night…

(ŭng-wŏn)
응원 Eung Won
Supporting

In K-pop, it refers to the "fan chants" during a song that show support for their idols, often accompanied by thunder sticks (bam bams) or glow sticks to create a wave of "fan light".

May: Light sticks? Check! Slogans? Check!
April: It's *eung wo*n time!

Eye Smile

The Shape of Eyes Becoming a Crescent While Smiling

The shape of the eyes becoming a crescent shape while smiling, thereby forming its own smile. This could be a stealthy way of flirting and showing affection.

Nina's *eye smiles* are so seductive and flirty that so many guys get fooled into thinking she likes them.

(öm-bba-ju-üi)
엄빠주의
Eom Bba Ju Eui

MOS (Mom Over Shoulder) / DOS (Dad Over Shoulder)

"엄빠 (*eom bba*)" is an abbreviation for "엄마 + 아빠 (*eom ma* + a *bba*)" meaning "mom + dad". Similar to NSFW (Not Safe for Work), it serves as a warning that the Internet content you are about to run into might be inappropriate (nudity, violence, profanity, etc.) to be accessed/viewed with your parents around you.

GF: Hey honey, I'm going to send you my bikini pic..So if you're home, *eom bba ju eui*!

(öm-ji-chök)
엄지척
Eom Ji Cheok

Thumbs Up

엄지 (*eom ji*, "thumb") + 척 (*cheok* - a word describing the motion of raising a thumb), hence it means "thumbs up."

I woke up with the worst hangover. Not remembering anything from last night, I texted my girlfriend saying, "Did I say something stupid last night?" and she just replied with an *eom ji cheok*... Don't know if she's being sarcastic or not... scary!

(üm-bang)
음방 Eum Bang

Music TV Show

Short for "음악" (*eum ak*, "music") + "방송" (*bang song*, "broadcast"). This is where you can watch your favorite idol groups perform live without having to go to a concert. Popular shows include *Inkigayo* (SBS), *Music Bank* (KBS 2), *M Countdown* (Mnet), and *Pops in Seoul* (Arirang TV).

Wow, I was surprised to see Lee Kwang Soo on an *eum bang* but was even more surprised when he started singing -- he really can sing!

(üi-nü-nim
의느님
Eui Neu Nim

Plastic Surgeon

A compound word made of "의사" (*eui sa*, "doctor") + "하느님" (*ha neu nim*, "god"). It refers to a plastic surgeon because they have the ability to change the life of a person through plastic surgery (from ugly to super hot), and they are likened to god because their ability is at the same level as the omnipotent god's divine power who controls our destiny.

Thank you *eui neu nim* for the beautiful new face you gave me...

음란마귀
Eum Ran Ma Gwi

Dirty Mind Illusion

"음란" (*eum ran*) means "obscene" + "마귀" (*ma gwi*) meaning "devil". Put together, it could be translated as "naughty devil", and it refers to the phenomenon of wrongly perceiving or interpreting completely normal things in a sexual way.

When I was filling out a job application, I blushed at the word "SEX", which was asking my gender. I must have an *eum ran ma gwi* in me.

음치 Eum Chi

Someone Who Can't Carry a Tune

"음" (*eum*) means "sound" and "치" (*chi*) means "stupid/ridiculous." Put together, it refers to someone who totally lacks musical talent and is not able to follow melodic lines when singing.

The most incredible fact about *eum chi* people is that they don't realize they are actually one until someone tells them.

응원봉
Eung Won Bong

Light Stick

"응원" (*eung won*, "cheering/support") + "봉" (*bong*, "stick"). A popular concert item the fans use to show their support and love during the performance of an artist. Fan clubs have their own "fan color," and members buy light sticks that have the corresponding color.

"Are lightsabers a type of *eung won bong*?" says a non-Star Wars fan.

Evil Maknae

It refers to the type of *maknaes* (the youngest member of a group) who doesn't possess the traditional/typical *maknae* qualities. They are often mischievous and naughty towards older group members, including the leader, but everybody just loves them because, after all, they are just adorable *maknaes*. It was also a nickname for Kyuhyun of Super Junior.

We have a new member in the band, and I have a feeling he will be an *evil maknae*… He is such a prankster!

EXID

EXID stands for "**EX**ceed **I**n **D**reaming" and is a five-member (Solji, LE, Hani, Hyelin, Jeonghwa) girl group formed by Banana Culture Entertainment. They debuted in 2012 with a song titled "Whoz That Girl," but they reached the peak of their career with the single "Up & Down," which climbed the charts four months after its release thanks to a fan-recording of a live performance that went viral. They created a subunit named "Dasoni," which consists of Hani and Solji in 2013. In 2016, they hosted a reality show on MBC Every1, titled EXID Showtime. Notable songs include "Ah Yeah," "Hot Pink," and "DDD".

All weak girl groups need to EXIT when *EXID* makes an entrance because they are the best!

EXO

EXO stands for "**EXO**PLANET" and is a nine-member (Xiumin, Suho, Lay, Baekhyun, Chen, Chanyeol, D.O., Kai, Sehun) boy group formed by S.M. Entertainment. They debuted in 2012 with a song titled "MAMA" and have become an international act since then. Their song "Growl" from the album "XOXO" (2013) instantly became a smash hit, helping them earn both Disc Daesang at the 28th Golden Disc Awards and Album of The Year at the 15th MAMA. The album sold over 1 million copies, and so did their second and third albums. In 2018, they performed at the closing ceremony of The 2018 Pyeongchang Winter Olympics. Notable songs include "Overdose," "Love Me Right," "Monster," and "Ko Ko Bop."

The reason people call *EXO* oppas from out of this world? Their name means *EXO* Planet!

EXO-L

EXO Fan Club

The name of the EXO fan club, and it means "**EXO**-L(OVE)." Their slogan is "We Are One", and the fan color is cosmic latte.

EXO-L doesn't meant Exo-Large. It means "Exo-Love!"

아이쇼핑 Eye Shopping

Window Shopping

A Konglish term for "window shopping," referring to the activity of looking at products in store windows without intending to buy any of them. Nowadays, surfing online stores without actually buying any of the items counts as well.

Hannah: Hm… who should I pick as my future husband? Suga? Jung Kook? G-Dragon?
Zack: Why do you even worry? They are not going to marry you!
Hannah: Oh come on… I'm just *eye shopping*! Don't ruin the fun ;)

팬카페
Fan Cafeé

Online Fan Forum

An online fan forum mainly consisting of message/bulletin boards, a photo gallery, and a chat room. Unlike the official homepage, its run by the fans. It's probably the go-to place for the latest news/rumors because you can interact with other fans on a real-time basis and see rare fan photos/clips. Most of the fan cafes are based on the Naver or Daum platform that requires you to sign up for a user ID in order to participate. They usually have a leveling up system, based on the amount of participation or contribution. The higher your level becomes, the more privileges you get, such as being able to see private posts that are reserved for a certain level of members only. The only downside is that most of them are managed in Korean, and user IDs are available only to Korean nationals and residents.

The only downside about *fan cafes* is that you can't sit down to have a cup of coffee.

(paen-shim)
팬심
Fan Shim /
Fan Heart

Feelings You Have Towards a Bias

A word composed of an English letter and a Chinese letter - **fan** + "心" (*shim*, "heart"). It includes the full emotional spectrum as a fan - admiration, excitement, compassion, anger, disappointment, etc.

Paul thinks she's following TWICE members purely out of *fan shim*, but everyone thinks he's a STAN!

Fansub

Subtitles Translated by Fans

It refers to the subtitles of a foreign film or a TV program that has been translated by fans, purely out of their fan heart. Often they are more complete than other subtitles because many of the translations require full knowledge of the story to be accurately translated - its best to be translated by someone who knows the story well.

Big thanks to all *Fansub* makers around the world! If it weren't for your help, at least half of the globe would have been missing out on K-pop!

(pi-shöl)
피셜 Ficial

Official

Originating from the English word "official," it indicates that the source of a story/rumor is a credible one. When used as a suffix, it describes where the story is coming from. For example, "뇌 (*noe*, "brain") 피셜" means it comes from one's brain, which is, of course, not a credible source, therefore deemed delusional.

Ricardo: Dude! Did you know that, if you don't do your homework, you get stopped at a K-pop concert!
Mo: What? For real?
Ricardo: Yeah! My mom told me that! It's mom*ficial*!

팬캠 Fan Cam

Footage Taken Directly by Fans

In contrast to those taken by professionals (e.g., photographers (paparazzi), journalists, reporters), this refers to moments (photos and videos) captured directly by fans (at concerts and fan events, you can see everyone is holding up their smartphones). Do not confuse this with the term "*sasaeng*", which refers to fans going to extremes (i.e., sneaking into a bias's home, which is a criminal offense).

Jin: Dang… Juno Juno has been charged with assault!
Bernard: Yeah, I heard everything was caught on that *fan cam* after the concert.

Fan Chant

Fans Chanting During a Performance to Show Support

Words chanted by the fans in the audience during a performance or a particular song to express their support and love. It is mostly the names of the singers and is usually shouted during the part where the singers are not singing.

Lee-Joo-Bin! Lee-Joo-Bin! One and Only Lee-Joo-Bin! The members of Lee Joo Bin's fan club, One and Only, shouted their signature *fan chant*.

Fan Club

Faction

An organized group of fans who engage in various activities to support their idol singers or groups. They usually have their own club name, meaning, color, and often have rival fan clubs.

I really like Eun Sung, so I joined the *fan club* Shooting Star! The name comes from her name Sung, which means star, and the official color is bright silver just like a star in the universe.

Fan Fiction

Fictional Stories Written by Fans Starring Their Favorite Idols

Fictional stories written by fans, starring their favorite idols. The storyline usually involves conflicts and romance.

Kayla is so talented at writing **fan fiction**. I asked her to write one with me and Junho in it. Of course, I was the love of his life in the story.

Fan Service

Something Idols Do to Please Their Fans

Something idols do to please their fans, both voluntarily and by request, such as singing a special song or making a cute gesture.

Seho Oppa! Please do the *bbuing bbuing* dance? Seho puts his fists up under his eyes and moves them in circular directions saying *bbuing bbuing*. Awwwww, Seho Oppa's **fan service** is the best!

Fan Wars

Brutal Warfare Between Fan Clubs

A brutal warfare between the fans of one idol group against the fans of another.

They totally ruined our Oppa's performance by creating a black ocean! Argggh! It's a **fan war**!

Fandom

Community of Fans

A community of fans who share a common interest, empathy, and camaraderie toward idols, groups, TV shows, movies, books, etc.

I think the TV show 'I Love You, You Love Me' has the biggest **fandom** among many reality shows because they have members from 5 different idol groups.

Fashionista

Someone Who Has a Great Sense of Fashion

Someone who has a great sense of fashion, such as GD of Big Bang. The opposite is "Fashion Terrorist".

My Oppa can make a really good model. Not only is he tall and slim, but he also understands fashion. He is such a *fashionista*!

Feels

Overwhelming Waves of Emotions

Overwhelming waves of emotions sometimes resulting in screaming and crying, which can't be easily explained or described with words.

The lyrics of J-Pay's new song are so romantic that watching J-Pay's MV gives me the *feels*, fooling my mind to think I am in love with him.

(hwa-i-ting)
화이팅 Fighting/ Hwaiting

"Cheers. Let's fight!" / Let's Go!"

Something said to promote a sense of unity. It can be said to show support for someone, especially in sports events. In a monologue, it is used to give the speaker a confidence boost.

Korea vs. Japan soccer game tonight! Team Korea *fighting*! Okay, I can do this… *hwaiting*! Hey sis, I heard you are having an exam today. *Fighting*!

Finger Heart

A Cute Way of Showing Affection

The act of crossing two fingers, thumb and index finger, to form a little heart shape. While there are many theories as to the origin of this hand gesture, no one is 100% sure who invented it.

Jeremy: Here you go! Sonya: Awww, is that a *finger heart*? Jeremy: Nope, just a booger.

가지마 Ga Ji Ma (ga-ji-ma)

"Don't Go"

A magical word used at the most dramatic moment of a K-drama or K-pop M/V. It has an enchanting power that glues together a couple on the verge of breaking up. It is most often used after an intense argument, and just when one decides to leave, the other summons up all their courage and says this, often followed by a back hug.

Girlfriend: We are over. Goodbye. It's been fun.
Boyfriend: *Ga ji ma*!
Girnfriend: Why?
Boyfriend: Can you spare me $5? I have no taxi money.

FT Island

F.T. Island stands for "**Five Treasure Island**" and is a five-member (Choi Jong-hoon, Lee Hong-gi, Lee Jae-in, Song Seung-hyun, Choi Min-hwan) rock band formed by FNC Entertainment. They debuted in 2007 with a song titled "Love Sick," which topped the K-pop charts for eight consecutive weeks. They won "Best New Male Group" at the MAMA in 2007, and Won was chosen as the "Best Rock Musician of The Year" at the Golden Disk Awards in 2011. Notable songs include "Love Love Love," "Thunder," and "Severely."

The only island I want to be stranded on is *FT Island*!

가성비 Ga Seong Bi (ga-sŏng-bi)

Cost-To-Benefit Ratio

Abbreviation for "**가격**" (*ga gyeok*, "cost," "price") + "**성능**" (*seong neung*, "performance") + "**비율**" (*bi yul*, "ratio"), used to determine the amount of benefits you get from spending a certain amount of money or the overall value for money spent. The higher it is, the more bang for the buck you get.

Wayne: Bought this K-CON package for just $30, and it includes unlimited access to concerts, fan signing events, and a backstage pass! Amazing *ga seong bi*! I can't believe I picked it up for just $30!
Dwayne: Dude, it says K-CON 2015... It's 2018 now...
Wayne: Aish!!!!!!!!!!

가심비 Ga Shim Bi (ga-shim-bi)

Price-To-Satisfaction Ratio

Short for "**가격**" (*ga gyeok*, "price") + "**심**" (*shim*, 心, "heart") + "**비**" (*bi*, "ratio"). Unlike the traditional, objective measure of "가성비" (*ga seong bi*, "price-to-performance ratio" = ("cost effectiveness")), it is a subjective measure where the amount of satisfaction you get from purchasing something is most important.

Although I paid a hefty price for it, I'm really glad I did. I got a great *ga shim bi* out of it.

★ ★ ★ ★ ★
GREAT DEAL

가시나 Ga Shi Na
(ga-shi-na)

Girl / Bitch

Originally a Kyeongsang-province dialect for "a girl," but nowadays, it has a slightly negative nuance like "bitch" and is used to address a girl in a demeaning/disrespectful manner. But of course, its casually used among girls who are close to each other. It's also the name of a song by Sunmi.

Doug: Yo! **Ga shi na**!
Jane: Did you just call me a bitc*?
Doug: Nooooooo - I was just singing a song by Sunmi!

개인기 Gae In Gi
(gae-in-gi)

Special Talent

"**개인**" (**gae in**, "personal/individual") + "**기**" (**gi**, "talent/skill"). That unique and special talent one possesses, such as impersonation and being able to take a selfie with a toe (this is EXID Hani's special talent, seriously).

Nowadays, entertainers must have at least a few **gae in gi**s to make them truly stand out from the others

갑질 GabJil
(gab-jil)

Abuse of Power/ To Go On a Power Trip

"**갑**" (**gab**) is the one with the upper-hand, and "**질**" (**jil**) is "doing something That's frowned upon." The arrogant and authoritarian attitude/actions to the degree of power abuse by someone of a higher position to someone of a lower position, such as boss-subordinate or client-contractor relationships.

Dory: Hey~ Who wants a free ticket to the BTS World Tour Concert?
May: Me! Me! Me!!!
Dory: Okay, then do my homework first and then do the dishes.
Mary: What?! It's **gab jil,** man!
Dory: So you don't want the ticket?
Mary: Can I do the dishes first?

겜방 Gaem Bang
(gaem-bang)

PC Bang / Game Show

Short for **겜** (**gaem**, slang word for "game") + **방송** " (**bang song**, "broadcast"). A type of broadcast/show dedicated to video games, reflecting the popularity of video games, which are formally known as "E-Sports" nowadays in Korea. Some of the most watched channels are OnGameNet and SPOTV Games (both cable TV networks), and Afreeca TV (Internet-based platform). It also means PC Bang or Internet cafes.

Did you know that Shawn from Swaggers Club used to be a pro gamer? You can find his game play clips on **gaem bang** channel.

(gae-gŭ co-dŭ)
개그코드 Gag Code

Type of Humor/ Humor Preferences

Also known as "humor code," its mainly used to describe any similarity/difference between people in the way they perceive whats funny.

I like pun jokes, but she likes sarcastic jokes... Our **gag codes** are so different.

(gae-gŭ man)
개그맨 Gag Man

Comedian

A Konglish term meaning comedian, but technically speaking, there are two different types of comedians in Korea. 1) Gag man - entertains people by talking only, such as telling jokes. 2) Comedian - entertains people by engaging in slapstick comedy. Recently, however, the boundaries have blurred somewhat, and they are used interchangeably.

Raina: You think I'd make a good actress?
Wonki: Bwahahaha! With a face like that? Hell no! Maybe a **gag man** because people will go LOL at your face!

(gab-ppa)
갑빠 Gab Bba

Pecks, Chest Muscle

A slang term that refers to (men's) pecs/chest muscle. The origin of the term is unclear, however. Although its a widely used term, you wouldn't hear it in formal conversations or on TV/Radio because its a slang word.

While you were at the bar building your beer belly, I've been working on building my **gab bba** at the gym!

(ga-zŭ-a)
가즈아 Gazua

"Lets Go!"

Originated from the Korean Bitcoin community as an outcry for wishing their cryptocurrency to go up in price after hearing exciting hyped-up news regarding the Bitcoin market. It's an enthusiastic, overly excited way of saying "가자" (**ga ja,** "lets go"). The more "아" (*ah*) you put after the word to make it more drawn-out, the more excited it sounds (e.g., "가즈아 아아아아아" = "lets gooooooooooooooo").

Tiara: I'm tired... Let's just stay home today.
Mark: What? They are having a happy hour at the bar! Unlimited cocktails!
Tiara: For real? **Gazuaaaaaaaaaaaaaaaaa!**

극딜 Geuk Deal (gŭk-dil)

Savage/Huge Damage/Nuking

"극" (*geuk*, "extreme") + "딜" (*dil*, short for "dealing damage"). A term originated in a massively multiplayer online role-playing game (MMORPG), where a player's attack makes huge damage to enemy characters.

> Joanna: Hey baby, don't I look like a cute little puppy? <3
> Victor: Yeah, definitely. You look like a baby pug.
> Joanna: Ouch... That's a *geuk deal*...

극혐 Geuk Hyeom (gŭk-hyŏm)

Extreme Hatred

Short for "극" (*geuk*, "extreme") + "혐오" (*hyeom oh*, "hatred"), but it doesn't carry such a strong connotation as its literal meaning. It's mostly used by teenagers in a playful manner.

> Kira: What the hell is this smell?
> Bo: It's me! I haven't showered for 10 days straight because I love my body odor, which is unique, and I believe others should have a chance to appreciate it.
> Kira: *Geuk hyeom*!!!

금손 Geum Son (gŭm-son)

Extremely Dexterous/Crafty

"금" (*geum*, literal meaning is "gold," but is idiomatically used to refer to something of very high quality) + "손" (*son*, "hand"). Describes someone who is extremely skillful and competent with their hands.

> Whoa! You fixed my broken iPhone! Thank you, Mr. *Geum Son*!

근황 Geun Hwang (gŭn-hwang)

Updates / What One's Been Up To Lately

One's recent activities or what one has been up to lately. This is often the first question of an interview with a celebrity who has come back from a hiatus.

> Tina: Long time no see! Give me your *geun hwang*!
> Mark: Nada mucho... It's been pretty much the same! Eat, Sleep, K-pop, and repeat! ;)

(gŭp-shik-che)
급식체
Geup Shik Che

The Way Teenagers Talk/Text

"**급식**" (*geup sik*, "school lunch (meals)")") +
"**체**" (*che*, "type/style (of text/writing).")
Specifically refers to teenagers because they eat
school lunches (meals). This style includes
excessive use of 1) acronym abbreviations
2) vulgar words 3) puns 4) slang words and
phrases. It all started as a way of secret
communication that wouldn't be detected by
adults.

ㅇㄱㄹㅇ, ㅂㅂㅂㄱ, and ㅇㅈ are examples of *geup shik che*.

(gi-dae-ju)
기대주 Gi Dae Ju

Rising Star / Up-And-Comer / Blue Chip

Literal meaning is "a stock that's expected to
rise in price = "blue chip" and is figuratively
used to refer to someone who's a rising star/up-
and-comer in the industry. It isn't necessarily
limited to young people.

Music Life chose Sparking Boys as the biggest *gi dae ju*
for 2019.

(gi-gye-chi)
기계치 Gi Gye Chi

Gadget Illiterate / Technologically Illiterate

"**기계**" (*gi gye*) means "machine" and "**치**" (*chi*)
means "stupid/ridiculous." Put together, it refers
to someone who is technologically illiterate.
It isn't necessarily limited to older
people—young people can be "기계치" as well.

What? You don't even know how to use an iPad? You
are such a *gi gye chi*!

(gi-ja-hoe-gyŏn)
기자회견
Gi Ja Hoe Gyeon

Press Conference

A meeting initiated by celebrities or their
agencies for the purpose of distributing
information to the media/press. It is when big
announcements are made, such as marriage,
disbandment, or retirement, but is also used for
promotional purposes, such as new movies or
new album releases.

At *gi ja hoe gyeon,* reporters asked very sensitive questions
about his marriage.

(gi-nyŏm-il)
기념일
Gi Nyeom Il

Anniversary

This is something you should always stay on top of, especially if you are a couple, because Korean couples feel obliged to count the days they have been together and to keep track of other important dates. Blocks of 100 days, as well as every yearly mark, are celebrated. Beware - not doing so will make you look not interested in / serious about the relationship and is often a legitimate reason for a break up.

Hyori: I can't believe you forgot what today means for us...
Chanmin: I'm sorry! I really don't know... Fill me in, please?
Hyori: It's our 39th day anniversary *gi nyeom il*!
Chamin: With all due respect... who in the world counts that?!

(gim-pŭ)
김프
Gim/Kim Peu

Price Gap Where It's Significantly Higher in Korea

Something Priced Way Higher in The Korean Market Than Other Markets in The World Short for 김치 (*kimchi*) + 프리미엄 (premium). It originated from the Korean Bitcoin community as a term describing the phenomenon where the same cryptocurrency trades at a significantly higher price (premium) in the Korean market (= kimchi) than any other market in the world. It's a reflection of the surging demand by Korean traders, and this price gap was seen as an arbitrage opportunity by many speculators.

What? Soju is $12 a bottle in the U.S.? It's only $2 in Korea! This is a reverse *gim peu*?

기프티콘
Gifticon

Virtual Gift Card Sent Via Smart Phones

"**Gift**" + "Emo**ticon**," a mobile voucher or virtual gift card sent via smartphones, using chat/messenger apps like Kakao Talk. It's a popular way to express one's gratitude or affection because you can simply purchase it on your phone and send it to another person instantly.

My little brother lives far away from me, so I sent him a McDonald's *gifticon* for his birthday!

고음 Go Eum
(go-ŭm)

High-Note

In the K-pop world, its the ultimate yardstick/standard used to judge the singing ability of a singer. The higher a singer can go, the more capable and talented they are perceived. IU made her name in the K-pop scene with her famous three-level high-note singing in her song "Good Day."

Daesung sounds so sweet when he hits *go eum*.

(go-jeong member)

고정멤버

Go Jeong Member

Regular Cast Member

"고정" (*go jeong*) means "fixed," so "**고정 member**" means those who are contracted to appear in every episode of a show that is composed of the regular cast (MCs, panelists) and special invited guests that could differ from episode to episode. In rare cases, special invited guests who make an outstanding impact on the show are cast and end up becoming regular cast members!

If we hit 3.5% viewer rating tonight, we will make you a *go jeong member*!

(go-kwŏl//jŏ-kwŏl)

고퀄//저퀄

Go Qual/ Jeo Qual

High Quality/Low Quality

"고" (*go*, "high") / "저" (*jeo*, "low") + "**qual**," short for "quality." Mostly used to describe the quality (resolution) of digital content (video clip/photo/music).

Yo... This pic is so grainy... Do you have a *go qual* picture?

(go-rae-ja-bi)

고래잡이

Go Rae Jabi

Circumcision

When the Korean word "포경" (*po gyeong*) is written in Chinese characters (捕鯨), it means "whale hunting" but also sounds the same as the word "circumcision" (homonyms). For this reason, people use the Korean expression "**고래** (*go rae*) "whale" "잡이" (*jabi*, "hunting") to indirectly refer to "circumcision.

Dad: Son! Lets go *go rae jabi*!
Son: Oh! Whale hunting!! I've never been fishing! Yay!
Dad: *giggles*

(go-so-mi)

고소미 Go So Mi

Lawsuit

"고소" (*go so*) is the Korean word for "lawsuit," and "고소미" (*go so mi*) is the name of a Korean cracker. Teenagers use it in place of "고소" just for fun and as a wordplay.

Someone should throw the back at this Internet troll and have him eat some *go so mi* for all the malicious comments he left on his post!

고스톱 Go Stop

Korean Card Game

It's a Korean variation of a Japanese Card Game *hanafuda* (花札)". The objective of the game is to score a minimum number of predetermined points, and when one reaches the threshold, they can either call a "Go" or a "Stop". If you call a "Stop", the game ends there, and the winning goes to the winner (caller). If a "Go" is called, the game continues, with the money doubling, tripling, and quadrupling depending on the number of "Go"s. Calling a "Go", however, puts the caller at risk because, if another player reaches the minimum threshold before the caller earns another point, then the caller would lose everything.

Won Hyo: Go!!! Stop!!! Oh wait, Go!!! No!! Stop!!!
Jenny: Dude, are you driving or playing **Gostop**?

골든타임 Golden Time

Critical Time Period That A Problem Can Be Resolved

A Konglish term referring to the most critical time period of an incident/situation, such as the window of opportunity to resolve a problem/rescue/capture someone or rectify a situation.

Five-second rule is a type of **golden time**. You drop food on the floor, but if you pick it up and blow off the dust within five seconds, you can still eat it.

(gol-cho) 골초 Gol Cho

Chain Smoker / Heavy Smoker

A slang, tongue-in-cheek term for a heavy/chain smoker, but its the type of character you can't easily see anymore on Korean TV because smoking scenes are always censored/blurred out.

Contrary to her innocent image, she's actually a **gol cho**!

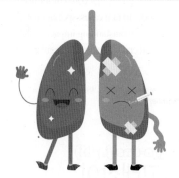

(gong-bang) 공방 Gong Bang

Recording With Live Audience

Short for "공개" + (*gong gae*, "open," "public") + "방송" (*bang song*, "broadcast"). It refers to the type of broadcasting where a show is recorded with a live audience on a stage open to the general public. It's extremely difficult to get an admission ticket to this type of event as they are usually complimentary, and competition is very fierce as a result.

I wish our *oppas* did more **gong bang** so we can see them perform live!

공카 Gong Ca
(gong-ka)
Official Fan Cafe

Short for "공식" (*gong sik*, "official") + "카페" ("**ca**fe"), a fan café officially recognized by the entertainment company. You can find lots of useful information and resources, such as tours, TV appearance schedules, and breaking news.

Francis: Wow! *Oppas* are coming back next month!
Kimmy: You're crying wolf again. I don't believe you!
Francis: You're wrong! It's from *gong ca*!
Kimmy: Oh!!!

공짜 Gong Jja
(gong-tcha)
Freebie

Something you get/receive without having to pay for it. There's a Korean saying: "If you like freebies too much, you will go bald." While the origin of the expression is unclear, some people believe it traces back to the post-Korean war era where people were so poor they had to go to a free barbershop to get a haircut, but because of bad hygiene, contagious diseases were spread, and people who got a free haircut lost their hair. Ever since then, it has been used as a warning and a reminder that there is no such thing as a free lunch.

The biggest perk of being a celebrity is getting *gong jja* stuff just because you are famous!

공익 Gong Ik
(gong-ik)
Public Service Worker

Korea has a mandatory military service that all able-bodied males over the age of 20 have to go through. The duration of the service is 21 months for the army, and 23 months for the navy and the air force. Any male idols who are in the military can't engage in commercial activities, such as appearing on TV or performing at concerts. However, for special cases, such as disability, he can be placed on alternative civilian service instead of regular military service. It is significantly less demanding, and the biggest perk is that you can commute from home because some of the duties include working at village/borough offices and subway stations (as a station employee/assistant).

Johnny never felt comfortable around people who talk about their time in the military because he was a *gong ik*. He always kept his mouth shut.

공주병 Gong Ju Byeong
(gong-ju-byong)

Conceited / Stuck Up / Narcissist Female

"공주" (*gong ju*) means "princess" and "병" (*byeong*) means "disease/sickness". Put together, it literally means "princess disease/syndrome" but refers to a narcissist female who's conceited/stuck up.

Eddie: You'd better stop treating her like a princess! She's going to have *gong ju byeong*!
Yonghyun: She already does... Too late!

(gong-jung-pa)
공중파
Gong Jung Pa

Public Broadcasting Network

There are two types of broadcasting networks. One is a public broadcasting network, or **O**ver **T**he **A**ir (**OTA**) network, which anyone with a TV and antenna can watch. The other is a cable TV network, which only the viewers who pay for the service can have access to. In a K-pop context, appearing on **공중파** *gong jung pa* means you have really made a name for yourself in Korea - or you will soon - because you are recognized as being worthy of being presented to the viewers all around the country and of its far-reaching power.

Until we make a *gong jung pa debut*, we have to keep trying hard!

Got 7

GOT 7 stands for "seven people with good luck," a seven-member (Mark. JB, Jackson, Jinyoung, Youngjae, BamBam, Yugyeom) boy group formed by JYP Entertainment. They debuted in 2014 with a song titled "Girls Girls Girls" and became famous for their dance style that includes elements of martial arts. They won Disc Bonsang's at the Golden Disc Awards in 2017 and 2018, as well as the "Hot Performance of The Year" award at the Gaon Chart Music Awards in 2018. Notable songs include "Hard Carry," "Never Ever," and "Fly."

Got 7? No! They are God 7 to me ;)

굿즈
Goods

Fan Merchandise

These are officially licensed items for sale by entertainment companies to promote their bands. They can be anything with the band's logo, name, and pictures of the members. Limited editions and signed items are often sold at a very high price.

On my last trip to Korea, I bought $1,000 worth of K-pop *goods*!

그린라이트
Green Light

Positive Sign In A Relationship

We all know a green traffic light means "go" and a red traffic light means "no-go," and the concept was borrowed by JTBC's relationship counseling show *Witch Hunt*, where the panels would listen to a story submitted by a viewer and determine whether the person in question is interested in the viewer or not. If the panel members believe he/she IS interested, then they would push the green light button and advise the viewer to take further actions.

She winked at me, and I took it as a *green light* and approached her. She told me there was something in her eye. What a letdown;(

구라 Gu Ra *(gu-ra)*

Lie / BS

A slang term for "lie/BS," which was originally something teenagers would use, but now it's being casually used by people of all ages. It's not, of course, used on TV/Radio or in formal situations.

Jen: I used to be a trainee for JYP!
Kyle: *Gu ra*! You can't even dance!
Jen: Not as an idol candidate. I was an aspiring comedian for JYP!

국뽕 Guk Bbong *(guk-ppong)*

Blindly Patriotic

"국" (*guk*) means "nation/country" and "뽕" (*bbong*) comes from the word "히로뽕" (*hi ro bbong*, Philopon (Japanese trade name of Methamphetamine), combined to mean something along the lines of "intoxicated with nationalism/patriotism". It's used as a self-deprecating term to describe a Korean who is blindly patriotic.

Dwayne: South Korea has the highest number of liver cancer patients.
Charles: Yeah! Because Korean people know how to drink! We are heavy drinkers!
Dwayne: Man, don't be a *guk bbong*. It's not a good thing!

국민 Guk Min *(guk-min)*

Very Popular

The word means "(Korean) people" or "(Korean) citizen," but its used idiomatically to describe something That's extremely popular on a national level, as it implies "something that is liked by everyone in the country." For example, "**국민** 여동생" (*yeo dong saeng*, "little sister") means "Korea's little sister (sweetheart)."

Kimbap is a *guk min* snack in Korea.

굴욕 Gul Yok *(gul-yok)*

Humiliation

The emotional state of feeling ashamed or losing respect for oneself. For example, live vocal fails are a major humiliation.

He thought he was a celebrity, but no one recognized him on the subway. What a *gul yok*!

과거 Gwa Geo
(gwa-gŏ)

Past/Story

It's one of the most frequently occurring themes in K-dramas, which is the apple of discord between a couple. A clichéd K-drama story goes like this: Someone with a past/story they want to hide finds the love of their life but is afraid of falling in love because their past/story would be a huge disappointment and make him/her want to leave them. But eventually, the love of their life finds out about the past and decides to embrace it wholeheartedly—and live happily ever after.

> Tony: Honey, I admit that I used to be a player, but *gwa geo* is just *gwa geo*! I'm a different person now.
> Alex: Past behavior is the best predictor of future behavior!

과로 Gwa Ro
(gwa-ro)

Overworking

A term referring to overworking, which often leads to hospitalization. For celebrities, popularity and fame are like a double-edged sword because the more popular one becomes, the busier one's schedule becomes, leading to burnout.

> If my job is to slack off, is being overly lazy a type of *gwa ro*?

과즙미 GwaJeup Mi
(gwa-jŭp-mi)

Bursting With Charm

"과즙" (*gwa jeup*, "fruit juice," "fruit nectar") + "미" (*mi*, 美, "beauty"). A slang term used to refer to someone's beauty/charm, which is metaphorically likened to that of fresh/refreshing fruits.

> Look at her dance! So cute and pretty! Full of *gwa jeup mi*!

광고 Gwang Go
(gwang-go)

Commercial

A term referring to all forms of advertisement, such as TV, radio, internet, and social media. For Korean entertainers, its a very important source of income, as securing a 광고 contract means a guaranteed income and a high probability of national fame.

> Son: Mom! I've got a *gwang go* contract! I'm a model now!
> Mom: What? A model? What kind?
> Son: You know those before/after diet commercials, right? I'm the "before" guy!
> Mom: The fat guy, right?
> Son: Yeah.
> Mom: You're a perfect fit for that role.

(gwang-tal)
광탈 Gwang Tal
Getting Eliminated
Quickly/Instant Elimination

Short for "**광속**" (*gwang sok*, "speed of light")
+ "**탈락**" (*tal lak*, "elimination"). It's a term
frequently used in competitive games or TV
shows (i.e., quiz shows or audition programs)
where a participant is eliminated immediately.

Okay - Let me apply for this job opening! Click submit! Done!
5 minutes later
Oh, I already got a rejection email. That was a *gwang tal*.

(gyŏ-tŏl)
겨털 Gyeo Teol
Armpit Hair

"**겨**" (*gyeo*) is the first word of "**겨드랑이**"
(*gyeo deu rang i*,"armpit") + "**털**" (*teol*) meaning
"hair" = "Armpit Hair". It's interesting to know
that Korean people find it embarrassing to have
their armpit visible, even guys - the reason guys
wearing sleeveless shirts on TV often cover their
armpit when they raise their hand.

Hide your *gyeo teol*. Korean girls don't like it haha.

(gye-ran-han-pan)
계란한판
Gye Ran Han Pan

Age 30

It literally means "a tray of eggs" but is
figuratively used to mean "age 30" because the
standard large egg tray carries 30 eggs in
Korean supermarkets.

I'm 29 and just a year away from becoming *gye ran han pan*.

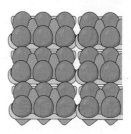

(gyŏl-bang)
결방 Gyeol Bang
Cancelled Episode

"**결**" (*gyeol*) means "lacking" and "**방**" (*bang*) is
short for "**방송**" (*bang song*, "broadcast/airing"),
so it means the airing of an episode of a
show/program is cancelled due to an unavoidable
reason, such as breaking news coverage and
special TV airing schedules. It really hurts the
fans when it happens to a show/drama that only
airs once or twice a week because you have to
wait that long for the next show.

Sonya: OMG I'm so pissed!
Tyler: Whats going on?
Sonya: K-popTonight is having a *gyeol bang*!
Tyler: WTF! I'm pissed too!

(gab/ŭl)
갑/을 Gab/Eul

Upper-Hand/Lower Hand

A term used to describe the power dynamic between two people, usually in contractual settings. *Gab* is the one with the upper hand, while *eul* is the subjugated party.

YOYO Entertainment is the **gab** while Honggi is the **eul**, bound by a contract. Honggi pretty much has to do whatever YOYO Entertainment orders him to do.

(gae-i-dŭk)
개이득 Gae Ideuk

Awesome Gain or Huge Profit

The term 개 *gae* literally means dog, which has many meanings aside from its original meaning. When used in combination with other words, it emphasizes the word, just like the F word in English. 이득 *ideuk* (not Iteuk from Super Junior) means "profit" or "gain".

Felix: I bought this laptop for $300 and sold it on eBay for $500!
Jose: Wow! That's some nice gain you made right there.
Felix: Not just a normal gain, it is **gae ideuk**.

(gae-chwi)
개취 Gae Chwi

Personal Preference

An abbreviation for "개인" *gae in* ("individual/personal") "취향" *chwi hyang* ("preference"). Although it has the term *gae*, it is not the *gae* used to emphasize (as in "개이득" *gae i deuk*). It is just an abbreviation for *gae in*. This word is strongly associated with the term *otaku*, someone who is overly obsessed with something (culture/subject).

Jenny: This is my detox juice! Coconut water, Tabasco, *kimchi* soup, and olive oil.
Mark: Ewwwwwwwwwwwwwww.
Jenny: Excuse me, can you please respect people's **gae chwi**?

갠소 Gaen So
(gaen-so)

Private Collection/Possession

A teen's way of abbreviating the word "개인" *gae in* ("personal") + 소장 *so jang* ("possession"). It refers to the downloading and storing of a rare picture of your favorite bias, with no intention of sharing it with others.

(Tony sees a sexy picture of his bias on the Internet)
Tony: **Gaen so**… Straight to my private collection…

감 Gam
(gam)

Hunch

An indescribable (but surprisingly accurate) gut feeling you get in a decisive situation. It could be the result of remembering a similar experience you had in the past or another mysterious reason (e.g., divine intervention?).

Hoon: I have a **gam** that she is not wife material. My **gam** is always right.
Joey: Sure. Your 3 ex-wives will agree with that.

감독 Gamdok
(gam-dok)

Coach (in Sports) / (Movie) Director

It refers to the person who oversees the production of a program or the management of a sports team.

The movie K-pop Legends was Baemin's debut work as a movie **gamdok**.

강추 Gang Choo
(gang-chu)

"Strongly Recommended"

An abbreviation for "강력추천" *gang ryeok choo cheon*. The word "강력" *gang ryeok* and "추천" *choo cheon* are Chinese words that mean "strong/powerful" and "recommendation", respectively. If a fangirl/fanboy's bias uses this on a product, it works as a strong endorsement that magically opens their wallet.

Murielle: Did you see? How was our oppa's new M/V?
Helen: One word. **Gang choo**!
Murielle: It must be another big hit!

강남 Gangnam

(gang-nam)

Wealthy District in Seoul

A wealthy district in Seoul. The literal meaning is "South of the River", and it is termed to refer to the south of the "Han River" that runs through the middle of Seoul.

*You want to go to Hongdae and get drunk on the cheap? Or, we can chill in **Gangnam** with style!*

Seoul

Han Gang

Gang Nam

간지 Ganji

(gan-ji)

"Fashionable", "Stylish", "Cool", "Swag"

Originating from the Japanese word *kanji* ("feeling" and "impression"), it is used to express admiration or awe.

*Tim: New Nike shoes, new Gucci hat, new Prada shades… In total, my **ganji** score increased by +50.*
Bo: And your bankroll decreased by -100,000,000.

강남스타일 Gangnam Style

Ultra-Mega Hit Song by Psy

An ultra-super mega hit song by Psy that became a world-wide phenomenon with its signature "horse riding dance".

*Op, op, Oppa **Gangam Style**!.*
Gangnam Style introduced K-pop to so many who had no idea where Korea was even located.

가온차트 Gaon Chart

The Only Official Music Ranking Chart

The only official music ranking chart certified by the KOCCA (Korea Creative Content Agency). It provides relatively trustworthy standards as it discounts mass purchases (downloads) when rating songs for chart position, a common entertainment company practice in an attempt to manipulate chart rankings.

*Color Pop just topped the **Gaon Chart**! This is big!*

(ga-sa)
가사 Gasa

Lyrics

One of the many essential elements that make up a good piece of music, and a well-written *gasa* can make a song go viral, especially when it is catchy. Idols who can sing the lyrics with their hearts are extremely talented and rare.

> Angel Mio, a singer-songwriter, composed the music and wrote the *gasa* for the song.

(ga-ship-nam)
가싶남 Gaship Nam

"Man Who I Want to Possess"

An abbreviation for "**가지고 싶은 남자**" *gajigo* ("to possess") *shipeun* ("want to~") *namja* ("man"). It can be used to describe a fan girl's fantasy or as a compliment paid to someone who is attractive. When used by a stan or sa saeng fan, things can get serious. This term frequently appears in fan fiction stories.

> Ursula: What do you want for Christmas?
> Miho: Jaemin oppa! I really want to possess him!
> Ursula: So he's your *gaship nam*!

(ga-yo)
가요 Gayo

Korean Pop Music

Originally used to refer to the whole category of "(Korean) popular music", but with the advent of K-pop, it became synonymous with "Korean Pop Music" over the globe. In Korea, the term "pop song" refers to Western music (e.g., Billboard Charts).

> My favorite *gayo* is Diamond 5's Eternal Love.

(ga-yo-dae-jŏn)
가요대전 Gayo Daejeon

Annual End-of-the-Year
K-pop Music Festival

An annual end-of-the-year K-pop music festival hosted by SBS (Seoul Broadcasting Services). In the past, awards were given to entertainers, but it evolved into a celebratory music event and the prize-awarding part is gone.

> It's the end of the year again… I am sad that I am getting older but happy because I can see all my Oppa's at the *Gayo Daejeon*!.

(gŏ-jin-mal)
거짓말
Geo Jit Mal

Lie

The mother of all evil. This is probably the single most frequently used term in melo K-dramas involving a love triangle, because it starts the entangled love line (without this, there would be no drama!).

Jinhee: I swear to god I didn't eat your cake!
Bonnie: **Geo jit mal**… What's that on your lip?
Jinhee: It's just some whipping cream that somehow got there. It happens to everybody!

(gŭm-su-jŏ)
금수저
Geum Soojeo

Someone Born with Privileges

Literal meaning is "gold spoon and chopsticks" but is used to describe someone born with privileges/perks. Its English counterpart phrase is "born with a silver spoon in your mouth". It also refers to an advantage that one didn't earn but inherited.

Layla: I really want to beat up that new girl…
Sam: Maybe you shouldn't.
Layla: Why?
Sam: She is a **geum soojeo** with a strong backing!
Layla: All right. I will let her slide then.

(gŭp)
급 Geup

All of a Sudden

Attached to the beginning of a noun, it is used to add a sense of urgency or unexpectedness.

Lad: Pack your bags! We are going to Hawaii today!
Gal: Oh wow, this is one **geup trip**!

GG

"Submission" "Give Up"

An abbreviation for "good game", it is used in online games as a means to (cyber) shake hands at the end of a match. At the same time, if the losing side says this first, then it is considered equivalent to admitting defeat. In MMA (Mixed Martial Arts), it is synonymous with "tapping out".

Girlfriend: Tell me exactly what you did last night! Why was your phone off? Do you want to die?
Boyfriend: **GG**…

기사 (gi-sa) GiSa

News Article

Something that can make or break a celebrity's reputation. If a negative reporter writes a nasty article about someone, it can seriously damage and potentially end a celebrity's career. Conversely, a good PR campaign, consisting of a series of well-written articles, can make a struggling entertainer an overnight media darling.

Jong: Did you see that *gi sa*? Maxus signed a deal with JIK entertainment.
Woo: Yeah, I did, but the journalist who wrote it is infamous for delivering false rumors.

GIFs

Short Animated Clip

A short, animated clip often containing funny or sexy moments of idols, such as bloopers or dance moves. It is termed so because the clip is created in the form of a **GIF** (**G**raphics **I**nterchange **F**ormat).

Hey, there is a site where you can see a whole bunch of *GIFs*! I am using one of those in my signature section on the K-pop board.

긴장 (gin-jang) GinJang

Tension, Nervousness

For K-pop fans, it is the feeling you get before the *dae sang* ("grand prize") is announced.

Oh my god… This is my first time seeing my Oppas in person! I am so *gin jang*ing right now.

걸크러쉬 Girl Crush

Intense Liking or Admiration that a Girl Develops Towards a Person of the Same Sex

An emotional reaction that occurs when the targeted subject possesses the values and characteristics to which the admirers aspire.

Carolyn: Tiffany is so adorable! Her voice is impeccable, and she can play 3 instruments… She is just perfect!
Rana: Are you in love with her?
Carolyn: No, I'm 100% straight. She is just a *girl crush*.

고소미 GoSoMi
(go-so-mi)
"To Sue"

Actually, the name of a biscuit snack cracker, but the word "고소" *goso* can mean "tasty", as well as "to sue", so people (usually teens) use it instead for fun.

Yoo: LOL! I left a dirty comment on her picture on Facebook.
Vince: Be careful! You can get a *go so mi* for that.

고소미
Go So Mi

고구마 Gogooma
(go-gu-ma)
Slow-Witted Person/Frustrating Situation

Literal meaning is "sweet potato", but it is used to describe a time-consuming situation without seeing fruition or someone who is insensitive or slow-witted because eating sweet potatoes without drinking a beverage causes similar feelings of serious congestion in your chest.

Seol: I really hate that new K-drama!
Jin: Why? You've been watching it every week.
Seol: The story just won't develop! It's been like that for 2 months… It's a *gogooma* drama…

갓 God
(gat)
The One and Only or The Best

When used in combination with another subject/object, it is converted into the superlative form, which implies it is the absolute best and untouchable. If your bias has a talent in a certain field, you add this term before their name.

Robert: Wow… Tyler is so good at playing StarCarft.
Kim: Dude, StarCraft is a *God*-Game! So much fun!
Robert: Yeah. I bet no one in our school can beat him.
Kim: Yup! We should call him *God*-Tyler!
Robert: All hail *God*-Tyler!

Golden Disk Awards
Prestigious Annual Awards Show

A prestigious annual awards show founded in 1986 presented by the Music Industry Association of Korea for outstanding achievements in the music industry in South Korea.

My Oppa has all-killed the K-pop charts three times this year. I bet he can finally win a grand award at the *Golden Disk Awards* this year!

고마워 Gomawo
(go-ma-wŏ)

"Thank You (informal)"

An informal way of saying "thank you".
Adding "yo" at the end makes it semi-formal.

Fan girl: Oppa! We really enjoyed your fan service! *Gomawoyo*!
Ido: My pleasure. *Gomawo* everyone!

공홈 Gong Home
(gong-hom)

Official Homepage

An abbreviation for "공식" *gong sik* ("official")
"홈페이지" **home**page. It is used when there are
many social media (SNS) outlets available, so
one knows where to go for official
updates/announcements. It is usually the
homepage of the entertainment company to
which your bias belongs.

Rabab: Yes! HEXO just announced their comeback!
Jihoon: Bull crap! Where did you hear that?
Rabab: On their *gong home*!
Jihoon: Dang… Then it must be real!

공식/비공식
(gong-shik/bi-gong-shik)
Gong sik/ Bi Gong Sik

Official/Unofficial

A term used to explain that something is authentic
and recognized by an authoritative entity.

Monica: Yes! I just won a ticket to our oppa's concert!
Hyeri: Really? Where did you get it?
Monica: Um… Fanclubs.com?
Hyeri: That is not a *gong sik* fan club site. It might be a
hoax.

공연 Gong Yeon
(gong-yŏn)

Concert, Recital

It can be either a paid event (e.g., Dream Concert)
or a public event (e.g., a guerrilla concert,
meaning "unannounced busking").

I went to see my Oppa's *gong yeon* yesterday. Their live
performance was out of this world.

(gun-dae-ri-a)
군대리아
Goondaeria

Hamburger Distributed to Soldiers in the Army as a Military Ration

A compound word made up of "군대" *goon dae* ("army") + "롯데리아" "lotte**ria**" (a hamburger franchise). The burgers are pretty much bare-bone basic, compared to those sold at restaurants, so it is often used to describe/make a joke of the poor treatment received in the army. If your boy bias joins the army, this is something he will be eating (in tears).

Girlfriend: Hey, honey, come try this I made for you.
Boyfriend: Nom nom nom.
Girlfriend: How does it taste?
Boyfriend: Reminds me of *goondaeria*…
Girlfriend: That… bad?

(gung-ye)
궁예 Goong Ye

Mind Reading

Originated from the name of a character in a Korean historical drama *Taejo Wang Geon*, where Goong Ye, a Buddhist monk, who claimed himself capable of reading others' minds. Since then, his name has become synonymous with "mind reading", and it is often used to call out someone who is nosy and pretends to know everything.

Eddie: I know what you are thinking. You want to ask that girl out, but you are afraid. Don't be a coward.
Nick: Don't be a *goong ye!* You are wrong. I'm gay!

(gung-di-pang-pang)
궁디팡팡
Goongdi Pang Pang

Spanking One's Bottom

A compound word made up of "궁디" *goong di*, a dialect for "hips, buttocks, ass" and "팡팡" *pang pang*, an adverb describing spanking sounds. Contrary to common usage, it is not used for corporal punishment but as a compliment after doing something praiseworthy.

Yuri: Our Oppa's just won the Golden Disk Award!
Miso: Awesome! They deserve some goongdi pang pang from me!

(go-su)
고수 Gosu

Highly Skilled Person

A compound word made up of two Chinese words "고" *go* ("high") and "수" *su* "a move (as in a chess game)" = "master player who knows many moves". It became a popular term among online gamers around the world, thanks to the ubiquitous Korean gamers who contributed to the burgeoning of the world's largest e-sports (Starcraft, LOL, Counter Strike, and etc.) leagues. It is the opposite of "초보"

Juno: Wow, did you know Jackie Kid has a black belt in Tae Kwon Do?
Mira: I didn't know he was such a *gosu* in martial arts!

게릴라 콘서트
Guerilla Concert

Unannounced Surprised Concert

Originally from MBC's variety TV show "일요일 일요일 밤에" *Ilyoil Ilyoil Bam Ae* ("Sunday, Sunday Night"), where the singer(s) are given one hour to promote their event in the street, with the goal of attracting an audience of over 5,000. Once the time is up, the singer(s) are blindfolded on the stage and nervously wait as the numbers are tallied. If it is less than 5,000, the concert is automatically canceled. Ever since then, it has been used to refer to any kind of unannounced concert event usually taking place on the street (including busking and fan service activities).

Charlie: I just saw AOB singing at the supermarket!
Jennifer: Holy cow! They must be having a *guerilla concert*! Why didn't you call me?

(gwaen-cha-na)
괜찮아
Gwenchana

"It's Okay"

Also something you say to mask your true emotions (anger, sadness, surprise etc.).

Hyoa: Ouch! I bumped my head against the window *cry*.
Min: *Gwenchana*?
Hyoa: It really hurts… but did our oppas see that?
Min: I don't think so.
Hyoa: *Gwenchana*, then!

(gwan-jong)
관종 GwanJong

Attention Whore

An abbreviation for "관심 *gwan shim* ("attention") "종자" *jong ja* ("kind/race")". This is somebody who incessantly seeks approval/validation from others. Some are obsessed with social media, such as Facebook and Instagram, and will go as far as making up stories just to get "likes".

Gyuri: Hey, you really went to that party? I saw your Facebook check-in.
Wonmi: Not really… I just fake-checked-in to get some likes, why not?
Gyuri: You are the biggest *gwan jong* I've ever seen…

(gwi-chŏk)
귀척 Gwi Cheok

Pretending to Be Cute

An abbreviation of "귀여운" *gwi yeo woon* ("cute") "척" *cheok* ("pretending"), which refers to "acting cutesy and coquettish".

Sonya: *Bbuing bbuing~* Oppa~ Aren't I so cute?
Adam: Stop the *gwi cheok*. Aren't you a little old for that?

(gwi-cha-ni-jŭm)
귀차니즘
Gwichanism

Lazism

The state of mind where you feel annoyed or bothered by almost everything presented before you. This is something a fanboy/fangirl would experience after their bias goes into hiatus. They lose the motivation to live, and this feeling of extreme annoyance kicks in.

Michael: Ugh… I'm so hungover…
Mom: Michael, can you take out the trash?
Michael: I can't. My religion prohibits it.
Mom: What? What religion?
Michael: **Gwichanism**.

(gwi-yo-mi)
귀요미 Gwiyomi

Cutie

A Korean slang for "a cute and adorable person" (귀여움 *gwiyoum* means "cuteness")

Awwwww when my Oppa was a little baby, he was such a **gwiyomi**!

(hae-jang)
해장 HaeJang

Easing a Hangover

A compound word made up of two Chinese words "해" *hae* ("to ease") and "장" *jang* ("intestine"). It refers to the act of eating food that has soothing properties, such as *seollong tang* (ox bone soup) and *boogeo gook* (dried pollock soup), but *ramyun* is probably the most sought-after hangover cure.

Doug: Holy *burp* molly *hic* I can still taste the alcohol in my mouth.
Danny: Me *burp* too. Let's go get some cheeseburgers for **hae jang**.

(haek)
핵 Haek

"Super"

Its literal meaning is "nuclear", but derived from the word "핵폭탄" *haek pok tan* ("nuclear bomb"), it is used by the younger generation as an adjective to make something the absolute superlative (because the nuclear bomb is the deadliest of all). Some of the common examples include "핵노잼" *haek no jam* ("absolute boredom") and "핵피곤" *haek pi gon* ("utter exhaustion").

Kimmy: LOL! I accidentally went into a men's restroom, and no one noticed it.
Robert: That is not just funny. That is **haek** funny!

하차 Ha Cha (ha-cha)

Quitting / Dropping Out

The literal meaning is "getting off a car/vehicle" but is figuratively used for someone dropping out/quitting a show. They can come in the form of voluntary quitting, such as health issues, but sometimes they are forced to—changes in drama script/scenario, or scandalous issues that prevent one from appearing in the show.

After our oppa made a *ha cha* from the show, the show's rating plummeted.

햄볶아요 Haem Bo Kka Yo (haem-bo-kka-yo)

"I'm Happy"

"햄 볶아요" (**ham** *bo kka yo*) means "I stir-fry ham (spam)" but is used in place of "행복해요" (*haeng bok hae yo*), which means "I'm happy." It's just a fun wordplay and an indirect/less embarrassing way of saying you are happy, especially because of the relationship you are in right now.

Cecil: Hey, what are you doing?
Victoria: *Haem bo kka yo*! I just got a new job!
Cecil: Congratulations! Is that why you are stir-frying ham?
Victoria: LOL no! It means "I'm happy!"

해외 Hae Oe (hae-oe)

Overseas

"해" (*hae*, 海, "sea") + "외" (*oe*, 外, "outside") = "overseas." If you are a K-pop fan outside Korea, this is one word you absolutely have to memorize because, when you hear this word along with the name of your favorite bias/band, it might mean they are coming overseas for a concert - possibly your country!

Timothy was disappointed after he learned that Manila wasn't part of TWICE's *hae oe* tour plans.

햇반 Haet Ban (haet-ban)

Instant Rice

It's actually the name of an instant rice product that has become an essential item for those who live alone by themselves, because rice is a staple food of Korean cuisine, but preparing it is just a pain in the neck, so That's when instant rice comes to the rescue. It's quick and convenient - just put it in the microwave, and after 90 seconds, you just made yourself a bowl of steamy hot rice! For that reason, the brand name became a household name in Korea.

Bernie: I didn't know you could cook! This is one yummy bowl of rice!
Alexandra: I have to come clean with you... It's actually *haet ban*! All I did was microwave it haha.

행쇼 Haeng Syo

(hang-syo)

"Peace Out"

A shortened word of the phrase "행복하십쇼" *haeng bok ha sip syo*, which means "be happy". It has become popular since G-Dragon started saying it on TV. It can be casually used for saying goodbye and can be translated as "peace out" in English.

My fans, it was a great pleasure having you today. Thank you so much and... *Haeng Syo!*

한복 Hanbok

(han-bok)

Traditional Korean Outfit

The traditional outfit of the Korean people. It is often worn on traditional holidays like Chuseok (Harvest Festival) and Seollal (Korean New Year), as well as festive events like weddings. It is characterized by vibrant colors and simple lines. All characters in *sageuk* (Korean historical drama) wear these.

Tony: Is that a *Kimono* Wonhee's wearing?
Mina: Nope, it's called *Hanbok*.
Tony: Woah, she looks doubly beautiful in it...

한류 Hallyu

(hal-lyu)

Korean Wave

"The Korean Wave" is the global phenomenon of Korean entertainment and popular culture spreading over the world through K-pop music, K-dramas, TV shows, and movies.

I thought *Hallyu* didn't exist, but every time I travel overseas, I happen to bump into a K-pop fan.

합격 Hap Gyuk

(hap-gyŏk)

Passing a Test, Acceptance

Success in exams, interviews, and the like.

Kimmy, how did the audition go? *Hap gyuk*?

힐링 Healing

(hēe-ling)

Alleviating (Mental) Stress

When you engage in an activity with the goal of easing the (mostly mental) pain/stress you are in, you use this term as a noun or an adjective. The term became popular thanks to SBS's hit TV Show *Healing Camp*, where guests are invited to pour out their troubles to the guest audience and unburden themselves.

Joann: I just can't get over the fact our oppa's going to the army... It is the saddest day of my life.
Hanna: We should definitely go on a *healing* trip.

허당 Heo Dang

(hŏ-dang)

"Mr./Ms. Clumsy/Sloppy"

A term describing someone who looks immaculate but is actually clumsy and incapable in areas where they were expected to excel. It's also a reference to someone who talks a lot and exaggerates their abilities but cannot back up their claims. Lee Seung Ki is best known for his *heo dang* character in *2 Days & 1 Night*.

Gyuho looks so smart, but it turns out that he is such a *heo dang*. He totally flunked the beginner's Korean class.

허세 Heo Se

(hŏ-se)

"Bluff"

A compound word made up of two Chinese words "허" *heo* ("empty") and "세" *se* ("strength"). It refers to the act of showing courage or confidence to impress others.

Mike: I will buy that Prada suit and Gucci shoes. Just put them on my credit card.
Employee: Sir, the credit card is declined.
Rachel: Ha! You and your *heo se*...!

흑기사
Heuk Gi Sa

Man Taking Penalty Shots for a Woman in a Drinking Game

Literally meaning "Black Knight", it is someone who solves a difficult situation for a woman but is mostly used in drinking games. The woman who is saved by "흑기사" owes him a favor and has to fulfill one request he demands.

Everyone: Shot! Shot! Shot! Shot! Shot!
Mary: I can't take it anymore. I drank too much already… Does anyone want to volunteer to be my *heuk gi sa?*

흑장미
Heuk Jang Mi

Woman Taking Penalty Shots for a Woman in a Drinking Game

Literally meaning "Black Rose", it is exclusively used in drinking games. It is the female equivalent of "흑기사".

Minkyu: Ugh… I lost again?
Brianne: Hey baby, I can be your *heuk jang mi* and take that shot for you. In return, you will have to kiss me!
Minkyu: I would rather die from alcohol poisoning.

흑수저
Heuk Soo Jeo

Someone Born Without Any Privileges

A term that contrasts sharply to the word "금수저" *geum soo jeo* (gold spoon and chopsticks). Literally meaning "clay spoon = "흙" *heuk* (clay) + "수저" *soo jeo* (spoon and chopsticks)", it refers to someone who was born without any competitive/comparative advantage over their peers. Hence, they are the low man on the totem pole.

Dennis: Hey, what are you doing this Friday?
Vince: Work, work, and work!
Dennis: Dang… do you have to work that much?
Vince: *Heuk soo jeos* like me have to work our asses off to survive, man.

호모 인턴스
Homo Interns

Young Job Seekers Who Are in the Vicious Cycle of Endless Internships

A satirical term describing the hardships that young Korean job applicants face. It refers to a vicious cycle of looking for a full-time job but having to settle for an internship position that is often unpaid. It is often likened to the life of K-pop trainees, where they have to spend countless hours with the goal of one day making a debut, which, of course, is never guaranteed.

*5 years and 10 internships. They are called **homo interns**.*

Hook Song

Addictive Song

A very addictive song that gets stuck in your head. It usually has repetitive lyrics or melodies that are catchy.

*I got the beats inside my head and can't get it out of there! Such a strong **hook song** they came out with.*

(hubae)
후배 Hoobae

Junior in a Certain Field

It refers to a junior who is less experienced or with less seniority in a certain field, regardless of age.

Although Kyuho is 3 years older than me, he is my hoobae because I debuted 2 years before him.

(hun-nam/hun-nyŏ)
훈남/훈녀
Hoon Nam/ Hoon Nyeo

Charming Male/Female

Someone who are not as handsome or beautiful as K-pop celebrities but still above average in terms of looks. However, it is their inner charm, such as kindness and thoughtfulness, that captures the heart of the people around them.

*That guy who helped an old lady cross the road is not only kind but handsome! A true example of **hoon Nam**.*

헐 (höl) Hul

"Whoa", "What the..."

Something you say when you are dumbfounded or lost for words.

Oyu: Layla, I accidentally spilled coffee on your Oppa's picture…
Layla: *Hul*…

현질 (hyŏn-jil) Hyeon Jil

Buying Video Game Items With Cash

The easiest and quickest way to upgrade your cybergame character. In many mobile games, the game developers let the users download the game for free but offer in-app purchases for those who wish to buy items with cash. Because it would take too much time to earn that item/reach a certain level, many people make an "investment" and seek instant gratification.

Oyu: Look at my character! It's got max attack and max defense!
Byeon: How? You just started playing yesterday.
Oyu: *Hyeon jil* is the answer, buddy!
Byeon: You know you could have bought a new car with all the money you spent online, right?

헌팅 Hunting

To Pick Up a Girl

A Koreanized English expression ("Konglish") used to refer to the act of making a casual acquaintance and asking someone for their contact information to schedule a date.

Minu: Hey! Let's go *hunting*!
James: Right on! Let me go grab my rifles.
Minu: WTH are you doing?
James: You said we are going *hunting*!
Minu: No, dude! I meant picking up chicks!

현웃 (hyŏn-ut) Hyeon Woot

Laughing in Reality

Contrary to LOL (Laughing Out Loud or "ㅋㅋㅋ"), which is the biggest lie on the Internet, the reader finds it so funny and hilarious that they burst out laughing in real life.

Daeho: LOL! Mina just farted while giving a presentation.
Max: LOL! I just had a *hyeon woot*. She must have been so embarrassed.

형 Hyung (hyŏng)

Older Brother

A term used by a younger male to address an older male sibling. It can be used for any older male with whom they share enough emotional intimacy. Sometimes the older male won't let the younger male call him this unless permission is given. It can be used in place of someone's name.

Hey, Tony, meet my little brother. Since he is 2 years older than you, he is a *hyung* to you.

형님 Hyungnim (hyŏng-nim)

Older Brother (honorific)

An honorific term for "*Hyung*", where "*nim*" can be translated as "sir" or "Mr.", and the bosses of 조폭 *jopok* (Korean mafia) are also called this.

Insoo: *Hyung*! Can I use your computer?
Inho: Only if you call me ***hyungnim***.

Hyungwhore

Person Who Loves to Hang Out with His Hyungs a Lot

A male K-pop idol, who is always seen in the company of *hyungs* (older males). It does not mean he is homosexual, but it is what he likes doing. Usually, the *maknae* members of a group show this tendency.

Yuno always hangs out with his *hyungs*. Many thought he might be gay, but he also has a girlfriend. So with that possibility ruled out, he is just a ***hyungwhore***.

이불킥 I Bool Kick (i-bul-kik)

Kicking Oneself

A compound word made up of "이불" *i bool* ("comforter") + "킥" (**kick**) = "kicking one's comforter". It refers to a situation where someone is lying in bed, waiting to fall asleep, and all of a sudden, something embarrassing they did in the past flashes through their mind, and they kick the comforter out of shame.

Maya: Remember the dude who threw up in front of everyone at band camp last year?
Jody: Yeah! I bet he is still ***i bool kicking*** today!

Hallyu Dream Concert

K-pop All-Star Concert

An annual concert held at the Seoul World Cup Stadium with varying themes each year. As the name suggests, its an event where you get to see all the hottest K-pop groups in one place, and for that, its one of the most difficult, if not impossible, events for which you can buy a ticket. However, it also had unexpected consequences: fan wars. Fans of rival groups boycotted and sabotaged another groups performance by shouting demeaning chants over them singing.

FIFA World Cup? Summer Olympics? I don't care. I would trade them all for the *Hallyu Dream Concert* in a heartbeat!

(han-gŭl)
한글 Hangul

Korean Alphabet

Invented by Sejong the Great in 1443, it consists of 19 consonants and 21 vowels. It's considered to be a very logical and scientific writing system because, as a phonogram, its highly capable of expressing sounds into writing, and its very easy to learn (although the Korean language is quite challenging to master).

Hangul is so much easier to learn than I thought! I mastered it when I was four! And yes, of course, I'm Korean.

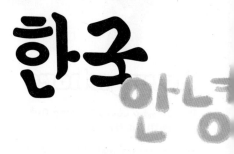

(han-sot-bap)
한솥밥
Han Sot Bap

Belonging To The Same Company

The literal meaning is "same rice pot," and it's used as part of an idiom "to eat from the same rice pot" = "living under the same roof," like family, and it refers to multiple groups/people belonging to the same company/agency.

Charlie signed a contract with YJP Entertainment! Now Charlie eats *han sot bap* with Twister Boys!

핸들
Handle

Steering Wheel (Of a Car)

A Konglish term referring to the "steering wheel" of a vehicle.

Watch out! Grab the *handle*! Our car crashed because he grabbed my love handle instead of the steering wheel…

해프닝
Happening

Funny / Strange Incident

A Konglish term referring to a funny/strange incident that happened totally by chance.

Holly was spotted at the biggest racist club in New York, but it was found to be just a **happening** - she thought it was a restaurant of the same name!

헬스 Health

Weight Training

Originating from the outdated English term "health club," which means "the gym," "**health**" means "weight training" because its whats done at the gym. Hence, "doing **health**" means "doing weight lifting."

Sam: Where's Hoonie?
Xenia: Hoonie went to **health**!
Sam: Huh? To get checked up at the hospital?
Xenia: No, he went to work out at the gym.

하드캐리
Hard Carry

MVP (Most Valuable Player)

Originated in massively multiplayer online role-playing games (MMORPG), like League of Legends, and refers to a player who outperforms all other members and "carries" them to victory single-handedly. It's also used in real-life situations, such as team sports and competitive TV shows, to praise and acknowledge that one outstanding player.

Valerie totally **hard carried** the team to the final because all the other members were still recovering from food poisoning.

(heart ppyong-ppyong)
하트뿅뿅
Heart Bbyonb Bbyong

Throwing Hearts at Someone/Something

"뿅뿅" (*bbyong bbyong*) is an onomatopoeia or a word that imitates the sound of something appearing/flowing out quickly in large amounts. Combined with "heart", it means throwing hearts at someone/something.

Whats up with the **heart bbyonb bbyong**? Do you need to borrow money again?

(hŭk-yŏk-sa)
흑역사
Heuk Yeok Sa
Shameful/Humiliating Memory

"흑" (*heuk*, "black/dark") + "역사" (*yeok sa*, "history"). Your shameful past that you wouldn't want anyone to find out about. It's similar to "이불킥" (*i bul kick*, "kicking oneself"), which refers to a situation where someone is lying in bed, waiting to fall asleep, and all of a sudden something embarrassing they did in the past flashes through their mind, and they kick the comforter out of shame.

LOL! This is my baby picture - OMG that haircut... my *heuk yeok sa*!

(ho-gu)
호구 Ho Gu
Pushover / Punching Bag

In the Asian board game *baduk*, or *go*, placing a stone right inside "호구 (*ho gu*)," or "tiger's mouth" is a sure, suicidal way of losing a point. For this reason, the word "호구" became synonymous with someone who's gullible, easily manipulated, and always taken advantage of by other ill-willed people.

Jenny borrowed $3,000 from me 2 years ago and never paid it back. She's asking for more money now. Does she really think I'm her *ho gu*?

(hŭng-bu-ja)
흥부자
Heung Bu Ja
The Life of The Party

"흥" (*heung*) means "fun/excitement/joy" and "부자" (*bu ja*) means "rich person." Put together, it means "someone who's full of fun/joy/excitement" = "life of the party." It's the type of friend you want to have around you when you are feeling depressed.

Megan started dancing at the funeral. Although we all know she is the biggest *heung bu ja*, that was too much.

(hoe-sik)
회식 Hoe Sik
Company Dinner / Get Together

"회" (*hoe*) means "to meet" and "식" (*sik*, 食) means "meal/to eat." Put together, it literally means "to eat in together," but it specifically refers to a company-sponsored dinner outing for employees. Its original purpose is building and promoting better teamwork, but junior-level employees usually hate it because being with their boss after work is quite stressful. Whats worse is that it usually doesn't end at dinner. It extends to 2-*cha* (2nd round) at a pub and 3-*cha* (3rd-round) at karaoke, and the worst part must be the fact that attendance is mandatory!

My party plan got ruined because of the stupid *hoe sik* tonight!!!

Wanna go home...

혼밥 Hon Bap

(hon-bap)

Eating Alone

"혼자" (*hon ja*, "alone/by oneself") + "밥" (*bap*, "meal"). A term that reflects a recent trend in the Korean lifestyle where people eat by themselves. The reason its a big deal is because Korea is a highly collective society, and eating with someone is a very important component and a social expectation. For this reason, if you are eating alone and your Korean friend bumps into you, then he/she would ask you why you are eating alone and might even be concerned, because Korean people would take it as a sign of not belonging to a group. Recently, however, due to the modern hectic lifestyle, an increasing number of people, especially the younger generation, chooses to eat alone, and it's becoming a new trend. Even restaurants come up with new menus targeting these solo-diners.

Today I've decided to do *hon bap* because I want to pig out, and I don't want my boyfriend to see me.

후드 Hood

Hoodie

A Konglish term meaning "hoodie," not to be confused with the English slang word meaning "the ghetto."

Hong: Hey, where is my *hood*?
Jack: You belong in the ghetto, bro!
Hong: Huh? I'm talking about my hoodie!
Jack: Oh, its on the sofa.

혼술 Hon Sul

(hon-sul)

Drinking Alone

"혼자" (*hon ja*, "alone/by oneself") + "술" (*sul*, "alcohol/drink"). Same concept as "혼밥" (*hon bap*, "eating alone"). Again, its a reflection of the modern, hectic Korean lifestyle - sometimes you just want to take a break from life and have a moment of self-reflection.

I'm watching my *oppas* getting the top award on TV! Perfect time for *hon sul*! Cheers!

Hottest

2PM Fan Club

It's the name of the 2PM fan club because 2PM is the hottest time of the day. Fan color is metallic gray.

Hottest is the fan club for the hottest K-pop band, 2PM!

(hu-bang-ju-ŭi)
후방주의
Hu Bang Ju Eui

NSFW (Not Safe For Work)

"후방" (*hu bang*, "rear/back side") + "주의" (*ju eui*, "caution") = "be careful of who's behind you." A warning that the Internet content you are about to run into might be inappropriate (nudity, violence, profanity, etc.) to be accessed/viewed in public places, such as the workplace or the bus.

(*Hu Bang Ju Eui*) oppas_doing_sexy_waves.mpg

(hwa-bo)
화보 Hwa Bo

(Promotional) Photoshoot

Literal meaning is "a material, print or digital, that contains paintings or pictures." Technically, a series of photos you put on Instagram counts as a "화보", but it generally refers to a promotional photoshoot of a celebrity for posters, magazine inserts, and other types of releases.

Everybody hates hanging out with Sena because everywhere she goes, she makes her friends take photos of her as if they were her dedicated photographer making a *hwabo* for her.

(hwal-dong)
활동 Hwal Dong

Activity

The opposite of going into hiatus or taking a temporary break. It refers to any kind of activity one engages in, such as TV appearances, concerts, and fan-signing events.

Good news! Oppas are making a comeback and starting their *hwal dong* next week!

(hye-ja)
혜자 Hye Ja

Merciful / Extremely Generous

The term became popular after the introduction of a celebrity-branded convenience store lunch box "*Hye Ja* Lunchbox," which offered generous portions of rice and accompanying side dishes at an affordable price. Since then, the word "*Hye Ja*" has become synonymous with something/someone very generous.

Ken: Oh dear... I think I broke your iPhone.
Jin: That's ok. We're friends.
Ken: Really? You are a real *hye ja* ㅠㅠ

현피 Hyeon Pi

(hyŏn-pi)

To Have a Fight in the Real World

It's "현실" (*hyun sil*, "real world/reality") + "피" (*pi*, short for "Player Kill"). Put together, it means "to have a fight in the real world" and refers to a situation in which two people who have had an argument on the Internet decide to have a real physical fight in real life.

How did we become best friends? We got into an online argument playing Overwatch and decided to do a *hyeon pi*, only to learn that he was a great guy! We hit it right off.

협찬 Hyeop Chan

(hyŏp-chan)

Sponsorship

Providing goods and services for free in return for brand exposure. Some celebs, however, have been criticized for abusing their fame/popularity to force companies to give them stuff for free! One example is they would rent expensive clothes to wear to a TV show and then never return them, insisting they did them a favor by exposing the brand. Companies usually just bite the bullet and let them have it their way.

Tony: Hey, I like your Ferrari. Can you give it to me as a *hyeop chan*? I have over 100 Instagram followers.
Ferrari Dealer: Please get out.

휴덕 Hyu Deok

(hyu-dŏk)

To Take A Break From Being A Fanboy/Fangirl

"휴" (*hyu*, "to rest") + "덕" (*deok*, "*otaku*" (geek, mania). The act of taking a break from being a fanboy/fangirl. It's different from "탈덕" (*tal deok*, "to quit being a fanboy/fangirl"), as it doesn't necessarily mean that one gives up being a fanboy/fangirl but is just a temporary state.

Sooni decided to *hyu deok* after spending all her money buying all the K-pop merchandise.

홀로족 Hyol Lo Jok

(hyol-lo-jok)

Someone Who Enjoys Life Alone

A compound word comprising "홀로" (*holo*, "alone") + "YOLO (you only live once) + "족" (*jok*, "people")." It refers to the people who value self-gratification and enjoy every moment of their single life, unbound by relationships with other people.

Aren't I the real *hyol lo jok*? I had a date with myself last night - I went to see a movie alone, had a nice romantic dinner alone, and took a bubble bath alone! Oh wait, I sound more like a loser.

(i-yŏl-chi-yŏl)
이열치열
I Yeol Chi Yeol

Eating Samgyetang on a Super-Hot Korean Summer Day

A four-letter Chinese idiom meaning "fighting fire with fire", which refers to the act of consuming boiling-hot, rejuvenating, stamina-restoring, and nutritious soups like *samgyetang* (chicken soup with ginseng) to beat the summer heat, usually during *"boknal"*, the dog days of Korea's summer.

Nana: Hot! Hot!
Wongyo: What is it that you are eating?
Nana: Oh, this is *samgyetang*. So hot!
Wongyo: Damn, why don't you get something cold, like ice cream?
Nana: No, this is called *i yeol chi yeol*! Our way of beating the summer heat!

Idolization

Dramatic Change or Transformation of Appearance (for the better)

A dramatic change or transformation of appearance for the better, mostly through weight loss, hairstyles, or even plastic surgery, thereby earning the "idol" status.

After losing 25kg, Aya became a totally different person, from *ajumma* to idol! What an *idolization* it is.

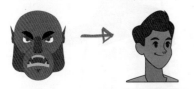

Idol

Young K-pop Entertainer

Young K-pop entertainers, who have come through many years of vigorous training in multiple areas, including singing, acting, dancing, and entertaining on TV shows. They work as a solo artist or as a group or, often, as both interchangeably.

Tim: Okay, so is Felix an *idol*?
Max: No way, I know that he can sing, but he is in his 50's and has no talent in other things…

(ik-ke)
익게 Ik Ge

Anonymous Bulletin Board

An abbreviation for "익명" *ik myeong* ("anonymous") + "게시판" *ge si pan* ("bulletin board"). Unlike its intended purpose to facilitate the exchange of honest opinions, it often turns into an incubator for numerous fan wars.

Marcus: Chris! You are in big trouble, my man!
Chris: What? Why?
Marcus: Why did you write that post talking trash about your ex?
Chris: Huh? I did… but I did it in the *ik ge* section…
Marcus: Man… there is no *ik ge* in our forum! You must have confused it with something else.

일진 Il Jin
(il-chin)

School Gangs

A group of school bullies (mostly in high school) who engage in violent and even criminal activities against weaker/vulnerable classmates. This is a serious social issue, and some idols/celebs have been severely criticized, as their history as school gang members have been disclosed after their debut.

> Fiora: Did you hear that Wendy was a notorious *il jin* in high school?
> Vera: No way, with such an innocent face?

인지도 In Ji Do
(in-ji-do)

(Brand) Awareness

A tool to gauge the level of brand awareness of something (i.e., a product, a political campaign, a celebrity, etc.) For K-pop fans, there are many factors used to gauge this, including chart rankings, the number of views on YouTube, the number of members of a fan club, etc. But the easiest method is taking the subway and seeing if anyone recognizes them.

> Hello Mini went out for a walk in a crowded park, but no one recognized her. She was slightly bothered by her low *in ji do*.

인강 In Gang
(in-gang)

Online Lectures

An abbreviation for "인터넷" (**Int**ernet) "**강의**" *gang eui* ("lecture"), a convenient means of acquiring knowledge among the younger generation. Many Internet-based companies offer courses to their subscribers.

> Murielle: My desire for learning is insatiable, but I have no time to go to school!
> Yura: Hey, just take *in gang* at home then!

인사 In Sa
(in-sa)

Showing Respect

The literal meaning is "greetings", but it has more subtle nuances. In Korean society, age plays an important role in determining someone's place in the social hierarchy. There are rules of politeness, and "인사" is one of them. It is more than making a bow. It includes keeping in touch with and looking after someone older or a superior at work, which boils down to a matter of showing respect.

> *In sa*, or showing respect to *sunbaes*, is the most important element for a good reputation.

(il-jin)

일진 IlJin

Bully / School Gang

Literal meaning is "first-class faction" but is used to refer to the school gang (bullies and delinquents). As in many other countries, bullying in school is a huge social problem, and a number of celebrities have been severely criticized after their "일진" past has been disclosed by the victim.

No *il jin* could touch me at school because I was notorious for never taking a shower.

(in-jŭng-syat)

인증샷
InJeung Shot

Flag / Proof Pic / Timestamp

"인증" (*in jeung*, "to certify", "to validate", "to confirm") + **shot**. It serves as an evidence photo of someone having done what they claim to have done or having been where they claim to have been because "pics or it didn't happen!"

Dad: I'm with the members of Big Bang.
Me: No way! Send me an *in jeung shot*!
Dad: Here you go!
Me: Oh... these are their wax figures ;(

(il-cha, i-cha, sam-cha)

1차 / 2차 /3차
il-cha, i-cha, sam-cha

1st, 2nd, 3rd Round (Stage) of Drinking / Bar Hopping

The word "차" (*cha*) means "round/stage", and in a nightlife context, it specifically refers to the "round/stage of drinking." Every different cha means changing the place of drinking or bar hopping. Hence, "2 (*i*) *cha*" means "bar hopping for the second round/stage of drinking," and "3 (*sam*) *cha* means "bar hopping for the third round/stage of drinking." Usually, 1 (*il*) *cha*, or the first round/stage, usually involves a meal and some drinks, like *soju* or beer, and 2 (*i*) *cha* could be *poktanju* (whiskey (*soju*) + beer); 3 (*sam*) *cha* could be more drinks at karaoke. The more rounds/stages you go through, the less you will remember the following day.

Okay, here is my plan for the weekend -
Il cha - eat, eat, eat
i cha - watch TV, play video game
Sam cha - sleep, sleep, sleep

(in-saeng)

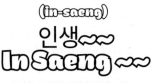
인생~~
In Saeng ~~

The Most/Best Ever

"인생" (*in saeng*) means "life" and is used by teenagers as a prefix to a noun to mean "greatest/best something ever in life." For example, "인생 콘서트" (*in saeng* concert) would mean "the best concert ever in life."

I went to the Super K-pop Concert last night, and it was my *in saeng* conce
Simply awesome!

INFINITE

INFINITE stands for "limitless," a six-member (Sungkyu, Dongwoo, Woohyun, Sungyeol, L, Sungjong) boy group formed by Woollim Entertainment. They debuted in 2010 with a song titled "She's Back," but they made their first appearance in an Mnet reality show "You Are My Oppa." Their single "Last Romeo" reached the #1 spot on the Billboard Twitter Emerging Artists chart in 2014 and had their own reality show titled Infinite Showtime on MBC Every1. Notable songs include "Paradise," "Destiny," "Back," and "The Eye."

Just like their name *INFINITE*, my love for the *oppas* are limitless.

(ing-yŏ)
잉여 Ing Yeo

Loser / Useless Being

Literal meaning is "surplus/extra", but the term is used by teenagers as a self-deprecating joke who label themselves as a "loser" because they are just another "surplus/extra" in society, whose existence doesn't matter that much.

I did nothing, literally nothing productive today. I feel like an *ing yeo*...

INNERCIRCLE

WINNER Fan Club

The name of the WINNER fan club and means "one who is nearest to the fans - the core layer that will help them." Fan color is nebula blue.

If you like WINNER, join the *Innercircle* to become part of the inner circle!

INSPIRIT

INFINITE Fan Club

The name of the INFINITE fan club. It's a compound word consisting of "**IN**(FINITE)" + "**SPIRIT**." It symbolizes the fans' love and loyalty, where they promise to be always supportive of INFINITE. Fan color is metal gold pearl.

What type of spirit will you be in your afterlife? I'll be *Inspirit!* Representing INFINITE!

입원 Ib Won
(ib-won)

Hospitalization

The worst thing that can happen to your bias - falling prey to a grueling schedule and getting hospitalized from burnout/exhaustion. It's the fans' worst nightmare because they can't see their biases perform on stage or appear on TV.

I heard the news that my *oppa* got ib won to the Korea hospital, so I broke my arm on purpose to get **ib won** to the room next to his!

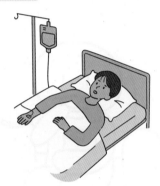

인기가요 Inkigayo
(in-kki-ga-yo)

Popular (K-pop) Songs/ Music Program by SBS

Literal meaning is "Popular (K-pop) Songs", but is also the name of a music program by SBS that airs every Sunday, featuring live performances by the hottest and most popular artists. This is a popular TV show in which the singers make a "comeback stage".

Tune in to channel 5! It's time for **Inkigayo**! Brothers are having a comeback stage today!

인기 Inki
(in-kki)

Popularity

A reference to the degree of popularity of an idol measured by various tools, such as the number of TV/Radio appearances, the size of a fan club, etc.

Jinpyo has so many friends. His *inki* knows no limit.

입덕 Ip Deok
(ip-tŏk)

Getting Hooked on an Idol

An abbreviation for a compound word made up of "입" *ip* ("to enter") "덕후" *deok hu* ("*otaku*" - geek/mania)" that refers to the moment one falls for an idol. This syndrome commonly afflicts someone watching a video clip of an idol that engulfs the "off-guard" audience with a "visual attack (handsomeness/cuteness overload)".

Mindy: When was your *ip deok* moment, Jen?
Jen: Oh, when his music video really wowed me.

(ip-gu member)
입구멤버
Ip Gu Member

The Very Member Who Made You Become Interested In The Group

"**입구**" (*ip gu*, "entrance") + "**멤버**" ("**member**"). It refers to that specific member who made you become interested in the group and eventually become a *deokhu*.

> The moment I saw Jackie on TV, I fell in love and joined the fan club for his band. He was my *ip gu member*.

(ja-sak)
자삭 Ja Sak

Self-Censorship

An abbreviation for "**자진**" *ja jin* ("self/voluntary") + "**삭제**" *sak je* ("deletion"). It is the act of someone deleting their already uploaded post/photo/file. The decision is usually made after 1) receiving feedback from other users or 2) belatedly realizing its appropriateness/awkwardness.

> Ikhyeon: Wow! I've got so many comments on my post!
> Rory: What are people saying?
> Ikhyeon: They are all telling me to *ja sak*…

재킷
Jacket

Album Cover

It's an English term that is more popularly used in Korea than other countries. The front of the packaging of a CD that features a photo or illustration and is known as album art for that reason.

> Cody: Don't you love their new *jacket*?
> Wanda: Oh yeah! I love leather jackets too!
> Cody: No, I meant their album cover haha.

자막 Ja Mak
(ja-mak)

Subtitles

It's what connects Korean culture with the rest of the world, but sometimes subtitles just don't do it justice because they are 1) poorly translated and 2) incapable of explaining situations/scenes that require cultural

> Sometimes it baffles me when they talk for 10 minutes in Korean, but the translated *ja mak* is only one sentence!

(ja-gi-ya)
자기야 Jagiya

Honey / Sweetie

"**자기**" (*ja gi*) means "sweetheart/honey" and "**야**" (*ya*) is a postpositional particle attached to a name, when calling someone, to make it sound friendly. Put together, "**자기야**" is an expression meaning "(Hey) Sweetheart."

Jenny: *Jagiya~ Jagiya~* <3
Mark: Hm... I have a feeling that you need something from me...

(jŏ-jak-gwon)
저작권
Jeo Jak Gwon

Copyright

The set of rights to which the owner of a particular work is entitled. In a K-pop context, its what earns the artists money through album sales and licensing of fan merchandise.

Are you reading a pirated version of this book? That's against *jeo jak gwon*! Hey, but its okay - as long as you learn Korean from it ;)

(jam-su)
잠수 Jam Su

Ghosting / M.I.A (Missing In Action)

Literal meaning is "going underwater/to submerge," and what happens when you go underwater? No one can reach out to you. Hence, it has two idiomatic meanings 1) ghosting: the act of breaking off a relationship by halting/refusing all communication and contact efforts with someone without any apparent warning or justification and 2) M.I.A (missing in action): someone, maybe your buddy, who has cut off contact with you intentionally (pissed at you) or unintentionally (e.g., too wasted).

After he threw up in my crush's car, he decided to *jam su*... Time heals everything...

(jŏ-jil)
저질 Jeo Jil

Pervert

Literal meaning is "low quality" but is more often used to mean "pervert."

Just because I'm not wearing any underwear doesn't mean I'm *jeo jil*!

(jae-bang-song)
재방송
Jae Bang Song

Rerun

A compound word made up of "**재**" *jae*
("re/repeat") + "**방송**" *bang song*
("airing, broadcast"). K-drama fans who missed
a live airing of an episode have to settle for this
and try to cover their ears before they finish
watching the episode to avoid a spoiler.

Slow Dude: Gooooooooooooooooooooooooal! Korea scores!
Oh my god!
Less Slow Dude: Dude, chill down, that's a *jae bang song*…
they lost the game…
Slow Dude: Oh.

Jailbait

Bias Who is Under 18

The danger of falling in love with an idol who is
under the age of 18, which is the legal age in
Korea. It became a popular term when Taemin
of SHINee debuted when he was only 16 in
2008, which led to countless *noona* fans falling
in love with him.

The reason the Miracle Kids are called the "*jailbait*
band" is because their average age is just 13.

(jaem)
잼 Jaem

Fun, Interest

Kids' and teenagers' way of saying the word
"재미" jae mi ("fun, interest"). It is used in
conjunction with other adjectives (e.g., "빅" big
"**잼**" *jaem* "fun" - "Much Fun", "노 no **잼**"
"No Fun". It is an effective conversation-ender.

Randy: Do you want to hear a joke? One time…
Jayna: No thanks, your jokes are *no jam*.

(jag-ŏp)
작업 Jak Eop

To Flirt With Somebody

Literally means "operation" or "work" but is
used figuratively to refer to the act of trying to
attract someone, mostly for amusement rather
than with serious intentions.

Rule #1 – Don't *jak eop* on a girl who has a boyfriend.

(jal-ja)
잘자 Jalja
"Good Night"

It is a sweet conversation-ender when talking to your loved one on the phone at night.

Yawn I feel so sleepy now. I'm going to bed early today. **Jalja** everybody~!

Jeju Island
Beautiful Island in the Southernmost Part of Korea

Jejudo 제주도, or **Jeju Island** is Korea's largest island off the southwest coast of the Korean Peninsula and is the most popular tourist destination for newlyweds, couples, and families. Palm trees, basalt, and beautiful beaches make exotic sights that are hard to see anywhere else in Korea. The iconic statues, *dolhareubang* 돌하르방(*dol* = "stone," *hareubang* = Jeju dialect for "grandfather"), famous for their bulging eyes, a long broad nose, and a hint of a smile, are carved from porous basalt (volcanic rock) and can be as tall as three meters. They are very popular among women because they are a symbol of fertility - There's a myth that if pregnant women touch the nose, they will have a son.

Why do all the couples in K-dramas have their first encounter in **Jeju Island**?

(jae-bal)
제발 Jebal
"Please"

Something you say when you want something dearly.

Dear god, **jebal** help our Oppa's win the award!

(jül)
즐 Jeul
"Whatever"

A term derived from an adjective "즐거운" *jeul geo un* ("fun, entertaining") used in expressions like "즐거운 게임 하세요" *jeul geo un* game *ha se yo* ("have a good game"). The shortened term, however, has evolved to become a conversation-ender. By saying *jeul* 즐 to someone, you express your intention of not wanting to engage in further conversation with the person, similar to saying "Have a Great Day, Sir".

Rex: Mimi! You know what you look like? A racoon! LOL
Mimi: **Jeul**!

지못미 Ji Mot Mi
(ji-mom-mi)

"Sorry I Couldn't Save You"

An abbreviation for "지켜주지 못해" *ji kyeo joo ji mot hae* (that I couldn't save you) "미안해" *mi an hae* ("sorry"). It is mainly used when someone looks funny (i.e., ugly funny) in a picture (e.g., a snapshot capturing an ugly moment). You are sorry because you 1) couldn't take a better picture, 2) weren't available to Photoshop it, or 3) just feel sorry that the person is ugly. You can also use this in drinking games when someone has to drink shots as a penalty for losing a game.

Hailey: LOL! Daniel looks like a sloth in this photo.
Xavier: *Ji mot mi* Daniel…

지름신 Ji Reum Shin
(ji-rŭm-shin)

Impulse Buying

A compound word made up of "지름" *ji reum* ("impulse buying") + "신" *shin* ("god") = "god of impulse buying". People use this imaginary deity as a scapegoat to blame for their lack of willpower (uncontrollable impulsiveness), as if their buying decision was the result of an unavoidable act of God (divine intervention). They usually come to their senses upon receipt of their credit card statement.

Sarah: Ben! Did you really buy this $3,000 bicycle with my card?
Ben: No I didn't. *Ji reum shin* did.

집 Jib
(jip)

Group's Full Length Album / Home

A term for 1) A group's full-length album, which usually contains upwards of 10 songs, while other works contain less than that (i.e., "mini album", "digital single", etc.). or 2) "Home".

Mr. A's 8th *jib* had 18 tracks and many other bonus materials.

직찍 Jik Jjik
(jik-tchik)

Photo/Video Taken by Me

An abbreviation for "직접" *jik jeop* ("in person") "찍음" *jjik eum* ("taking"). For celeb shots, it is a product of truly zealous fans' passion as they wait for days and days to get a glimpse of their bias, or it is the result of pure luck. You can also use this for any photo/video you have taken in person and you have all the rights pertaining to the final material.

Keira: Check out this photo, girls!
Judy: Wow! Is this a *jik jjik*?
Keira: Yup! I went to our oppa's concert and took it myself.

진상 Jin Sang (jin-sang)

Eyesore/Karen (Female)

Someone who has a nasty temper and makes a fuss over the most trivial things. It is similar to "drama queen", but it mostly refers to customers who demand outrageous favors (e.g., forcing the store to accept a return of a non-returnable product) because they believe they are the boss.

Joohee was screaming and even pushing the poor restaurant server over a strand of hair found in her meal. No one knew that she could be such a *jin sang*.

짜가 Jja Ga (tcha-ga)

Counterfeit / Knock Off

"가짜" ga jja ("fake") spelled backward, but it is most often used to refer to a counterfeit product.

Mingyu: *Bling Bling* Look at ma Lorex!
Juno: You mean Rolex?
Mingyu: LOL it is Lorex 'cause it is a *jja ga*, my man!

iPhome

짜 Jjang (Zzang) (tchang)

The Best / Awesome / Incredible

A word that appeared among the younger population in the 1990's, it has been widely used among all generations recently. It is not, however, used in formal/official settings, such as TV news.

My son got straight A's! My son, *Jjang*!
My Oppa just showed off his dancing skills. *Jjang*!

찌라시 Jji Ra Shi (tchi-ra-shi)

Tabloid Tales

A style of journalism that focuses on sensational topics (i.e., vivid crime stories, celebrity gossip, and junk food news) in order to distinguish themselves from other media. Although often criticized for overly sensational topics, they always find a significant share of readers, who appreciate the stories that can't be found elsewhere.

According to a *jji ra shi* circulating on the Internet, the youngest member of the group VODKA sleeps with his thumb in his nose.

좋아요 Jo A Yo (jo-a-yo)

"Like"

It refers to the "like" or "heart" button on Facebook and Instagram, which serves as a self-esteem booster for many.

Some people believe a post that receives less than 10 *jo a yos* is a shame.

LIKE

조공 Jo Gong (jo-gong)

Giving Gifts to One's Bias

Original meaning is "tribute", but in K-pop lingo, it refers to the act of giving gifts to a bias. Excessive *jo gong* issues often make headlines.

June made his *jo gong* to his favorite member of the girl group 4 Wonders through the fan club, but he is not sure if it will ever make it to her.

존댓말 Jon Daet Mal (jon-daet-mal)

Formal/Honorific Way of Speaking

The Korean language has different styles and forms of speaking. It is the polite form in which you basically attach "~요" *yo* and "~습니다/ㅂ니다" *~seup ni da/~up nida*" to the end of a sentence. It is determined by the social hierarchy (age, position at work/school etc.)

Byeongjin: Hey man, *gomawo*!
Ronald: Dude, you should use *jon daet mal* to me! I am a *hyung* to you!
Byeongjin: Oh, sorry. *Gomawoyo, hyungnim*!

(jon-nye/jon-jal)
존예//존잘
Jon Ye/Jon Jal

Pretty/Handsome as Hell

An abbreviation for "존나" *jon na* ("~as hell") + "예쁘다" *ye bbeu da* ("pretty") / "잘생겼다" *jal saeng gyeot da* ("handsome/good looking"). It's a teenager's term and should never be used in an official setting or to someone with whom you are not friends.

Boyfriend: Honey, I am going to call you *jon ye* from now on. You want to call me *jon jal*?
Girlfriend: Pay me.

(ju-jang-mi)
주장미
JooJang Mi

Episode Preview

An abbreviation for "주요" *joo yo* ("important") "장면" *jang myeon* ("scenes") "미리 보기" *miri bogi* ("to view in advance"). It is a handy feature if you don't have much time to watch a full episode, but it can also be a spoiler.

Too curious about the ending, but with too much homework to do, Jordan watched the *joo jang mi* of the last episode.

JYP

Jin Young Park

These are initials of **J**in **Y**oung **P**ark, one of Korea's most successful and influential music artists. He is also the CEO of the entertainment company **JYP** Nation.

I like *JYP* as a singer but more as a businessman.

JYP Entertainment

One of Big Three Entertainment Companies

One of the Big Three entertainment companies in Korea. Its artists include Wonder Girls, GOT7, miss A, 2 AM and 2 PM.

Did you know that *JYP Entertainment* got itself covered for 24 hours because they have 2 AM and 2 PM?

(jŏn-guk-gu)
전국구
Jeon Guk Gu

Mr./Ms. Nationwide

A term used to describe someone who has made a name for themselves, known by everyone in the nation.

I've been put on the FBI's Most Wanted list. I'm **jeon guk gu** now!

(jŏng-shin-sŭng-li)
정신승리
Jeong Shin Seung Ri

Sour Grapes

"**정신**" (*jeong shin*) means "mentality" + "**승리**" (*seung ri*) means "victory". Put together, it literally means "mental victory" but is used as an idiomatic expression to describe the act of pretending that one doesn't want something or self-rationalization because one cannot have it, similar to the English expression "sour grapes."

Mark: Well, the reason I'm not dating the members of TWICE is because I'm too busy!
Vicky: That's **jeong shin seung ri** right there.

(jik-gu)
직구 Jik Gu

Buying Something Directly from Overseas Internet Store

Short for "**직접**" (*jik jeop*, "direct") + "**구매**" (*gu mae*, "purchase"). Purchasing something directly from an overseas Internet store because its generally more expensive to buy the same item from a retailer in Korea, as the middlemen (importer and distributor) and the retailer jack up the price to make profit.

LOL I've gotten so fat, and they don't have my size in Korea. I had to **jik gu** my T-shirt from overseas.

(jin-tung)
진퉁
Jin Tung

Authentic / Genuine

A slang term for something "authentic/genuine" and is the direct opposite of "**짝퉁**" (*jjak tung*), which means knockoff/fake/imitation.

Everybody thought her Gucci shoes were **jin tung** until someone looked very closely to find out that it actually says Gucd.

(jip-sa)
집사 Jip Sa

Cat Servant

Literally means "butler/steward," but among cat lovers, it means "cat servant," because they know cats CAN'T be owned but only served and pampered. Your life goal as a "집사" is to keep them happy and satisfied at all times!

*If my oppa was a cat, I'd volunteer to be the **jip sa** in a heartbeat!*

(tchak-sa-rang)
짝사랑 Jjak Sa Rang

Unrequited Love / Crush

Actually from the word "외짝사랑" *oe jjak sa rang* where "외짝" (*oe jjak*) means "not a pair" and "사랑" *sarang* means "love," but "외" has been dropped out and "짝사랑" has been more popularly used to mean "unrequited love or crush," which is a clichéd theme for K-pop songs and K-dramas.

*I've been in **jjak sa rang** with her for over 5 years, and I finally decided to man up and ask her out!*

(tcha-jang-myŏn)
짜장면 JjaJang Myeon

Korean-Chinese Black Bean Sauce Noodles

A Korean-Chinese noodle dish topped with a thick *chunjang* sauce (blackbean), diced pork (or seafood), and vegetables. It's commonly believed that it first appeared in Incheon Chinatown in 1905 at a restaurant run by an immigrant family from the Shandong Province of China. Although there is a dish in China with the same name, its different in many ways, and for this reason, its considered a Korean-Chinese dish. It is one of the most popular, if not THE most popular, food in Korea because its affordable, convenient, and tasty. There is even a day called "Black Day", an unofficial, more of a tongue-in-cheek day of consolation, observed each year on April 14th by singles in Korea. It is related to Valentine's Day and White Day. On these days, people who have not received gifts gather together wearing black and eat black-colored food, such as 짜장면 *Jja jang myeon*, as a means of sympathizing with each other.

*Oh! It's Black Day tomorrow! Let me call my buddies and have **jja jang myeon** all together... Forever alone!*

(tchak-tung)
짝퉁 Jjak Tung

Knockoff / Fake / Imitation

A slang term referring to a knockoff or an imitation of an expensive product. It's also spelled as "짭퉁" (*jjap tung*), and they are used interchangeably.

*I bought this **jjak tung** Prada bag from eBay, and everyone thinks its authentic.*

(tchŏk-bŏl-nam)
쩍벌남
Jjeok Beol Nam

Manspreading

"쩍" (*jjeok*) means "wide," "벌" (*beol*) is the first word of "벌리다" (*beol li da*, "spread"), and "남" (*nam*), meaning "male/man". Put together, it literally means "wide spreading male," but it refers to the act of men sitting in public transport, such as subway/metro, with legs wide apart, covering more than one seat, but its also broadly used to refer to a male with no manners. The English equivalent is "manspreading."

So rude! That **jjeok beol nam** is taking up 5 seats ;(

(tchŏl-ŏ)
쩔어 Jjeol Eo

Freaking Awesome / Epic / Unbelievable

Similar to "대박" (*daebak*, "jackpot," "awesome" in meaning. It has a dual nuance, depending on the situation (positive as well as negative).

Wow! I just got a ticket to a BTS concert! Unbelievable... **Jjeol eo**!

What? You went bar hopping last night? You just got arrested for DUI a few days ago.... **Jjeol eo**...!

(tcho-lep)
쪼렙 Jjo Leb

Noob / Newbie

"쪼" is a mutated version of the first word of "초보" (*cho bo*, "beginner") + "렙" (*leb*) is a short form of "레벨" (level). A slang term for a beginner, whose nuance is similar to that of "noob" in English.

Flower Boys got a new member named Toby! He's a **jjo leb**!

(tchol-at-da)
쫄았다 Jjol At Da
Got Cold Feet / Intimidated

"쫄았다" is a Gyeongsang province dialect for "scared" and is used to refer to the state of becoming nervous and intimidated to the point at which you want to change your mind. It should never be used in formal settings but is perfectly fine between friends.

I worked so hard for today's interview, but I got really **jjol at da** when I sat before the interviewer.

(tchok-bak)
쪽박 Jjok Bak
Going Bankrupt

"쪽" (**jjok**) refers to the state/shape of something split in half, and "박" (**bak**) means "gourd." So what good is a gourd when it's split in half? Absolutely useless -hence it's used as an idiom to describe someone who has lost all their money.

I went to Vegas dreaming of a jackpot but ended with a **jjok bak**...

(jo-hap)
조합 Jo Hap
Combination

It's similar to "케미" (compatibility/match) in meaning. It refers to the combination of two or more people/items. The better "조합" a group has, the better chance of success it has. The tricky part of it is, though, you never know what the combination will look like until people/objects are put together. They might create a synergy or cause a cacophony.

Tony: We should go out cause we will make a good **jo hap**!
Dana: Doubt it. No wonder you failed chemistry in high school.

WE GOT CHEMISTRY

(jo-sŏn-shi-dae)
조선시대
Joseon Shidae

Very Old Fashioned / Very Long Time Ago

"조선시대" (*Joseon shidae*, "The Joseon Period/Era") refers to the historical period of the Joseon Dynasty, a Korean dynastic Kingdom founded in the 14th century and lasting until the 19th century. The Kingdom had a set of values reflecting on the teachings of Buddhism and Confucianism, and many of the ideas are considered archaic nowadays, so the term "조선시대" means something VERY outdated and old-fashioned that just doesn't belong in the world we currently live in.

9PM is my curfew... My parents must think they are living in *Joseon shidae* .

(jo-yŏn)
조연 Jo Yeon

Supporting Actor

Someone who plays the role below 주인공 (*ju in gong*, "protagonist") in a film, drama, play, or music video. For this position, directors look for actors who precisely match the profile of the character they have created, rather than someone who's well-known and popular. This is a great opportunity for unknown actors to make a name for themselves!

You are not the boss of me! I'm the shot caller here! Don't act like I'm your *jo yeon*!

(jong-gyŏl-ja)
종결자
Jong Gyeol Ja

Best In The Business

Literal meaning is "terminator" but is idiomatically used to refer to someone who's the best in the business because, if he/she is the best, then the game is over when he/she appears.

Wow... did you really design this? I think this is the best work I've seen in my life... You're truly a design *jong geyol ja!*

(jon-bŏ)
존버 Jon Beo

HODL (Hold On For Dear Life)

Short for "존나" (*jon na*, "f***ing") + "버텨라" (*beo tyeo ra*, "persevere," "hang in there"). A slang term originated from the Korean Bitcoin community when referring to keeping and holding onto a cryptocurrency rather than selling it when the price fluctuates and the future looks uncertain, hoping it will go up in their favor. The English equivalent is HODL (hold on for dear life), which many believe is actually a typo for HOLD because people got too excited and made a mistake while typing.

Doug: Ugh... I'm having the worst hangover...
Juan: *Jon beo*, my friend... It shall also pass...

주인공 Ju In Gong *(ju-in-gong)*

Main Character / Protagonist

The main character, whom the (crazy) stories revolve around. Some of the common examples in K-dramas with a Cinderella-type storyline is a young son or a daughter of the company's chairman. They are cocky, arrogant, and believe money can buy anything, including love, but they gradually change after meeting that new employee who teaches them the value of true love...

Hey! It's my birthday! So I'm the *ju in gong* of this party!!!

주작 Ju Jak *(ju-jak)*

Made-Up Story

"주" *(ju,* "self") + "작" *(jak,* "work," "production"). A fictitious story one intentionally makes up to gain attention, cause controversy, or just for fun.

Ha! The whole story about Jim getting kidnapped turned out to be a ju jak! He did it to get people's attention...

주연 Ju Yeon *(ju-yŏn)*

Leading Actor

Someone who plays the role of 주인공 *(ju in gong,* "protagonist") in a film, drama, play, or music video. Usually, its extremely difficult for rookie actors to get this role, as directors prefer well-known, popular actors with proven track records of commercial success.

Movie directors try to cast K-pop idols as a *ju yeon* for their movies because it guarantees a great number of tickets sold from the fandom.

중2병 Jung 2 (i) Byeong *(jung-i-byŏng)*

Edgelord

"중2" *(jung-i)* means "8th Grade(r)" + "병" *(byeong)* means "sickness". Put together, it means "Eighth Grader Syndrome" but is idiomatically used to refer to someone who tries so hard to appear overly cool, apathetic, rebellious and unique by posting shocking and cringe-worthy stuff in an attempt to gain attention. It's termed so because such state of mind is similar to that of a teenager who's going through puberty.

Oh dear... He posted a "Whats the meaning of life?" post again on Instagram... He should see a doctor for his *jung i byong*!

중박 Jung Bak
(jung-bak)

Modest Success

We all know "대박" (*dae **bak***) means "jackpot" where "대 *dae* (大)" means "big/large," and "중 *joong* (中)" means "medium/middle." Hence, "**중박**" means a moderate success that is not big but not small.

The new song they came out with was a ***jung bak***. Not a huge hit but not a total bust, either.

중독 Jung Dok
(jung-dok)

Addiction

The act of doing something repeatedly, such as putting your bias' song on auto-repeat mode and listening to it 24/7.

I have a huge K-pop ***jung dok*** problem, and the doctor said there's no cure for that!

중고신인 Jung Go Shin In
(jung-go-shin-in)

Someone Who Came Into The Spotlight In Their Late Career

"중고" (*jung go*, "used") + "신인" (*shin in*, "rookie"). Someone who's been in the industry for quite a long time but hasn't come into the spotlight until recently, causing people to think they are a rookie.

No wonder Rocky didn't look nervous on stage at all - he's a ***jung go shin in*** who debuted back in 2009!

줍줍 Jup Jup
(jup-jup)

Buying Something That Went Down In Value

Short for "줍기 줍기" (*jup gi jup gi*, "to pick up, to pick up"), which originated from the Korean Bitcoin community as an expression referring to the act of purchasing cryptocurrency that went down in value, with the hope of it soaring in the near future. Since then, it has been widely used in MMORPGs, where players pick up unattended items lying on the ground.

Kim: Whats all that stuff?
Jeremy: Some old lady dropped a bunch of stuff in the supermarket parking lot, and I went ***jup jup!***
Kim: That's no good, man! That's stealing!

newbie

좌표 Jwa Pyo (jwa-pyo)

URL Address

Literal meaning is "coordinates" but it is used to mean the URL address of a photo, movie clip, data, file, and the likes on the web.

Joy: Damn! Look at this article bashing our *oppas*!
Diane: WTF! Give me the *jwa pyo*! There will be blood...

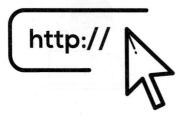

케미 Ke Mi (ke-mi)

Compatibility / Match

Short for the English word "Chemistry," it refers to the degree of compatibility/match between the two, as in the case of having "love chemistry" when one falls in love with another. So if you have good 케미, it means you, too, are a good match, and bad 케미 means the opposite. It can also be used for things other than people, like milk and cookies, shakes and fried chicken, and beer (yummy 치맥 *chimaek*! as well as between the members of a group.

My boyfriend and I fight every day. We must have a bad *ke mi*...

KCON

K-pop Expo

Annual Hallyu (Korean Wave) convention organized by Mnet Media, CJ E&M, Powerhouse Live, and Koreaboo in order to promote K-pop and Korean culture, as well as facilitate mutual cultural understanding among people around the world. It's held in various locations across the world and is composed of reception, K-pop concerts, and discussion sessions with panelists. The latest events were held in New Jersey, Los Angeles, and Sydney in 2017. The Los Angeles event, which was held at the Staples Center, attracted more than 85,000 attendees.

The fun part about attending *KCON* is you can meet your fellow K-poppers

킬링파트 Killing Part

Most Impressive Part Of A Song

In a K-pop context, it refers to the most impressive part of a song, which is usually a title song with very catchy and addictive lyrics/dance moves.

"Oppa Gangnam Style" is probably the most famous *killing part* of a K-pop song.

smooth like butter

(Ka-tok)
카톡 Ka Tok

Messaging App Virtually Used by Every Korean Smartphone User

It refers to Kakaotalk, a chatting/messaging app that holds the dominant position in Korea.
It is the most widely used means of communication today.

Jim: Call me when you get home, buddy!
Tony: I have no talk minutes. I will *ka tok* you!

(Gamsahamnida)
감사합니다
K/Gamsa Hamnida

"Thank You (formal)"

Formal way of saying thank you, which is equivalent to saying, "I appreciate it."

Amy met the man who saved her life, but all she could say was "*Kamsa Hamnida*".

(Kal-toe)
칼퇴 Kal Toe

Leaving Work On Time

An abbreviation for "칼" *kal* ("knife") "퇴근" *toe geun* ("getting off work"). Literally means "leaving work on time, sharp as a knife".
It is what Korean office workers dream of, but in reality, they often find themselves working overnight.

Being able to *kal twae* is something that all Korean office workers dream of doing.

(Ke-ba-ke)
케바케 Ke Ba Ke

Case by Case / YMMV (Your Mileage May Vary)

An abbreviation of an English phrase 케이스 바이 케이스 "case by case" that means "results may vary depending on the situation".
It is frequently used with the term 사바사 *sa ba sa* ("person by person"). When giving advice to someone, make sure to mention this so you are not held accountable for any unexpected outcomes.

Michelle: Why did he get the job and I didn't? It's not fair!
Mark: Well, oftentimes who gets the job is *ke ba ke*.

키보드 워리어
Keyboard Warrior

Someone Who Expresses Anger/Hate on the Internet

The individuals who display bad temper through malicious comments, cyber-bullying, etc., mainly because they are incapable of doing it in real life, and the Internet provides anonymity.

Getting bullied at school and rejected by a girl, Minu became a **keyboard warrior**, and expressed his anger through harsh comments on others' social media.

(kim-ttŏk-sun)
김떡순
Kim Tteok Soon

Kimbab, Tteokbokki, Soondae

The most popular trio of Korean street foods, so popular that they are abbreviated to resemble the name of a real person.

Although Jenny doesn't have a boyfriend, she wouldn't cry because her best friend, **Kim Ddeok Soon**, is always by her side.

(Kim-chi)
김치 Kimchi

Staple Korean Food

A staple of Korean cuisine. A traditional fermented Korean side dish made of vegetables, such as *baechu* (napa cabbage), with a variety of seasonings. The most representative Kimchi is *baechu* **Kimchi**. This tangy and spicy fermented side dish made of vegetables with a variety of seasonings has become an inseparable part of the Korean lifestyle, to the point where people view it as part of their identity. It's also a word you say to induce a smile when taking a picture, similar to saying "cheese" or "whiskey" in English.

Kimchi is so Korean that it even has "Kim" in it.

(king-wang-tchang)
킹왕짱
King Wang Jjang

The Bestest

A compound word made up of "**King** +
왕 *wang* ("King") + **짱** *jjang* ("best")".
A set of 3 superlatives, thus it is the best possible
thing in the entire universe.

Girlfriend: How much do you love me?
Boyfriend: A lot!
Girlfriend: That's it?
Boyfriend: No, *king wang jjang*!

킹카/퀸카
Kingka /
Queenka

Male Hottie/Female Hottie

A male/female hottie who is not only good-
looking but also rich and well-educated. The
terms are believed to have originated from
playing cards ("**King Car**d" and "**Queen
Car**d", which are both high in value).

I think the *queenka* of the group QTQT is Myo. She is from
a *chaebol* family and always gets straight A's in school.

(kkam-nol)
깜놀 Kkam Nol

Startled

An abbreviation for "깜짝 놀라다" *kkam jjak
nol*ada ("very surprised"). This is the type of
response you would have if your favorite bias
announced retirement.

Nina: Mina, can you come pick me up at the hospital…
Mina: Why? What's wrong?
Nina: I ran out of taxi money, and this is the farthest the
driver would take me.
Mina: **Kkam nol**!

(kkap)
깝 Kkab

Acting Crazy and Overly Energetic

Slang for someone acting crazy and overly
energetic to the point where they are thought to
be insane. Jo Kwon of 2 AM popularized this
term with his outrageous dance moves, earning
the name "*Kkab* Kwon".

Last night in the club, I saw so many kids doing the
kkab dance. I am pretty sure they were on something.

(kkwal-la)

꽐라 Kkwal La

Wasted

The state of being wasted. There is a hypothesis that it is related to koala bears because they eat eucalyptus leaves, which are believed to contain chemicals similar to alcohol, thereby saying that koala bears are always drunk and spend most of their time sleeping.

Sam: People call me Koala! I think that is a cute nickname.
Tony: You drunk head! I bet they meant ***Kkwal La***…

(kong-ga-ru)

콩가루 Kong Ga Ru

Messed Up Family

Literal meaning is "bean powder family" but is figuratively used to describe a family that is so unstable and fragile that, when the air is blown near it, everything will just fall apart and collapse, just like bean powder. It is one of the most stereotypical families in *mak jang* (drama with unrealistic and outrageous storylines) K-dramas.

Judy comes from a ***kong ga ru*** family. Her mother lost all her money on gambling and her dad just went to jail for drug trafficking.

(kong-da-bang)

콩다방 Kong Da Bang

Coffee Bean

A compound word for "**콩**" ***kong*** ("bean") + "**다방**" ***da bang*** ("coffee shop, tea house"). This is one of the largest coffee franchises in Korea along with Starbucks and Café Pascucci, where people willingly spend more for a cup of coffee than they would for lunch.

Amy: ***Kong da bang*** at 7 tonight, right?
Doug: What the what?
Amy: Coffee Bean.

김밥천국

Kimbap Cheon Guk

Korean Restaurant Franchise with Unbeatable Cost-to-Benefit Ratio

"김밥" (*Kimbap*, "Korean seaweed rice roll") + "천국" (*cheon guk*, "Heaven"). Its literal meaning is "kimbap heaven," but it's actually a franchise with a huge selection of menus, including *kimbap*, omelet, *ramyon* noodles, tofu stew, and many others. It's super popular, especially among teenagers who are strapped for cash because they have an unbeatable cost-to-benefit ratio. Their foods are served quickly, portions are big, and most importantly, they are easy on your wallet!

What kind of heaven serves yummy Korean food?
Kimbap Cheon Guk does!

(kka-bang-gwon)

까방권

Kka Bang Gwon

Indulgence/Protection From Getting Bashed

"까" (**kka**) comes from the slang word "까임" (***kka im***), which means "bashing," and "방지권" (***bang ji gwon***) literally means "the right to prevent/protect," or "indulgence." Something That's (virtually) given to a celeb who does/achieves something exceptional/exemplary. For example, if a Korean player scores the winning goal in the World Cup, then excited Korean fans would say he is protected from getting bashed in the future.

Ji-Sung Park scored the winning goal at the FIFA World Cup, and he earned a ***kka bang gwon*** for the rest of his life!

Kiss Me

U-KISS Fan Club

The name of the U-Kiss fan club. It stands for 1) answer to the question "If U-KISS asked who they should kiss...?" and 2) U-KISS & ME (fans). Fan color is pearl fuchsia.

Jenn*y: Kiss Me! Kiss Me!*
Mark: Oh I'd love to! I love you too!
Jenny: I'm talking about the U-Kiss Fan Club I'm joining today!

(kkang-pae)

깡패

Kkang Pae

Top Level

Literal meaning is "bully" or "gangster," but its used among teenagers as a suffix to mean something is of top level because a bully/gangster will beat anyone in their way! For example, "어깨 깡패" (*eo kkae*, "shoulders" *kkang pae*) means someone with a super well developed set of shoulders.

Man! You solved the puzzle already? You're an IQ ***kkang pae***!

(kkŏm-ttak-ji)
껌딱지
Kkeom Ttak Ji

Glued At The Hip / Attached At The Hip

Literal meaning "gum stuck on something", but its idiomatically used to refer to a person who follows another person around very closely and constantly, like a little child following his/her mom.

> Dude! You are a stalker! Not a **kkeom tak ji**!

(kkŭt-pan-wang)
끝판왕
Kkeut Pan Wang

Best In The Business / Master

"끝판" (**kkeut pan**, "final stage" in video games) + "왕" (**wang**, "king"). The last boss of any video game, which is the strongest and thus most difficult to defeat. In a K-pop context, it refers to someone/something That's the best in the business.

> Did you see their new choreography? It's a real dance **kkeut pan wang**!

LEVEL 99

(kkon-dae)
꼰대 Kkon Dae

Fogey / Stick-In-The-Mud

A slang word for an old-fashioned and stubborn person with zero flexibility, who thinks he/she is always right and others are always wrong and therefore constantly resists change, even for the better. Although it refers to an old person, it could also be used for young people who possess all the qualities mentioned above.

> Jimmy is only 15 years old and thinks girls shouldn't be allowed to vote or be educated! What a stupid **kkon dae**!

(kkot-baem)
꽃뱀 Kkot Baem

Gold Digger / Female Con Artist

Literal meaning is "flower snake" but is idiomatically used to refer to a female con artist who seduces men using sex as a bait and using it to blackmail them to get money afterwards.

> After Jenny got a new Prada bag from her boyfriend, she dumped him immediately. Everyone knows she's a **kkot baem**.

(kkot-gil)
꽃길 Kkot Gil

Sunshine and Roses / Sunshine and Rainbows

Literal meaning is "flowe(ry) road" but is idiomatically used to wish someone all the best in their coming days because walking on the flower(ry) road is something that symbolizes happiness. There are many theories on the origin of the expression, but the most plausible one is that JYJ fans came up with it as an homage to the part of the lyrics of the song "Fallen Leaves": "after the flower withers, we will start again."

Yes!!! I'm finally graduating and already got a new job! I have *kkot gil* laid out before me ;)

콩글리쉬
Konglish

Korean-Style English

A term referring to Korean-style English, with English loanwords that have been appropriated into the Korean language in ways that are not readily understandable by native English speakers.

When I got to the U.S., I realized that much of my English vocabulary was actually *Konglish* words!

(ki-yop-ta)
KYOPTA / KYEOPTA

Cute

"귀엽다" (*gwi yeop da*, "cute") spelled/transcribed and widely used by non-Korean speakers.

Han: Awwwwwwwww! Is that your baby daughter? She's so *KYOPTA*
Toby: That's my pet pig.

(kong-kkak-ji)
콩깍지
Kong Kkak Ji

Blinded by Love

Literal meaning is "bean pod" and comes from the expression "눈에 콩깍지가 씌다" (*nune kong kkak ji ga ssui da* "one's eyes are covered with a bean pod"), which is figuratively used to denote the phenomenon where one is blinded by love.

I don't know what you see in her... She's not wife material! Ugh! I wish I could remove that *kong kkak ji* for you...

꽃미남
Kkot Minam / Flower Boy

Incredibly Beautiful Young Male

꽃 *kkot* ("flower") + 미남 *minam* ("handsome man") = an incredibly beautiful young male whose beauty (mostly looks) is comparable to that of a flower.

How can a man be so beautiful? Taeyong is such a *flower boy*.

(i-su-man)
이수만
Lee Soo Man
The Founder and Chairman of SM Entertainment

The founder and chairman of SM Entertainment. Having produced countless star idols, he is considered a pioneer in establishing the K-pop idol system that is widely popular today in the 1990s, earning the nickname "the father of K-pop".

Oh, so SM Entertainment is named after the founder *Lee Soo Man*?

(le-jön-söl)
레전설
Legen Seol
Legendary Figure

"레전드" legend and "전설" *jeon seol* ("legend") combined as one word to make it sound funny because "gen" of "legend" and "*jeon*" of "*jeon seol*" sound the same.

After winning all five music charts, which is the first in the music industry, BTBT became a *legen seol*.

(li-jü-chi-jöl)
리즈시절
Leeds Sijeol
Heyday / Prime
One's Best Days

The time when Ji Sung Park and Alan Smith were teammates at Manchester United (English Premier League Football Club). At that time, Alan Smith wasn't getting many playing opportunities like he did at Leeds United Football Club when he was in his prime. For that reason, "during his days at Leeds" became synonymous with "someone's best days". The word 시절 *sijeol m*eans "specific time in the past").

Hector: I keep losing StarCraft matches these days! I miss my *leeds si jeol*…
Enzo: What *leeds si jeol*? You have only won once so far, and it was because the opponent got disconnected.

립싱크 Lip Sync
Pretending to Sing

The act of pretending to sing while simply matching lip movements to pre-recorded vocals. It is a godsend for many who lack singing talent.

Ingu failed the audition because he attempted to *lip sync*.

Leader

Idol Member Who is in Charge and Oversees the Group

A member of an idol group who is in charge of organizing and managing its members. Although not in all cases, the oldest of the members usually takes on this role.

Awesome Sophomores have 15 members, and it is extremely difficult to guess who the *leader* of the group is.

(lot-te world)

롯데월드

Lotte World

Korea's BiggestAmusement Park

Lotte World is a major recreation complex in Seoul, South Korea. It consists of the world's largest indoor theme park, an outdoor amusement park called "Magic Island," an artificial island inside a lake linked by a monorail, shopping malls, a luxury hotel, a Korean folk museum, sports facilities, and movie theaters. Opened on July 12, 1989, Lotte World receives 7.3 million visitors each year.

Forget Disneyland. We have *Lotte World* here in Korea!

L.E.G.O/L.E.G.G.O

EXID Fan Club

The name of the EXID fan club. It stands for 1) Lets go (together with the fans) and 2) LEGO: Lets build memories together, piece by piece like LEGO. Fan colors are PANTONE 7499C, PANTONE 7423C, PANTONE 272C.

Hoon: I joined *L.E.G.O*!
Daniel: Aren't you a little too old to play with Lego?
Hoon: No, dude! It's the EXID Fan Club!!! Up, Down, Up, Up, Down!

Lets Git It

"Lets Go!"

An expression frequently used by Jay Park and Dok2 on Show Me The Money, which became popular among the younger generation hip hop fans who started using it to express excitement.

Ticket sales for Big Bang + BTS + EXID collaboration concert will begin in 5 minutes... *Lets git it*!

(ma-tong)

마통 Ma Tong

Credit Line

"마" (*ma*) is the first sound of the English word "minus", and "통" (*tong*) is the first syllable of "통장" (*tong jang*), meaning "bankbook/bank account." Put together, it refers to something similar to "credit line," which means you are allowed to borrow money from the bank at a certain rate up to a set limit.

OMG... I'm doomed... I just put $3,000 into Bitcoin from my *ma tong*, and its value shrunk to zero. WTF!!!

로케 Locae
(lo-ke)

Location Shooting

The practice of filming in the actual setting or location in which a story takes place, rather than on a stage set up to emulate the environments of the actual location.

The new K-drama about lovers in Russia was *locae'd* in Moscow.

Love Call
러브콜

Offer

The act of asking someone to appear on a show or star in a film, CF, or movie, or sign a contract in general.

Thanks to the recent success of her CF, Shu has been receiving countless *love calls*.

Love Line

Map of Love Relationships Among Characters in K-dramas

A map of complicated relationships among characters in K-dramas. For example, if Soomi and Tak have been having something going on and finally decide to go out, then they have just formed a *love line*.

Hey sweetie, do you want to form a love line with me?

맹구 Maeng Goo
(maeng-gu)

Idiot/fool

The name of a comical character from an extremely popular 90's comedy, best known for his foolishness. Since then, the name has become synonymous with "someone foolish" or "idiotic".

Kim: I just lost $500 at the casino.
Nina: You *maeng goo*! Didn't I tell you that you have no chance of winning against the house?

막장 Makjang

(mak-jang)

K-drama With Crazy Storylines

Slang for something that can't get any worse. It is widely used to describe K-dramas that have seriously outrageous and unrealistic storylines (e.g., birth secrets, adultery, accidents, memory loss, fatal illness, etc.) to the point that it becomes ridiculous. It does, however, attract a significant number of fans, due to its addictive nature, speedy development, and surprising plot twists.

Dude, you went out with this girl, and now you are dating her sister? You are living a **makjang** life!

막내 Maknae

(mang-nae)

The Youngest Member of a Group

The youngest member of an idol group, who is often the life of the party. They also assume the role of taking care of little favors and chores for the group.

Anybody can tell that Grace is the **maknae** of the group because she is the most energetic, innocent, silly girl of all.

MAMA

Mnet Asian Music Awards

An annual event and one of the major K-pop awards events hosted by CJ E&M through its music channel subsidiary Mnet in which many high-profile actors and celebrities from China, Hong Kong, Japan, and Taiwan also participate.

This year, **MAMA** will be held in Shanghai, China. I wonder who will win the top award.

말도안돼 Maldo Andwae

(mal-do-an-dwae)

"Nonsense!"

Literally means "does not even make any sense". It can be used as a rejection when somebody asks for an outrageous favor or as an exclamation when something beyond belief actually happens.

TV: And the winner is... XOLO!
AAA fans: **Maldo andwae**... This award is rigged!

만렙 Man Leb

(man-lep)

The Highest Level

An abbreviation for a compound word of a Chinese word "만" *man* ("full") and an English word "레벨" level, shortened and pronounced as "렙" *leb*. It refers to someone who has reached the highest status in a field, such as an online game. It can also be used to describe someone who is full of "geekiness".

Jim: Level 99! Level 99! I did it! Yes!
Andrew: Congrats, mate! You just reached *man leb*!

Sarah: My boyfriend just abandoned me and ran away when a fake tiger approached us.
Jenny: Dang... His cowardice hit *mal leb*!

Lv. 100

Manner Hands

Trying Not to Touch Someone While Taking a Photo Together

A kind and considerate act where a male's hand stops short in an attempt not to make contact with a female's shoulders or waist. It is also known as "hover hands" as the hand literally hovers over the area.

Look how Keegan is doing his *manner hands* while taking pictures with his fans! He looks like a magician.

맛있어 Mashisso

(ma-shi-ssŏ)

"Delicious"

Literally meaning "delicious" but can also be used as an expression of euphoria when eating something that pleases your taste buds.

Oh my god, did you make this? *Mashisso*!

Manner Legs

Lowering Height to Match That of Another

A kind and considerate act to accommodate height differences. It is usually done by the taller male spreading his legs sideways while standing, thereby lowering himself to achieve a mutually desired goal (e.g., kissing, hugging, etc.).

I love it when Jiho does the *manner legs* to kiss her! That's so sweet of him.

맞선 Mat Seon (mat-sŏn)

Formal Blind Date Arranged by Parents

A formal blind date prearranged by parents.
In K-dramas, parents (usually the rich guy's mother) often use this tactic to break up a relationship because they think the girl (who usually comes from a poor family) is not good enough for their son.

I think it's about time I got married. My mom set me up for 5 *mat seons* this month!

마음 Maum (ma-ŭm)

Mind/Heart

It refers to the personality/characteristic that a person is originally born with but also can mean one's emotions.

You stole my *maum*, and you can have it. I am so in love with you.

멜론 Melon

Music Streaming Service

An Internet-based music streaming service where you can listen to music for a fee.

Mina: How much are you paying for *Melon*?
Doohee: The fruit or the streaming service?

Melo Drama

Romance Drama

Originally, it refers to a gripping drama genre full of exciting/sad events and often accompanied by exaggerated/forced acting. While it is not limited to love stories but includes various topics, such as revenge, success, and forgiveness, the term is almost exclusively associated with "romance drama" in Korea.

Juno's story of finding the love of his life is such a *melo drama*.

멘붕 Men Bung
(men-bung)

Mental Breakdown

The psychological state of total chaos caused by something utterly beyond belief.

I had the biggest **men bung** when I heard my Oppa's been having a secret affair with the member of GBGB.

멘트 Ment

Pick up Line

Originated from the word "comment", but in Korea, it refers to something sweet and charming one says to seduce the opposite sex.

Dohoon: Hey girl, you look like a traffic ticket!
Jenny: Excuse me?
Dohoon: You got FINE written all over you!
Jenny: Is that a **ment**? Don't flirt with me, Mr.!

먹튀 Meok Twi
(mŏk-twi)

Eat and Run / Dine and Dash

Literally meaning "eat and run/vanish". It's used to describe an overpaid contract, especially in sports, where a player shows a poor level of performance after signing a blockbuster contract. In business, it refers to an entity that does not fully carry out the mutually agreed terms after signing a contract and securing its share of the money.

Fing: Hey, can you lend me $50? I will pay it back in a week with interest.
Mei: Hell no! I heard you **mweok twied** with Jenny's money last week!

미쳤어 Mi Chyeo Sso
(mi-chyŏ-ssŏ)

"Crazy"

An expression used to describe various emotions, such as surprise, joy, or anger, depending on the situation.

You drank that whole bottle of Soju? *Mi Chyeo Sso*?

(mi-jon)
미존 MiJon

Scene Stealer

An abbreviation for "미친" *mi chin* ("crazy") "존재감" *jon jae gam* ("presence"). It refers to someone with an overwhelming swag, who dwarfs everyone around them.

The movie wouldn't have been complete without him. Yes, he is such a *mi jon* no one else can imitate.

(mi-nam/mi-nyŏ)
미남/미녀 Mi Nam / Mi Nyeo

Good Looking Male/ Beautiful Female

A compound word made up of two Chinese words - "미" *mi* means "beautiful" "남" *nam* means "male" and "녀" *nyeo* means "female".

Wow, that *mi nyeo* is a real head-turner. She is the most beautiful girl I've ever seen!

(mil-dang)
밀당 Mil Dang

Psychological Tug of War

A fierce psychological warfare that usually takes place among couples as they attempt to protect their ego and hope to secure the upper hand in the relationship. Not everyone is good at playing this game, and if not played well, the rope can snap and recoil.

Sabrina: He hasn't called me for 3 days. Should I?
Jim: No, Sabrina – I am 100% sure he's playing *mil dang* with you. Don't give in!

(mi-an-hae)
미안해 Mianhae

"Sorry"

Informal way of saying "sorry". It can only be used between people with emotional intimacy, such as friends and family. An older person can say this to a younger person if the age difference is wide (e.g., a grandpa to a grandson). Adding "yo" makes it more formal.

Jenny: Oppa, I deleted your Instagram account by mistake… *Mianhae*…
Oppa: What? How?! I can't believe you just did that!
Jenny: *Mianhaeyo...*

민낯 Min Nat
(min-nat)

Bare Face

A face without any makeup on. Synonymous with 쌩얼 *saeng eol*.

Oh hi, who are you? Oh, it's you! Didn't recognize you without any makeup on. Your *min nat* is quite different from the picture.

미니 앨범 Mini Album
(mi-ni aeb-beom)

Album that Contains about Half or 1/3 of the Songs of a Full Length Album

A short album that contains less than 10 songs but more than one (known as a single album). It usually includes remixes and instrumental versions of the songs.

Nora: When will our *oppa's* hiatus end? It's been 2 years already.
Nancy: I know, right? They should release a *mini album* or something at least!

미워 Miwo
(mi-wŏ)

"Hate You"

A cute way of saying "I hate you".

Why didn't you call me? Oppa *miwo miwo miwo miwo*!

목소리 Mok So Ri
(mok-so-ri)

Voice

Can also be used figuratively to refer to someone's opinion or assertion.

Kyumin has the sweetest *mok so ri* among all K-pop singers.

몰카 Mol Ca

Hidden Camera

An abbreviation for "**몰래** *mol lae* ("secretly") + **카메라**" ("**camera**"), referring to the act of filming someone unbeknownst to them. The term originated from MBC's popular comedy TV show "일요일 일요일 밤에 (*Ilyoil Ilyoil Bam Ae* – "Sunday, Sunday Night", where Lee Kyung Kyu, a famous comedian, set up a hidden camera to see how celebrities would react to a hilarious situation. Recently, however, the term has been more frequently used to describe criminal activities, and a handful of celebrities have fallen victim to such crimes (i.e., leaked private clips).

After Jason's *mol ca* on his private life leaked, many of his sponsors canceled CF contracts.

몰라 Mola
(mol-la)

"I Don't Know"

Can be used to avoid answering certain questions that can cause embarrassment.

Uhyuk: How much do you weigh?
Mina: *Mola*! How can you ask a lady that kind of question?

몰컴 Mol Com

"Using Computer Secretly"

An abbreviation for "**몰래** *mol lae* ("secretly") **컴퓨터** comp**uter**, meaning secretly using your computer when you are not supposed to (e.g., after bedtime). You engage in this thrilling activity after you make sure your parents are fully asleep. During this time, the whirring sound of your computer feels like the loudest sound in the entire universe, and the time it takes to fully boot up feels like an eternity.

Kim: Ugh! My oppa's live performance will be on YouTube past my bedtime…
Hyeri: You should *mol com* tonight.
Kim: Last time I was caught and got grounded.

몸짱 Momzzang /Momjjang

(mom-tchang)

Someone With Killer Body

Someone with an awesome body, usually muscular for males and a slim, well-toned body for females.

Man, I am so fat, and my personal trainer told me it will take full 2 years to transform me into a *momzzang*.

무플 Moo Peul

(mu-pŭl)

"No Comments Received (for something you posted on the Internet)"

무 *moo* "nothing" + 플 *peul* from "reply". This happens when people think your post is not worth commenting on, or it is so controversial that no one dares to get involved.

Minho: Do you know what is worse than *ak peul*?
Donny: What is it?
Minho: *Moo peul*. It makes you feel like a nobody.

무대 Moodae

(mu-dae)

Stage

The stage on which K-pop singers perform.

Centurion looked like a little boy when he was on a TV show, but when he is singing on *moodae*, he is such a sexy man.

무개념 Moo Gae Nyeom

(mu-gae-nyŏm)

Shameless

무 *moo* ("nothing", "non-existent" + "개념" *gae nyeom* ("concept", "idea"), referring to someone who is clueless about what's going on around him/her, similar to 진상 *jin sang*.

Laughing out loud at someone's funeral is a prime example of *moo gae nyeom*.

모태 솔로 Motae Solo

(mo-tae-sol-lo)

"Forever Alone"

A compound word made up of "모태" *motae* ("within the womb") and **solo**. It is used to refer to someone who has never dated anyone and has been single their entire life.

As a *motae solo*, Junhee had no idea what kissing feels like, so she devised a brilliant plan - to fake a drowning and get mouth-to-mouth.

MR

Backgorund Music

An acronym for "music recorded". It refers to the music portion of a song. MR-removed means leaving only the vocal part of the song, which is a nightmare for some, as it is the ultimate tool to gauge someone's true vocal skills.

Haha, did you hear the **MR** version of Kori's song? She really can't carry a tune in a bucket.

Music Bank

Weekly Live Music Show by KBS

A weekly live music show by KBS (Korea Broadcasting System), where a winner is announced using a combination of factors, such as the digital music charts, album sales, the number of times the song is played on TV/Radio, and viewers' choice charts.

I look forward to watching *Music Bank* this week because my favorite *Oppas* are performing live!

Tex

Most popular means of communication in Korea, especially among the younger generation, thanks to the wide propagation of smartphones. Due to the overwhelming popularity of chatting apps like Kakaotalk, 문자 *munja* mostly refers to text messages you send and receive using a phone number (e.g., Apple's iMessage), as opposed to using chatting apps.

Munja has completely replaced talking on the phone as the most used means of communication.

MV

Music Video

Each music video has a different "theme" according to the "concept" of the song. In the K-pop industry, a great portion of the production money goes into making high-quality music videos.

8Players' new **MV** has over 3 million views now on YouTube.

맴매 Maem Mae

(maem-mae)

Corporal Punishment

A baby-word expression meaning "corporal punishment" spoken to infants/little kids when trying to discipline them by giving them a physical punishment as a penalty for unacceptable behavior. Examples include spanking or whipping.

Mom: Jody, did you break the mirror?
Jody: Nope, it was a ghost who did it.
Mom: Now you are lying! Come here! You need some *maem mae*!

메이킹 Making

Behind The Scenes / Making-of

A Konglish term that refers to a documentary film/footage featuring the production of a film or TV program, such as how its made and their untold stories.

I just saw the *making* of the new music video, and I could confirm the rumor that the members do not get along with each other.

막방 Mak Bang

(mak-bang)

Last Episode of a Show/Program

"막" (*mak*, "last") + "방" (*bang song*, "show/broadcast"). The very last episode of a show/program. It's a very moving moment in which you can see how much each member of a show has progressed/grown, given that the show wasn't abruptly shut down due to low ratings.

The *mak bang* of the popular show made every viewer cry.

MAMAMOO

Mamamoo stands for "**MAMA** (mother) + **Moo** (sound babies make) = organic/instinctive music" and is a four-member (Solar, Moonbyul, Wheein, Hwasa) girl group formed by Rainbow Bridge World. They specialize in retro, jazz and R&B style music and debuted with a song titled "Mr. Ambiguous" in 2014. They appeared on Immortal Song 2 in 2015 and won the competition with Korean trot singer Bae Ho's "Backwood's Mountain." They performed at KCON NY in 2016, as well as SXSW K-pop Night Out. Notable songs include "Ahh Oop!" "You're the Best," and "Yes I Am."

Mamamoo is the cutest band name I know.

(man-tchit-nam)
만찡남
Man Jjit Nam

Unrealistically Beautiful (Handsome) Man

Abbreviation for "**만화**를 **찍**고 나온 **남자** (**man**-hwa-reul **jjit**-go na-on **nam**-ja)", which literally translates as "a man who looks as if he has just come out of comic books" because of his incredible looks.

People call me *man jjit nam*, not because I look cool like a superhero but more like an ugly villain who gets his ass kicked by a superhero.

(man-su-ru)
만수르
Man Su Reu

Super Rich

Actually the name of Sheikh Mansour bin Zayed Al Nahyan, the deputy prime minister of the United Arab Emirates, minister of presidential affairs, and member of the ruling family of Abu Dhabi. In Korea, though, he's more famously known for his wealth, and the name "**만수르**" (Mansour) has become synonymous with "super-rich."

If I was as rich as *man su reu*, I'd invite my *oppas* over to my house and have them perform just for me.

(map-so-sa)
맙소사 Map So Sa

"My Goodness!" / "Oh Dear!"

An interjection or more of a sigh of grief used to express frustration/surprise.

Map so sa... Is that BTS?

OMG!

맛점 Mat Jeom (mat-jŏm)

"Have a Nice Lunch!"

Abbreviation for "**맛**있는" (*mat it neun*, "tasty") + "**점**심" (*jeom shim*, "lunch"). As its used mostly among the younger generation as an Internet slang expression, it shouldn't be used in formal settings, to people older than you, or your superiors.

Oh! It's lunch time already! *Mat jeom*, ya'll!

(mat-pal)
맞팔 Mat Pal

Following Each Other on Instagram

Short for "맞" (*mat*, "each other) + 팔로우 (*pal*, "follow"), it refers to following each other on Instagram. Note: there is no F sound in Korean.

Hm, you look like a nice guy! Lets *mat pal* on Instagram!

(mŏk-bang)
먹방
Meokbang / Mukbang

Eating Show

"먹는" (*meok neun*, "eating") + "방송" (*bang song*, "show/broadcast") is a live online show/broadcast in which a host, better known as a BJ (broadcast jockey), eats a large quantity of food (pizza, hamburger, *kimbap, tteobokki, jjajangmyeon,* you name it…) while interacting with their audience through a chat screen that appears at the side. While it sounds weird, people find it entertaining because you can get vicarious gratification from other people eating food, or, conversely, it makes you feel healthy by watching other people overindulge in food. Many popular show hosts make lots of money by receiving star balloons (cyber currency used In AfreecaTV) and from advertisement deals. This type of show/broadcast has gained popularity around the globe, encouraging many foreign YouTube celebrities to jump on the bandwagon.

Wow... I can definitely be a super star if I start my own *mukbang* channel because I can really pig out!

(me-rong)
메롱 Me Rong

Nana-Nana Boo-Boo

A phrase used to tease someone, delivered while sticking your tongue out, for more humiliation.

HAHA! I ate that last slice of pizza! *Me rong!*

Meolody

BTOB Fan Club

The name of the BTOB fan club, named so because the group name is "Born To Beat," and the melody is what you need to make music as they complete each other. Fan color is slow blue.

Melody and *BTOB*! We are one!

미드 Mi Deu

American TV Dramas

"**미국**" (*mi guk*, "America/USA") + "**드라마**" (*d*rama). American TV Dramas. Many Korean people watch them as a means of studying English.

The biggest difference between *mi deu* and K-dramas is that, in K-dramas, the story always involves a complex love line among the characters.

미리 크리스마스 Mi Ri Christmas

"Merry Christmas in Advance"

"**미리**" (*mi ri*, "in advance") + **Christmas**. A pun joke/ expression for saying "Merry Christmas" ahead of the actual holiday.

Son: I want a new iPhone for Christmas!
Dad: Hold your horses, son! It's only April now.
Son: *Mi ri Christmas*!

미세먼지 Mi Se Meon Ji

Fine Dust / Toxic Air

Literally "fine dust," a type of air pollution caused by fine particulates that mainly come from exhaust fumes from internal combustion engines (e.g., cars), smoke from factory chimneys, and so on. It's particularly worse in the winter season due to yellow dust blowing in from the Mongolian desert. This is why you see a lot of people wearing a mask while outside.

Did you know that farting actually releases poop particles into the air, causing *mi se meon ji*?

밀월여행 Mil Wol Yeo Haeng

Secret Trip (With A Lover)

"**밀**" (蜜, *mil*) and "**월**" (月, *wol*) are both Chinese words meaning "honey" and "moon," while "**여행**" (*yeo haeng*) means trip/travel. So its original meaning is "honeymoon (trip)" but is very often mistakenly used by many Korean speakers/media who use it to refer to a "secret trip (with a lover)" because there is another Chinese character "**밀**" (密) that means "secret/to hide," which they confuse with the other "**밀**" (蜜) that means "honey."

I lied to my friend and decided to have a *mil wol yeo haeng* to Vegas with my girlfriend, but my friend saw me at the airport... The cover's blown!

민폐 Min Pye
(min-pye)

Public Nuisance

"민" (*min*) means "people" + "폐" (*pye*) means "nuisance." Put together, it means "public nuisance," and its an important concept in a collective culture like Korean because the whole is considered more important than its parts. Some "민폐" examples are: taking up two parking slots, bringing your pet to someone else's place without asking first, and talking on the phone in the movie theater.

I have a habit of eating so loudly, and yes, I know it's a *min pye*.

몰빵 Mol Bbang
(mol-ppang)

Putting Everything in One Basket

A slang term for "putting everything in one basket" or "concentrated investment," or "going all-in."

I'm butt ugly, slow-witted, and have no sense of humor, but I'm as healthy as a horse! God must have done a *mol bbang* on my health... ;(.

MooMoo

MAMAMOO Fan Club

The name of the MAMAMOO fan club. It stands for the meaning of becoming a listener of Mamamoo's music. "Moo" also means "radish" in Korean - this is why the fans hold radish-themed light sticks at concerts.

MooMoo sounds as cute as the band, MAMAMOO.

몸치 Mom Chi
(mom-chi)

Someone Who Has "Two Left Feet"

"몸" (*mom*) means "body" + "치" (*chi*) meaning "stupid/ridiculous." Put together, it refers to someone who is simply unable to dance well due to having awkward or clumsy footwork.

Join any K-pop entertainment company as a trainee and they will convert any *mom chi* into a crazy dance machine!

모닝콜
Morning Call

Wake Up Call

A Konglish term for "wake-up call," termed so because you usually get a call in the morning. However, its used regardless of time because it is used synonymously with "wake-up call."

Me: Hey Siri, give me a *morning call* at 9 AM.
Siri: Consider it done!

MSG

Exaggeration

MSG (monosodium glutamate) is an artificial seasoning That's added to food to make it taste better. In Korean variety shows, people use the term to refer to someone who makes up or exaggerates stories to make their stories more interesting.

Miguel: So I was like going 120 miles per hour, and then this dude on a bike was tailgating me, so close to the point where I could count his nose hairs!
Dan: Hey man... That's impossible...! You're putting too much *MSG* on your story!

모자이크
Mosaic

To Blur Out / Censor

As the name suggests, it is the act of "pixelating" a portion of a photo/film and is a type of censorship. In Korea, The Korea Communications Standards Commission has a set of rules and regulations for censorship: 1) Weapons - large swords in ancient dramas are just fine, but a small butterfly knife a bank robber is waving in the air is blurred out, as it might cause excessive shock, anxiety, or disgust to viewers. 2) Cigarettes - smoking on TV is not family-friendly and is a negative influence on teenagers. 3) Tattoos are censored for a reason similar to #2. 4) Brand names and logos that stand out too conspicuously are also blurred out or have black duct tape put on top of them. The main reason is to prevent any possible lawsuits by hiding brand names and logos that are not associated with the show.

They'd better put a *mosaic* on my *oppa's* face because he's too handsome, and it might offend other people.

(mu-myŏng-si-jŏl)
무명시절
Mu Myeong Si Jeol

Days of Anonymity

"무명" (*mu yeong*) means "unknown, anonymous, unpopular" + "시절" (*si jeol*), meaning "time period." Put together, it refers to the time/days of anonymity one has to go through before rising to stardom. K-pop trainees usually have to go through a vigorous/arduous period of time before their debut, which still doesn't guarantee success.

Every K-pop super star had a *mu myeong si jeol*, even G-Dragon!

무리수 Mu Ri Su

(mu-ri-su)

Going Too Far / Overambitious Attempt

"무리" (*mu ri*) means "impossibility" and "수" (*su*) means "move." The term originated in *baduk*, or go (board game in Asia), and refers to a bad, useless move made as a result of being overly ambitious. A close English expression is "biting off more than one can chew."

I texted my crush, "Hey, do you know who you look like? My future wife!", and she replied, "No. No. No." Oh boy... what a *mu ri su* I made.

Muggle

Non-Otaku / Non-Fan

Originating from the Harry Potter books by JK Rowling, it means "non-magical person" or "normal person." In a K-pop fandom context, it refers to someone who's not a fan/*otaku*.

K-pop Fan: Oh! You're wearing a Korean T-shirt! Are you a K-pop fan too?
Dude: Huh? I got it from a flea market. I don't even know what it means lol.
K-pop Fan: Oh, so you're just a *muggle*.

문찐 Mun Jjin

(mun-tchin)

Someone Who Can't Keep Up With The Latest Trends

Short for "문화" (*mun hwa*, "culture") + "찐따" (*jjin tta*,"loser"), someone who is enormously behind the times and just can't keep up with the latest trends.

These days, you might want to start listening to K-pop because, if you don't, people might think you are a *mun jjin*.

물타기 Mul Ta Gi

(mul-ta-gi)

To Cloud The Issue

Literal meaning is "to dilute with water" and is used idiomatically to mean "to cloud the issue," which is obfuscating/distracting the listener from the topic at hand by introducing irrelevant information.

Wife: Honey! What's this "Gentlemen's Club" on your credit card statement?
Husband: Oh! By the way, did you hear that credit card users have an average debt of $450?
Wife: Oh really? That's quite high!
Husband: (Yess! *mul ta gi* worked!)

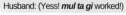

(mut-ji-ma)
묻지마 Mut Ji Ma

With No Apparent Reason / Careless

Literally "don't ask" or "no questions asked," so when used as a prefix to a noun, it mostly refers to the act of doing something for no apparent reason. For example, "**묻지마 폭력**" (*pok ryeok*, "violence") means assaulting someone for no apparent reason. Another meaning refers to the act of doing something haphazardly and carelessly. For example, "**묻지마 투자**" (*too ja*, "investment") is investing without carefully assessing the risks involved.

Not knowing the rules of Black Jack, I made a series of mut ji ma bets and lost everything.

(myŏng-pum)
명품 Myeong Pum

Designer Brands

Literal meaning is "masterpiece," but it generally refers to expensive luxury goods, such as Louis Vuitton, Hermes, and Cartier. While it's a matter of preference, some people spend beyond their means just to show off but are often frowned upon for their vanity (snob!). People who want them but can't afford them often choose an alternative route by purchasing counterfeit products that cost a fraction of an authentic product.

BTS' new album is truly a *myeong pum*... It's like a Hermes bag of K-pop.

(mwŏng-mi?)
뭥미? Mwong Mi?

"What the…"

A slang for "What the…?" It is mostly used among teens and netizens on the Internet.

Suzy texted me saying *mwong mi*? I didn't know what the hell she was referring to so I texted her back saying mwong mi?

(myu-ming)
뮤밍 Myu Ming

Music Video Streaming

Short for "**뮤직 비디오 스트리밍** ("**mu**sic video strea**ming**"), which is the act of watching a certain music video on YouTube because doing so works in favor of the band who sang the song—the number of times a music video is played is counted towards the chart. Fans do this to help their favorite band rank high on the chart.

Hey everyone, our *oppa's* new song is currently #4 on the chart. Let's start *myu ming*!!!

엔빵 N Bbang

(en-bbang)

Going Dutch

This expression originates from a mathematical formula "something divided by n," where n is the number of people in this case. Hence, it means dividing the total amount on the check by the number of people, so everybody can pay the same amount of money on an outing.

Q: Who picks up the tab when Super Junior goes out to dinner?
A: They all do **N Bbang** because, with so many members, the bill can get so huge!

내게로 와 Nae Ge Ro Wa

(nae-ge-ro wa)

"Come to Me"

Asking someone to be either 1) physically or 2) emotionally close to the speaker. If the latter, it means "come into my heart" and implies the speaker's intention to capture the heart of the listener. It is, therefore, a powerful yet cruel spell one can cast on someone who's already almost enchanted.

Husband: Honey, **nae ge ro wa** <3
Wife: Ok baby <3
Husband: Oh, can you grab the remote on your way?
Wife: You bastard…

마이 스타일 My Style

"My Type"

One's ideal type of person.

Nira: Oh! Oh! Johnny is so **my style**!
Alexa: I hope he feels the same way.

냉무 Naeng Moo

(naeng-mu)

"End of Message"

An abbreviation for "내용" *nae yong* ("content") "무" *moo* ("nothing"). Its English counterpart is EOM (end of message) used in the subject line of a post or email to indicate to the reader there is no more content to expect.

No example here. **Naeng moo**!

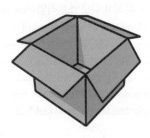

네이버 Naver

Korea's Almighty Internet Portal

Korea's largest Internet portal site. It provides a myriad of services, such as web search, shopping, blogs, news, music, directions, and so on. Its presence is so significant that many K-pop idols dream of ranking on Naver's real-time search results.

Abe: Bro, can you Google this for me?
Nielson: Forget Google. Everybody **Navers** in Korea, mate!

Netizen

Internet User

A compound word made up of "Inter**net**" and "citi**zen**". Some of them are notorious for their mob mentality, where they leave an endless amount of negative comments on news articles, sometimes causing an end to one's career or even leading to suicide.

Hong Sung got arrested for stealing at the supermarket. I can't wait to see all the harsh comments the **Netizens** have come up with.

(nŏm-sa-byŏk)
넘사벽
Neom Sa Byeok

Something Unbeatable/Unbelievable

An abbreviation for "**넘**을 수 없는 *neom eul soo eop neun* ("unclimbable") **사차원의** *sacha won eui* ("fourth-dimensional") **벽** *byeok* ("wall")". It is used to describe someone or something beyond one's control (unbeatable) or comprehension (unbelievable), and it can be used both as a compliment and ridicule.

Doyle: So I had 3 shots of Vodka, 1 bottle of Soju, and 2 glasses of wine, and I'm still sober.
Mina: When it comes to drinking, you are **neom sa byeok**.

(nyu-pe)
뉴페 New Pe

New Member

Its literal meaning is "New Face" **뉴** new **페이스** *pe i seu* ("face" but there's no F sound in Korean). While it is similar to "Newbie", it doesn't necessarily mean someone is inexperienced. It refers to someone who joins a group for the first time, regardless of their experience.

Ning: Boring! Aren't we getting any **new pe**'s to our band this semester?
Jenna: I got a major overhaul through plastic surgery. Does that count as a **new pe**?

(nak-shi)

낚시 Nak Si

Fooling Someone

Literal meaning is "fishing", some say that it originated from the English word "phishing". It is used to describe deception/trickery used to achieve the desired outcome (e.g., scamming). It is also associated with the word "fishing" because the person who falls prey resembles a hooked fish. This is something to look out for on April Fool's Day.

Judy: Jack, if you do me a favor, I will give you kisses!
Jack: Don't **nak si** me, girl. I know you will give me Hershey's Kisses!

(nam-dae-mun)

남대문 Nam Dae Moon

Zipper

Literally means "South Grand Gate", which refers to one of the four grand gates located around the city of Seoul, but due to the fact that the word 남 (*nam*) also means "Male", it is figuratively used to refer to the "Men's Grand Gate" = the front zipper of a (man's) pants.

Keira: Hey! **Nam dae moon**!
Jim: Hm? You want to go to the South Grand Gate?
Keria: No! Your zipper is open!

(nam-chin/yŏ-chin)

남친/여친 Nam Chin/ Yeo Chin

Boyfriend/Girlfriend

Abbreviation for "남자" *namja* ("man/male") 친구 *chin*goo ("friend") and "여자" *yeoja* ("woman/female") 친구 *chin*goo ("friend"). To some, they are imaginary creatures, like a unicorn, which do not exist in the real world.

Nora: I have a lot of guy friends, but no **nam chin**… I wonder why?
Jenna: Maybe because you have so many guy friends that people automatically assume you have one?

(nam-sa/yŏ-sa chin)

남사/여사친 Namsa/Yeosa Chin

A Male/Female Friend

While "남자 친구 *namja chingoo*" and "여자 친구 *yeoja chingoo*" mean boyfriend/girlfriend, "남사 *namsa*" and "여사 *yeosa*" are short for "남자 *namja* ("male") *saram* ("human") and "여자" *yeoja* ("female") 사람 *saram* ("human")". Hence, it is used to make clear that the person being referred to is just a friend that happens to be of that gender.

Monica: Hey, you two make a cute couple!
Tom: No, no, no – She is just a **yeosa chin**!
Jennifer: Exactly! He is not my type. He is a **namsa chin**!

(noe-sek-nam)
뇌섹남
Nwae Saek Nam

Man with a Smart Brain

An abbreviation for "뇌가" *noe ga* ("brain is") "섹시한" *sek si han* ("sexy") "남자" *nam ja* ("male"). It is used to describe a man who is smart and witty, making him "sexy" on the inside. Hence, someone who does not look particularly attractive can still earn this title.

Sohyang: You know that new guy in our math class, right? I heard he got a perfect score on his SAT!
Gloria: Wow – I didn't know that she was such a *noe saek nam*!

NG

"Blooper" "Retake!"

An abbreviation for "**N**o **G**ood". It is what the director/producer says during a filming of a movie or a show when an actor makes a mistake (e.g., forgetting their line or bursting into laughter). The portion is discarded, and the scene is filmed again until a good take is achieved.

NG! You were not supposed to close your eyes when you kiss her!

뉴비 Newbie

Someone Who is Inexperienced in a Particular Field/Activity

If a new K-pop idol has just debuted, he/she is a newbie in the music industry and has a lot of *sunbaes* to show respect to.

Jun: Hi guys, I am a former professional baseball player!
Taro: Welcome! But yoga is completely different from baseball You are a *newbie* yogi!

(no-an)
노안 Noan

Face That Looks Older Than Actual Age

The exact opposite of 동안 *dong an*.

Andy is only 22, but he has the face of a 40-year-old man. What's more amazing is, his whole family looks older than their actual age. I guess they all have *noan* DNA running in their blood.

(no-kwa-bang-song)
녹화방송
Nok Hwa Bang Song

Airing of a Pre-recorded (Show)

A compound word made up of "녹화" *nok hwa* ("recording") + "방송" *bang song* ("airing, broadcast"). This is the format used by most TV shows that have a script to follow and in which NGs can be redone.

Yoshi: I wonder how they keep a straight face when making such funny jokes?
Ina: Because it's a *nok hwa bang song*! I bet they had lots of NG's.

(nol-to)
놀토 Nol To

"Saturday-Off"

Literal meaning is "playing Saturday". The term came into existence in 2012 when public schools in Korea adopted a five-day school system, making Saturday an off-day for students.

Kimberly: Just 10 seconds left...
Mary: Huh?
Kimberly: Yay! It's *nol to*!
Mary: You didn't have to wake me up for that...

(nun-chi)
눈치 Nun Chi

Tact, Common Sense

Literal meaning is "eye measure", and it's an essential social skill that is a combination of various elements, such as being able to read others' emotions quickly and make necessary adjustments accordingly. It's especially important in a high-context and hierarchical society like Korea. Those who can't are considered a potential threat due to their unpredictability (e.g., talking about someone's ex at their wedding).

(At a Korean business lunch)
CEO: What should we have for lunch? I'm thinking about getting... *Kimbap*. Feel free to get whatever you want!
Subordinates 1,2,3,4,5: That's a great choice, sir! I'd like to have *Kimbap* as well!
New Intern: Wow! You guys love *kimbap* so much! I'd like to have a cheeseburger, fries, lightly salted, and a milk shake please!
Subordinates 1,2,3,4,5: (Have some *nun chi*...Ugh...)

(nu-na)
누나 Noona

Older Sister

A term used exclusively by a younger male to an older female, but it can't be used to a stranger unless permission is given or until enough emotional intimacy has been established. It can, however, be used by a younger male to address an older female in a relationship.

Hey *Noona*! Where is mom?

누나 로맨스
Noona Romance

Older Woman Falling in Love With a Younger Guy

In K-dramas, it often starts with a strong denial/rejection by the female character but gradually develops into a romantic relationship when the female character gives in and accepts reality.

What? There is no way I'm having **noona romance** with him! He is way younger than me, and I like him only as a *dong saeng*. Hm, on second thought, he *is* kinda cute.

누나킬러
Noona Killer

Young Male Capable of Making Noonas Fall in Love With Him

A young male who is capable of making *noonas* fall in love with him, using various tactics, such as *aegyo* and eye smiles.

Andrew is so popular among *noonas* because of his cuteness. He is such a **noona killer**.

(no-rae)
노래 Norae

Song

A song and the act of singing.

Norae and *choom* are the 2 most sought-after talents in idol groups.

(no-rae-bang)
노래방
Noraebang

Karaoke

Literally means "singing room". It's a place where many people go for 2-*cha* or 3-*cha* (2nd round or 3rd round of drinking). People go there to let their hair down and bring out their "party animal" side. It's usually the final destination for a company group dinner.

Ya! Let's go to **Noraebang**! I am so drunk, and I have to sing my favorite song!

(en-po-se-dae)
N포세대
N Po Se Dae

Gloomy Young Generation

"**N**" refers to "number of things," + "**포기**" (*po gi*, "to give up") + "**세대**" (*se dae*, "generation"). A self-deprecating satirical term used by the younger generation who are fed up with - and feel hopeless about - the current socio economic state of South Korea, where the unemployment rate is high and working conditions are sub-par, therefore they have to "give up N (number) of things", such as dating, marriage, having kids, or getting a job in order to maintain at least the average standard of living. A similar term in Europe is "the 1,000 Euros generation," or "Mileurista " in Spanish, where the young people in their 20s and 30s have to make a living out of a low monthly wage of 1,000 Euros.

Don't be an *N po se dae*! All our K-pop *oppas* are part of the generation too, but they are working so hard to make their dreams come true!

(nae-bi)
내비 Nae Bi

GPS Navigation System

Short for "**내비**게이션 ("GPS **Navi**gation System"), which helps drivers find directions in an automobile by using a satellite device to determine the car's position on the road. There are various "**내비**" apps for smartphones in Korea if you ever visit. Some of the popular ones are "네이버 맵 (Naver Map)" and "카카오 맵 (Kakao Map)", which also provides directions for walking.

I have no sense of direction and need a personal *nae bi* every time I leave the house.

(na-ya-na)
나야나 Na Ya Na

"Me, It's Me"

An expression that literally means "me, its me" and is the Korean name of the song "Pick Me" by Wanna One.

Bouncer: Let me see your ticket, please.
Me: *Na Ya Na*!
Bouncer: If you don't have a ticket, you can't get in.
Me: Sorry!

(nae-han/bang-han)
내한/방한
Nae Han/ Bang Han

Visiting Korea

It means coming to/visiting Korea but most frequently used by the media when world famous celebrities visit Korea, usually for a concert tour, movie promotion, and the like.

If Ariana Grande makes a *bang han*, I'd love to see her perform with Big Bang!

WELCOME TO KOREA

(nae-ro-nam-bul)
내로남불
Nae Ro Nam Bul
Double Standard

Abbreviation for "**내**가 하면" (*nae ga ha myeon*, "If I do it") + **Ro**mance + "**남**이 하면" (*nam i ha myeon*, "if someone else does it") + "**불륜**" (*bul lyun*, "adultery"). Used to criticize someone who applies differing sets of principles for similar situations.

If I stalk my oppa, it's because I love him so much! If YOU stalk my oppa, it's because you're a *sasaeng*. Yes, this is *nae ro nam bul*.

(nae-sung)
내숭 Nae Sung
Acting Coy / Playing Innocent

Used to describe a person, usually a female, who pretends to be innocent/naïve/shy, especially around a crush.

Jeremy: If we kiss, we have to get married.
Ryan: Oh come on, don't give me *nae sung!* We're just playing a drinking game!

(nam-u/yŏ-u-ju-yŏn-sang)
남우/여우주연상
Nam Woo / Yeo Woo Ju Yeon Sang
Best Leading Actor Award / Best Leading Actress Award

An award given to outstanding actors/actresses at the "청룡영화상"(*cheong ryong yeong hwa sang*, "The Blue Dragon Award") and the "대종상" (*dae jong sang*, "Grand Bell Awards") events.

I bumped into a robber but fooled him into thinking I really had no money while, in reality, I had over $300, cold cash! I deserve a *nam woo ju yeon sang*!

(nŏm)
넘 Neom
Very

A short slang form of "너무" (*neo mu*, "very"), mainly used in chats because it saves you time. It should never be used in formal/official documents.

You are so funny! *Neom* funny!

(no-chul)
노출 No Chul
Showing Skin

Literally "exposure," "revealing" but in a K-pop context it is mostly used to refer to the act of showing skin, both unintentional (scandalous headliner or a funny blooper) and intentional (self-promotion by showing off one's body). Either way, too much 노출 is a big no-no.

Summer! The season of *no chul* is here! I better stay home.

(no-dap)
노답 No Dap
Dead End / Helpless

"답" (*dap*) means "answer," so when put with "no," it literally means "no answer" but is idiomatically used to refer to a dead end, a helpless situation, or someone who is just tactless and is absolutely clueless about whats going on around them.

Wait up... You said you were on a diet and ate the whole pizza? Man, you are really *no dap* ...

(nok-ŭm)
녹음 Nok Eum
(Audio) Recording

The act of recording audio, such as radio talk shows, podcasts, and songs for an album. Bonus fact: there is an urban legend/myth in the music industry that, if a singer hears the sound of a ghost while recording a song, the song will be a huge hit.

Our oppas are busy having a *nok eum* session in the studio! Can't wait to listen to their new song!

(nok-hwa)
녹화 Nok Hwa
(Video) Recording

The act of recording visual materials, such as a variety show, onto a storage medium so it can be watched again or aired on TV at a later time. It's not used for radio shows because technically it only refers to the recording of visual materials. For audio materials, "녹음" (*nok eum*) is used.

Cassandra was so nervous during the *nok hwa* session and made so many mistakes before the camera.

(nu-ri-jip)
누리집 Nu Ri Jip
Home Page

"누리꾼" (*nu ri kkun*, "Netizen (Internet User) + 집 (*jip* "home page"). It's a 100% Korean word for "homepage" because, in an effort to encourage the use of Korean words rather than imported foreign terms, the National Institute of the Korean Language announces Korean versions of such terms. For this reason, you would encounter this type of word on TV/Radio or government home pages often but not as much in real life conversations.

News Anchor: Please visit us at our *nu ri jip* at www... Viewer: WTH... Can't they just use what's actually said in real life? HOMEPAGE!

(nu-gu)
누구 Nugu
Unknown / Not Popular / Obscure

Means "who" in Korean, but in a K-pop fandom context, it refers to someone/group who hasn't made a name for themselves yet but doesn't necessarily mean they are less talented than other accomplished K-pop acts. Many of them just need strong promotions and higher brand awareness. Many fans also support these "minor" groups and take strong pride in doing so, because they have faith that their nugu is the next up-and-coming K-pop act.

When they first debuted, everyone was like *nu gu*? But nowadays, they all go "WOW".

(nu-ri-kkun)
누리꾼 Nu Ri Kkun
Netizen (Internet User)

A 100% full Korean word for Netizen (Internet user).

An anonymous *nu ri kkun* left a malicious comment on a K-pop idol's latest post, and the fans tracked him down and got him arrested!

(nun-chi)
눈치 Nun Chi
Tact / Being Self-Conscious

Literally "eye measure," a concept unique to Korean culture that signifies the importance of being able to listen to and gauge others' moods. In Western culture, it could be described as the concept of emotional intelligence, such as being perceptive, tactful, or self-conscious. In a high context culture like Korean, such unspoken ways of communication are of central importance in interpersonal relationships.

Charlie: Hey, everyone's walking on eggshells around Tony because his girlfriend recently dumped her...
Henna: Oh, hey Tony! I have two tickets to KCON! Do you want to take your... Oh shoot! Never mind... Sorry!
Charlie: Come on, girl! Have some *nun chi*! You're so oblivious...

(nun-ting)
눈팅 Nun Ting

Lurking

"눈" (*nun*) means "eye" and "팅" (*ting*) comes from the word "채팅" (chat**ting**). Put together, it means "chatting with eyes" and refers to the act of reading/keeping up with the posts/conversations in Internet forums/chat rooms without actually getting involved.

The reason I only do *nun ting* is because I want to keep a low profile in the forum.

(nun-chi Game)
눈치게임
Nun Chi Game

Timing Game

A popular Korean drinking game in which the game leader initiates a game by saying "1" then every player must say the following number, without saying the same number with other players at the same time or being the last player to say the last number. If you do, you lose the game and have to drink a penalty shot. While the rules seem really simple, its a cliff-hanging game thanks to its high-paced nature and having to read other people's minds.

When I'm driving, changing and merging lanes feel like a *nun chi game*.

(o-gu-o-gu)
오구오구
O Gu O Gu

Coochy Coo / There, There

An onomatopoeia that phonetically imitates the sound an adult makes to appease/compliment a baby/kid/pet animal. As it has a cute feeling associated with it, its often used between a couple as a way of teasing each other, but one should exercise caution when using it as it can give the feeling that one is talking down to/looking down on the listener. It's essentially the same as "우쭈쭈".

Husband: Yes!!! After spending countless hours, I finally beat the final boss!
Wife: *O gu o gu*, great job... (sarcasm) Quit playing video game and go get a job already!
Husband: Gosh... the real final boss is here...

(nyang-i)
냥이 Nyang I

Cat

A nickname for "고양이" (*go yang i*, "cat"), and there are many different types of them. 1) 개냥이 (*gae nyang i*) = "개" (*gae*, "dog") + "냥이" ("cat") = "cat dog" = "puppy cat," or a cat that behaves like a dog. 2) 길냥이 (*gil nyang i*) = "길" (*gil*, "street") + "냥이" ("cat") = "street cat."

Are you a *nyang i* person or a dog person?

(o-jing-ŏ game)
오징어 게임
OJing Eoh Game

Korean street game / Squid Game

It is the name of a Korean street game and also the title of the world-famous Korean Drama series on Netflix. This street game was popular among Korean children until around the 1980s, and the name "Squid" comes from the fact that the shapes marked on the ground to play the game were similar to the that of the squid. The namesake drama (English title "Squid Game") is about people competing for their lives to become the final winner of a mysterious game with a prize of 45.6 billion won (about 37 million USD). It topped the charts in all countries Netflix has entered.

It seems like *o jing eo gam*e is the talk of the town! It sure creates a lot of watercooler talk after a new episode is released!

(o-jing-ŏ)
오징어
OJing Eoh

Ugly Face

Literally meaning "squid", but recently, it has been used to refer to someone hideous after a hilarious anecdote circulated on the Internet. The story goes like this: a couple went to a movie starring Won Bin, who is one of the best looking actors in Korea. While watching the movie, the woman thought he wasn't so good looking. After the movie, however, she turned and looked at her boyfriend, and all of a sudden, there was a "squid" sitting next to her.

People avoided being in the same picture with Marco because his overwhelming visual always made them look like an *oh jing eoh*.

(o-gŭl)
오글 O Geul

"Cringing"

Literal meaning is "(fingers/toes) curling", which describes your body's natural response to something stimulating, both positive and negative (e.g., fear, shame, joy, etc.). In Korean, however, this is exclusively used to describe a situation that makes you feel embarrassed, or awkward. Hence, it is an expression of aversion.

Mini: That new boy in our science class is such a dork. He proposed to his girlfriend during gym class and got rejected.
Arthur: That is so *o geul o geul*… I feel embarrassed.

Once

TWICE Fan Club

The name of the TWICE fan club, meaning
1) If fans love the group even once, then TWICE will repay the love with twice their love.
2) In order for there to be TWICE, there needs to be ONCE. Fan color is apricot and neon magenta.

There has to be **ONCE** in order for TWICE to exist.

원룸
One Room

Studio Apartment

A Konglish term for "studio apartment" because they are composed of just the living room. Newly-built onerooms come with optional features, such as a flat-screen TV, washer, and air conditioning system.

I'm just a poor student living in a **one room**, but mark my words, I'll be living in a penthouse in the very near future, like Gatsby!

(op-chi)
옵치 Op Chi

Overwatch

A team-based MMOFPS (multiplayer online first-person shooter) video game by Blizzard that is hugely popular, especially among teenagers in Korea. Just walk in to any PC Bang (PC cafe) in Korea to see a bunch of excited little kids playing the game together.

The *PC bang* was full of little kids playing *op chi.*

오픈카
Open Car

Convertible

A Konglish term meaning "convertible (car)," termed so because the roof of the car can open up completely. It's something that many guys dream of having.

The reason I bought this *open car* is to pick up girls, but the only thing I've picked up so far is a speeding ticket.

오해 O Hae (o-hae)
Misunderstanding

The mother of all conflicts. This is probably the single most frequently used theme in melo K-dramas involving "love lines (map of love relationships among characters in K-drama)" because it gets the entangled love line going (without this, there would be no drama!).

Aaron: WTF? You already had a boyfriend when we kissed?
Jenna: Oh no... That's just an *o hae*... I can explain.
Aaron: Ok, go on.
Jenna: Oh! A Unicorn!
Aaron: Where?
Jenna disappears.

오지다 OJi Da (o-ji-da)
"Sick!"

A term that has been used widely by teenagers very recently, and for this reason, its thought to be a slang expression, but its actually a word included in the Korean dictionary, meaning "something very satisfying."

Triple Crown? Again? *O ji da*...

오리발 O Ri Bal (o-ri-bal)
Playing Innocent

Literally "duck foot," originating in a Korean sayi,ng "pull out a duck foot after eating a stolen chicken," which basically means you are playing innocent in front of people while you are actually guilty of what you are accused of.

Edward: Hey! Did you touch my wallet?
Conrad: Huh? What wallet?
Edward: Don't give me an *o ri bal*, man! It's all caught on camera!

오피스텔 Officetel
Office With Living Amenities

A compound word comprising "office + hotel." A multi-purpose building with residential and commercial units. A type of studio apartment or studio flat with basic furnishings included. Its main purpose is to help occupants live and work in the same building, minimizing commuting time; a significant portion of tenants are working professionals.

For a busy professional like me, *officetel* is the perfect housing solution, but I'd trade it for a girlfriend in a heartbeat.

Original Sound Track

A track specifically composed and sung for a soap opera (drama) or a movie. It is usually played as background music during important scenes, such as when romance suddenly develops (e.g., kissing) or at the end of the show with the credit roll.

These days, **OSTs** are sung by many famous singers.

"Oh No!"

Can be translated as "What should I do?" Also used to express amazement, embarrassment, and confusion.

I forgot to do my homework! *Otoke*!
Jenny: Hey, I got 2 tickets to the Dram Concert~!
Michael: What? *Otoke*?

OTL

"Frustrated", "Discouraged"

Emoticon that symbolizes a man kneeling down with both hands on the ground, where **O** is the head, **T** is the arms, and **L** is the legs. It is a simple yet powerful way to convey complex emotions.

Soo: Why the long face?
Minho: I drunk-dialed my ex last night *OTL*.

OTP

One True Pairing

Your most favored and preferred pairings of people within a group. Describes two people who especially get along really well with each other, regardless of whether romance is involved.

Jenny and Tony are *OTP* – they are like brother and sister, but they are also like boyfriend and girlfriend.

(o-ba-i-tŭ)
오바이트
Oba Iteu
To Throw Up

Konglish for "overeat", but it is used to refer to the general act of vomiting.

Miso: Oh crap! I just *oba iteu*!
Christina: Oh no! Did you drink bad milk or something?
Miso: No, I accidentally saw a picture of your bare face.

올드미스 Old Miss
Woman Who is Old and Not Married

Indirect/less offensive way of saying "spinster". Keep in mind that this is different from "돌싱" *dol sing* because it refers to someone who has become single through a recent divorce.

Ju Ju: Hey, why is your aunt so cranky today?
Sena: I dunno… maybe she's having her *old miss* hysteria!

(o-ji-rap)
오지랖 Oh Ji Rap
Being Nosy

Being overly curious and meddlesome, such as gossiping and prying into each other's affairs.

Umi: Hey! You should be a rapper!
Joe: Rapper? What rapper?
Umi: The *Oh Ji Rap*per! 'Cause you have a finger in every pie.

(o-ppa)
오빠 Oppa
Older Brother

A term used by a younger female to address an older male. It can be used between siblings or anybody who has emotional intimacy with the recipient. Guys are known to love hearing this from their dong saeng girls, as it gives them a sense of superiority and dominance. Many girls use this to their advantage, by calling someone oppa and asking for favors because it generally yields a higher success rate.

Daisy: Sam, can you do the dishes for me?
Sam: Hell naw.
Daisy: *Oppa*~! Pweeeeease~! (Baby voice)
Sam: Oh, ok.

(ŏ-mŏ)
어머 Omo
(Eo meo)!
"Oh My!"

Spontaneous response that comes out in amazing, embarrassing, surprising, and scary moments. It is only used by females, and if used by a male, he could be suspected as gay.

Yun: Did you hear that? Carla farted on the show.
Michelle: *Omo*! That is so hilarious.

아웃오브안중
Out of An Joong

Out of Consideration

"안중" *an joong* literally means "in the eyes", so if someone or something is out of "안중" or "out of sight", someone or something is of no importance.

Yurim: I lost so much weight, and I feel awesome! I think I look so beautiful! I don't have to beg him for attention anymore. I can get someone better than him.
Phillip: Whoa, girl! He is so out of *an joong* now!

(pal-bul-chul)
팔불출
Pal Bool Chool

Someone Who Habitually Brags About Their Significant Other

Literally someone who was born one month prematurely, but it has been figuratively used to describe someone who is dull. In real life, it also refers to a married man who keeps bragging about his wife all the time.

Beginning this year, no *pal bool chools* are allowed at the high school's reunion because there are still people who are not married.

P방 P Bang

PC Bang (Internet Café)

Kids' and teenagers' way of saying "*PC Bang*", the place where all the liberated souls (read: students) gather to indulge in their freedom. Their freedom ends at 10PM, the time when the "shut down" rule becomes effective.

Tony: Yay! School's over! Lets go to our sacred haven!
Zack: Huh? What do you mean?
Tony: *P bang*, my friend, *P bang*…

PD

Program Director / Producer

The person in charge of making TV shows and programs. In Korea, PDs exert an absolute authority regarding casting, and as a result, they exert an enormous influence in showbiz. Also, successful PDs earn as much, if not more, as top celebrities because TV stations are willing to pay top dollar for them.

If you want to earn a spot in that variety TV show, you really have to suck up to Kim *PD*.

파마 Pa Ma
(pa-ma)

Perm

A Konglish term meaning "perm," and there are lots of different types of perm available in Korea, including baby perm, parting perm, magic perm, and foil perm, depending on the material used and what the outcome looks like.

These days, guys also get *pa ma*.

팩폭 Paek Pok
(paek-pok)

Brutally Honest Remarks

Abbreviation for "팩트" (*paek teu*, "fact (there is no "f" sound in Korean)) + "폭격" (*pok gyeok*, "bombing"). The act of talking to someone in a direct way and not in a roundabout way. It's similar to "돌직구" (*dol jik gu*, "very straightforward comment (question)".

Shauna: My boyfriend dumped me because I'm too good for him, and he couldn't handle me.
Marco: Nope, it's the opposite - He was too good for you! You will never find anyone like him in your life.
Charlie: Whoa... That's a *paek pok* right there!

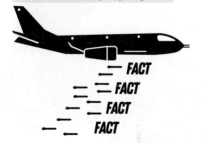

FACT
FACT
FACT
FACT

패완얼 Pae Wan Eol
(pae-wan-ŏl)

"Face Completes the Look"

Short for "패션의 완성은 얼굴 (fashion *eui* ("fashion") *wan seong* ("completion") *eun eol gul* ("face")" = "what completes fashion is face" = "face completes the look." It describes the importance of having a good-looking face because its not about the clothes/accessories you put on - you'd look fashionable/attractive no matter what you wear as long as you are good-looking. It's the face that matters.

Ismael: Hey! How's my fashion?
Dick: Your fashion is awesome, but you know the term pae wan eol? It's your face that matters, man. You don't have it.
Ismael: You're just jelly.

팬싸 Paen Ssa
(paen-ssa)

Autograph Signing Event

Short for "팬" (*paen* (note: there is no "f" sound in Korean), "fan") + 싸인회 (*sa-in-hoe*, "autograph signing event"). It's a dream come true moment for K-pop fanboys/girls because its a rare opportunity to meet their bias in person, and they are welcome to bring their belongings on which they wish the autographs to be signed.

MAMAMOO held a *paen ssa* at the StaplesCenter in LA, and over 3,000 fans showed up.

Pedo Noona

Older Female with an Interest in Younge Male Idols

A compound word made up of "**pedo**phile" and "**noona**". It refers to an older female with an interest in a younger male idol in an inappropriate and even sexual way.

Be careful, Patricia is an infamous **pedo noona**! I heard her boyfriend just graduated from high school.

(ppe-ppe-ro de-i)
삐삐로 데이
Pepero Day

"Valentine's Day in November (11/11)"

November 11th, the day when people exchange **Peperos** (chocolate-covered long biscuit sticks, similar to Pocky) because the numbers look like four sticks (11/11). It's similar to Valentine's Day, but many think it is just another marketing gimmick (and an insult to all singles).

To celebrate **Pepero Day**, Wendy bought 5 packs of **Pepero** and finished them in one sitting.

(ping-pŭ)
핑프 Ping Peu

Finger Princess

Short for "**pin**ger (no F sound in Korean) **p**rincess". It refers to someone who sits on their ass in front of a computer all day and orders people around by sending chat messages.

Brother: Hm? Got a message from sis…
Sis: Hey, can you get me a cup of coffee?
Brother: What the… Hey! Don't be a **ping peu** and get your own coffee!

피켓팅 Picketing

Blood Splattering/Splashing Ticket Sale

피 **pi** "blood" + "'tic**keting**". It's a term used to describe how difficult and even brutal it is for K-pop fans to get a ticket to a TV music show in Korea. Its intensity is, therefore, likened to that of a battlefield.

Jenny got hospitalized as a result of the **picketing** war she participated in. The blood-covered ticket is a Medal of Honor to her.

Plastic Prince

Good Looking Male Who Achieved Flower Boy Status Through Plastic Surgery

A good-looking gorgeous male who achieved "flower boy" status through plastic surgery.

Tony came back to showbiz after his 2-year break. During that time, he went through a massive transformation involving plastic surgery. He looks really beautiful, but he can't deny the fact that he is a *plastic prince*!

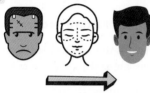

Plastic Surgery

Surgically Altering One's Physical Appearance

The practice of surgically altering one's physical appearance. Double eyelids, fuller forehead, reshaping chin, and getting a nose job are among the most popular.

Mom, Dad, today I decided to become a changed person… through *plastic surgery*!

(po-jang-ma-cha)
포장마차
Pojangmacha

Outdoor Korean Street Food Pub

Literal meaning is a "covered wagon". It's an outdoor Korean street food pub involving a small, tented spot that is either on wheels or a street stall. It sells a variety of popular street foods, such as *tteokbokki*, *mandu*, and *anju* (bar snacks), and because you can grab a bite and get drunk on the cheap, they're clustered around office buildings. In K-dramas, this is a place where people go to drown their sadness or anger in bottles of *soju*. Other clichéd settings include subordinates confronting their boss about something or one making "drunk love confessions (asking out)" to a secret admirer (with the help of alcohol!).

After work, Dohwan and Yonggi got together and headed straight to *Pojangmacha*, where they emptied 8 bottles of *soju*.

(po-syap)
포샵 Po Shop

Photoshop

The omnipotent computer graphics/image editing software that turns ugly into pretty and skinny and fatty into supermodels.

Alexis: Summer is just around the corner!
Minjoo: We need to hit the gym and get in shape!
Alexis: Girl, no need to do that.
Minjoo: Why?
Alexis: I just learned how to use *Po Shop*!

(pum-jŏl-lam/nyŏ)
품절남/녀
Poom Jeol Nam/Nyeo

Married Man/Woman

A compound word made up of "**품절**" *poom jeol* ("sold out") + "**남/녀**" *nam/nyeo* ("man/woman"). Someone who just became an unavailable player/participant in the dating market.

Juan: What… Hector and Susana are getting married?
Victor: Yup, they are a ***poom jeol nam/nyeo*** couple.

PR

"Picture Request"

A term used on fan sites when users request pictures of an idol or a specific event.

Toya: Got some pics at the concert last night!
Cecilia: *PR*! Can you send them to my *Ka Tok*?

Prince of Asia

Lee Kwang Soo

A nickname originally given to the actor and singer Jang Geun Suk for his overwhelming popularity in Asia (especially in Japan). Recently, however, Lee Kwang Soo has taken over the title, thanks to a successful TV show "Running Man" that is incredibly popular in Asia (especially in China and Hong Kong).

When I went to Hong Kong, so many people surrounded me asking for my autograph. It must be because I look like Lee Kwang Soo! Now, I kinda know what living as the ***Prince of Asia*** would feel like.

(pal-lang-gwi)
팔랑귀
Pal Lang Gwi

Gullible

Literally "flappy ear," and as you might have guessed, it refers to someone who's gullible and easily persuaded to believe something.

What? Bitcoin is going up in price? Oh, it's not? What? Gold is going up in price? I can't decide where to put my money! Too many options, and I have a *pal lang gwi*!

(pŭ-sa)
프사 Peu Sa

Profile Pic

Short for "프로필" (*peu-ro-pil*, "profile") + "사진" (*sa jin*, "picture"), the main picture That's displayed on your social media account.

I've changed my *peu sa* to that of an ajumma so my ex wouldn't bother me again.

Pink Panda

APINK Fan Club

The name of the APINK fan club. "Pink" comes from the group name, and "panda" comes from the nickname "Kung Fu Panda" of their former manager Lee Jeong-ah. After the launch of their official fan club, it changed to "PANDA". Fan color is strawberry pink

I quite enjoyed the movie Kung Fu Panda, but I find being part of *Pink Panda* more fun and exciting!

(po-ka)
포카 Po Ca

Photo Card

Short for "포토" (*poto*, "photo") "카드" (**card**), it is the little piece of paper, often laminated, that has a photo of idols printed on them. They are a very popular fan merchandise and are sold in decks of all different quantities. Older K-pop bands don't have photo cards on the market, so some K-pop fans choose to go the DIY route and make their own.

I've been collecting *po ca* of my oppas for over 4 years now. I can make a little book with them

(po-jang)
포장 Po Jang
Sugarcoating

Literal meaning is "packaging/(gift) wrapping" but idiomatically means "the act of making it sound nicer than it actually is," usually with an ulterior motive to rip someone off.

Dean: My height is optimized for picking up valuables on the ground quicker than anyone else.
Chan: Don't *po jang* yourself! Just say you are damn short, haha!

(pok-mang)
폭망 Pok Mang
Complete Failure

"폭" is short for "폭풍" (*pok poong*, "storm") + "망" is short for "망하다" (*mang ha da*, "to fail"), so when combined, it refers to a disastrous situation or a total fiasco that went completely the opposite to what was expected.

I invited over 100 guests to my birthday, and only 2 people showed up... *pok mang*!!!

(pok-tan-ju)
폭탄주 Pok Tan Ju
Boilermaker / Depth Charge

"폭탄" (*pok tan*) means "bomb" and "주" (*ju*) means "alcohol/drink". Put together, it literally means "bomb shot" and is made by mixing two drinks, usually a shot glass of soju dropped into a glass of beer. It's termed so because it will make you get drunk very quickly, as powerful as a bomb. It's similar to "boilermakers" or "depth charges" and is pretty much a ritual drinking activity at "회식" (*hoe sik*, "company dinner/get together").

Anthony got totally knocked out after his 3rd glass of *pok tan ju*.

Prima Donna
F.T. Island Fan Club

The name of the F.T. Island fan club. It's named after the song from their first album "Prima Donna," and it symbolizes the fact that their fans are their heroines. Fan colors are sunshine yellow and black.

Debbie: I'm a *Prima Donna*!
Sean: Huh? You know how to sing opera?
Debbie: LOL no! I'm a member of F.T.Island Fan Club!

프로 Pro

Per Cent

Short for the Dutch word "pro cent", which means "per cent" in English, first widely used in Japan, later making its way into Korea through the period of Japanese Occupation in the early 20th century.

> I applied for an internship position at Apple. The likelihood of getting accepted is about 30 *pro*.

펑크 Punk

1. Flat Tire 2. No Show

A Konglish term meaning "flat tire" because it comes from the English word "puncture." It also means a "no show" or not showing up for an appointment/meeting/reservation because doing so "punctures" your plans!

> I inadvertently made a *punk* to a dinner with my girlfriend because I had a punk in my tire on the way to the restaurant.

Produce 101

Korean Girl Group Survival Reality TV Show

A Korean girl-group survival reality TV show produced by CJ E&M and Signal Entertainment Group. It was a groundbreaking show when first introduced because it was Korea's first agency-collaboration unit girl group project ever. In the show, a total of 101 trainees from several companies are brought together to create a pool of candidates, and the final 11 are selected to form a unit girl group. As a result of the show, the unit girl group I.O.I was born.

> *Produce101* selected the best 11 from their pool of 101 candidates.

(pye-in)
페인 Pye In

Crock / Good For Nothing / Addicted to Something

Literally "ruined man," in a K-pop context, it refers to someone who has become totally nonfunctional as a human being due to being ejected (e.g., after being dumped), addicted (e.g., drugs, video games), or just too lazy to do anything productive ("couch potato").

> Ever since he got dumped by his girlfriend, he's been living the life of a *pye in*.

(pyo-jun-ŏ)
표준어
PyoJun Eo
Standard Language

In South Korea it means the "standard language" and is defined as "the modern speech of Seoul widely used by the well-cultivated" by the National Institute of the Korean Language, and its the style you would expect to hear in Korean TV shows and K-pop songs.

Is "*Daebak*!" a ***pyo jun eo***?

"Crying"

An emoticon used to symbolize crying.

After watching the new K-melodrama, I was literally ***Q_Q.***

R.I.P

Symbolizes the black ribbon put on as a token of condolences at funerals, and Korean people place it in the name section of their profile screen on chat apps.

►◄ Ice Bucket Challenge (2016-2016). You were fun.

퀵서비스
Quick Service
Express Courier Delivery

A Konglish term referring to "express courier delivery." As mentioned in "8282 (*bbal li bbal li* - "quickly, quickly"), Koreans LOVE having things done quickly, and "quick service" is a great example). Essentially, it is a motorcycle express service equipped with a loading area + trunk in the back, with a row of smartphones placed on the dashboard, along with a hands-free kit attached to the side of the driver's helmet. They deliver documents and parcels that are not too big or heavy, all within a couple of hours within Seoul.

Shoot! Forgot to submit my application! I'd better call ***quick service*** because it's due in 3 hours.

(ra-bok-i)
라볶이 Rabokki
Ramyeon + Tteokbokki (Topokki)

It's a heavenly combination of "라면" (*ramyeon*, "instant ramen noodles") + "떡볶이" (*tteokbokki*, "spicy stir-fried rice cakes in gochujang sauce"). A super popular street food commonly sold in *bunsikjip* (snack bars), but you can easily make it at home by simply adding *ramyeon* noodles to any *tteobokki* recipe you already have.

Don't say you know Korean food unless you tried ***rabokki.***

레알 Rae Al (rae-al)

"For Real"

It's a teenage slang for an English word pronounced in a Spanish style, as the Spanish football team Real Madrid is hugely popular in Korea. It can also be used to express surprise or to assert that something is genuine or true.

Mario: I aced the math test!
Yasiel: *Rae al*?
Mario: Yeah, dude, for real!

Red Sun

Hypnosis

Popularized by a Korean hypnotist who says this to his client while inducing hypnosis on a TV show. For this reason, when someone says this, they pretend they are hypnotized (just for fun).

Hey man, you talk too much! Let me put you to sleep. *Red Sun!*

Rainism

Anything That is Influenced or Touched by Rain (Bi)

The title of the song by Korean singer Bi (Rain). It is used to describe anything influenced or touched by him or the act of someone trying to imitate him.

Jeong put on a black leather jacket and dark sunglasses and started doing the Rain dance. He sure has serious *Rainism* going on.

Repackaged Album

Full Album that is Re-released with a New Title Track

A full album that is re-released with the addition of a new title track, along with other bonus tracks and remixes.

Because of the disagreements over the contract, New Boys couldn't release a new album. Instead, the company put a *repackaged album* on the market.

RED VELVET

Red Velvet stands for "unique concept & great music," a five-member (Irene, Seulgi, Wendy, Joy, Yeri) girl group formed by S.M. Entertainment. They debuted in 2014 with a song titled "Happiness." Their albums, "Ice Cream Cake" (2015), "The Red" (2015), "The Velvet" (2016), "Russian Roulette" (2016), "The Red Summer" (2017), and "Rookie" (2017), all topped the Gaon Album Chart, and they became the K-pop girl group with most #1 albums in the chart. Additionally, "The Red," "Rookie," and "The Red Summer" topped the Billboard World Albums. Notable songs include "Dumb Dumb," "Red Flavor," and "Peek-a-Boo."

I'm eating this red velvet cake as a way of showing support for **RED VELVET**.

ReVeluv

Red Velvet Fan Club

The name of the Red Velvet fan club, short for "Red Velvet Luv," which symbolizes their wish to have a relationship in which they love and care for each other. Fan color is coral pink.

ReVeluv sounds French, but it's not.

(ro-mang)
로망 RoMang

Fantasy/Wish

Originated from the word "romance," it has a slightly different meaning in Korean language because it refers to something not necessarily related to love that one wishes/is eager to have. For example, having a full-blown home theater system is every man's "로망".

My *ro mang* is to have a backstage pass to a TWICE concert and have dessert time with the members.

(ri-mo-còn)
리모컨
RiMoCon

Remote (Control)

A Konglish term meaning "**remo**te (**con**trol)," something that magically disappears when you need it the most. He/she who controls it in the house "wears the pants in the house".

I wish I had a *ri mo con* to control my unruly nephew.

런닝맨
Running Man

Super Popular Variety TV Show

An SBS Korean variety TV show that first aired in 2010 and is labeled an "urban action variety," as the MCs and guests are given a set of missions to complete at a landmark in order to win a race. Recently, it has gradually transformed into more of a general variety show format, in which MCs and guests play games. The show has established a strong global presence, being translated and fansubbed into various languages immediately after each episode airs. The show was chosen as one of the 20 TV shows of 2016 by Business Insider.

> I think **Running Man** is the most hilarious Korean variety show.

사춘기 Sa Chun Gi *(sa-chun-gi)*

Puberty

That period of time in life when teenagers become adults through dramatic bodily/emotional changes. When boys start keeping their room door locked/closed, and girls start caring more about their looks, its a surefire sign of puberty! Congratulations!

> Although I'm in my 30's, I feel like I'm in my **sa chun gi** again when I see my favorite K-pop idols perform.

런닝셔츠
Running Shirts

Tank Top

A Konglish term for "tank top/sleeveless shirt," believed to have originated from the fact that its worn as an undershirt by athletes when running, hence "running shirts."

> Don't come to church wearing a **running shirt**!

사기캐 Sa Gi Kae *(sa-gi-kae)*

Overpowered Character

"사기" (*sa gi*) means "scam/fraud" and "캐" is the first word of "캐릭터 ("cha**racter**)." Put together, it refers to an overpowered character in a video game, almost to the degree of scam/fraud because they dominate the game. The term is also widely used in the real world, generally among teenagers, to refer to someone who is superior to others in many aspects.

> Don't you think G-Dragon is a **sa gi kae**? He's smart, sexy, cute, and artistic.

S Line

Curvaceous Female Body

A curvaceous female body. When standing sideways, the shape of the body with a flat stomach and curvy backside resembles the Latin letter "S".

The first thing I need to get the **S Line** is to cut down on the sweets.

사바사 Sa Ba Sa (sa-ba-sa)

"Differ From Individual to Individual"

An abbreviation for "**사람**" *saram* ("person") **by** 사람 *saram*. This is similar to "Case By Case", and its closest English equivalent is "YMMV (Your Mileage May Vary)".

Molly: How is the new Korean restaurant in K-Town?
Kwon: Well, sometimes good, sometimes so-so.
Molly: Why?
Kwon: I guess It's **sa ba sa** – some days, there is a good chef on duty, but other days, there must be a horrible chef on duty.

사랑해 Sa Rang Hae (sa-rang-hae)

"I Love You"

It is probably the most spoken (abused) phrase throughout K-pop songs and K-dramas.

No, I don't hate you. **Sa Rang Hae**!

사이다 Sa I Da (sa-i-da)

"Hits the Spot"

Opposite of "고구마" *go gu ma* ("a stuffy or suffocating situation" or "someone who is insensitive or slow-witted"). It originated from the word "cider", a carbonated Korean soda similar to Sprite or 7UP because drinking it makes you feel refreshed. It is a powerful antidote for "고구마".

Mindy: **Sa i da**… I need **Sa i da**!
Hoon: Whats wrong?
Mindy: The male character hasn't confessed his love to the female character in the past 6 episodes, and its driving me crazy!

(saeng-bang-song)
생방송
Saeng Bang Song
Live Airing

A compound word made up of "**생**" *saeng* ("live/alive") + "**방송**" *bang song* ("airing, broadcast"). It is a format used by major weekly music shows (e.g., Music Bank). Because everything is performed live, mistakes made on the stage will be broadcast unedited. This is something many "vocally weak" idols are afraid of, but it is a great opportunity for those with superior "vocals" to show off their talents.

Yeonhee: I feel anxious from watching Music Bank…!
Tim: Why?
Yeonhee: Because its *saeng bang song*… I worry about my oppas making a mistake on the stage!

(saeng-ŏl)
생얼 Saeng Eol
Face Without Any Make-up on

생 *saeng* means "bare", and **얼** *eol* is an abbreviation for **얼굴** *eol gool*, "face", hence "bare face". To some girls, this is their worst nightmare.

Mark: If I were a cop, I would arrest you!
Jennifer: Awww, so you can keep me in your jail?
Mark: No, for having a weapon of mass destruction.
Jennifer: What weapon?
Mark: Your *saeng eol*.

(saeng-pa)
생파 Saeng Pa
Birthday Party

An abbreviation for "**생일**" *saeng il* ("birthday") "**파티**" (**party**).

Mary: Tomorrow's my birthday!
Jin: Where the *saeng pa* at, bro?

(saeng-sŏn)
생선 Saeng Seon
Birthday Gift

Acronym for "**생일**" *saeng il* ("birthday") "**선물**" *seon mool* ("gift"). It is widely used by teens because it sounds funny (because it also means "fish").

Hanna: I hope you brought *saeng seon* for my birthday.
Min: Huh? Fish?
Hanna: No! Birthday gift!

쌩유 Saeng You
(saeng-yu)
"Thank You"

A funny variation of saying "thank you", which was first used by a comedian, Yoo Jae Seok. Instead of pronouncing the "th" sound, you substitute it with a strong S sound.

After 10 years of living in Korea, Brandon, a native New Yorker, started feeling confused about whether to say, "Thank You" or "**Saeng You**".

사극 Sageuk
(sa-gŭk)
Historical Korean Drama

사 *sa* "history" + 극 *geuk* "play". A historical Korean drama set in a period earlier than modern-day Korea (the 1900's).

Charlie will be acting as a 13th-century bladesmith in an upcoming **sageuk**.

삭발 Sak Bal
(sak-bal)
Shaving One's Head

Something male idols have to go through before joining the army for their military obligation. It is an emotional moment because cutting one's hair symbolizes disconnection from the outside world. In Korean culture, it is also a popular method of demonstrating one's discontent and determination (e.g., in a strike or a riot).

Victoria couldn't stop crying as she watched her oppa, Chanyong, was getting a **sak bal** because it meant a 2-year-long farewell.

삼촌팬 Samchon Fans
(sam-chon-paen)
Uncle Fans

It refers to the fan demographic (males aged 30-40) that follows girl group idols. They are known for their ability to spend more on *jo gong* because most of them have full-time jobs.

Thanks to their overwhelming cuteness, Hello Ladies have tens of thousands of **samchon fans** over the age of 40.

(sang-nam-ja)
상남자
Sangnamja

Macho Man/Tough Guy

A man who possesses the stereotypical male characteristics, such as physical strength, mental toughness, and paternal (fatherly) instincts, in contrast to "flower boys".

Mason drank 2 bottles of Soju in one sitting to make him look like a *sangnamja*, but he only became an alcoholic.

(se-jel-ye)
세젤예 SeJelYe

"The Most Beautiful in the World"

An abbreviation for "세상에서" *se sang e seo* ("in the world") "제일" *je il* ("number one") "예쁜" *ye bbeun* ("beautiful").

Evil Queen: Mirror, mirror, on the wall, who is the prettiest of all?
Mirror: You. You are the *se jel ye*.
Evil Queen: You are promoted to Deluxe Mirror.

(sa-saeng)
사생 Saseng

Overly Obsessive Fan

사생 *sasaeng* comes from the word 사생활 *sasaenghwal* "private life". Combined with the word **fan**, it refers to the overly obsessive fans who engage in outrageous and even dangerous behavior toward their idols, including stalking them and breaking into their homes. They are compared to stalkers and peeping toms.

Did you hear? Marcus broke into HIHI's home and stole their photo album! That's a serious crime and something only a *saseng* would do.

셀카 Selca

Selfie

An abbreviation for "**sel**f-**ca**mera". It is the act of holding one's camera and taking a shot of oneself. With a little touch-up using a photo editing app, you can become an "얼짱" *ulzzang* ("best looking face").

Heemin takes one too many *selcas*. Her Instagram is full of photos of her face.

선수 Seon Soo

(sŏn-su)

Player

Literally meaning "someone who is highly skilled at something", such as an athlete, but it is also used to refer to a "player" who flirts and is good at seducing someone.

Youngmi: Be careful with Jinho! He's such a *seon soo*!
Yena: I like athletes! What does he play?
Youngmi: No! It means he's a player and a womanizer!

샤방 Sha Bang

(sya-bang)

"Bling Bling", "Dazzling"

A term used to describe someone's radiating beauty. A cliche example: a girl tosses her hair in slow-mo, with some sort of celestial lights and glittering CG surrounding her, making everyone's jaws drop in amazement.

Joon: Wow! Why are you so *sha bang sha bang* today?
Bonnie: I have a date today, so I spent some time preening myself.

스샷 Seu Shot

(sŭ-syat)

Screen Capture

An abbreviation for "스크린" screen "샷" shot. It is the act of capturing the displayed image on a device's monitor (e.g., computer, smartphone, etc.).

George: I got a message from my crush!
Winnie: I don't believe you. Send me a *seu shot*!

식신 Shik Shin

(shik-shin)

Food Hogger

A compound word made up of two Chinese words: "식" *shik* ("to eat") "신" *shin* ("god" or "demon"). It refers to someone who shows exceptional ability devouring a massive amount of food at a super-human speed. Jeong Joon Ha of the Infinity Challenge was a famous "식신".

Wanso only weighs 100 pounds, but she is a formidable *shik shin*. She eats 5,000 calories a day.

(shim-kung)
심쿵
Shim Koong

"Heart Racing"

An abbreviation for "심장" *shim jang* ("heart") "쿵쾅" *koong kwang* ("sound of the heart beating/racing") = "Heart is Racing/Beating Rapidly". This is a spontaneous reaction by your central nervous system that occurs upon seeing your *bias*.

Nero: Oh, wow! We almost got run over by a car!
Nick: *Shim koong*…

(shi-nui-a-dul)
신의아들
Shineui Adeul

Someone Who is Exempt from Mandatory Military Service

"신의" *shin eui* means "God's" and "아들" *adeul* means "son", so its literal meaning is "son of God". It is used to refer to someone who is exempt from Korea's mandatory military service, especially for no apparent reason but through various means not available to the general public. This "privilege" is often abused by the rich and the powerful (i.e., a politician, *chaebols*, and so on), which causes many social problems.

Dana: So, why did he not go to the army?
Russ: News says he was diagnosed with "happy virus"
Dana: That's B.S.! There is no such thing, right?
Russ: I guess he's just a *shineui adeul*.

(shin-gok)
신곡 Shin Gok

New Song

A compound word made up of two Chinese words: 신 *shin* ("new") 곡 *gok* ("song"). It is the subject of extreme anticipation by fanboys/girls because it means their idols are coming back from a hiatus.

Fans all over the world have been waiting for UIUI's *shin gok*, which incorporates the elements of jazz and funk.

셧다운
Shut Down

Cyber Curfew

Also known as the "Cinderella Law", it is a regulation that went into effect in 2011. It prohibits children of age 16 and under from playing online games between the hours of 12:00 A.M. and 6:00 A.M.

Kid 1: Who's our biggest enemy?
Kid 2: Teachers? Parents?
Kid 1: No! It's the *shutdown* rule!

싸인회 Sign Hwae

(ssa-in-hoe)

Signing Event

A dream come true moment for K-pop fanboys/girls because it is a rare opportunity to meet their bias in person, and they are welcome to bring their belongings for the bias to autograph.

The **sign hwae** by Jamie J attracted more than 10,000 people because everybody wanted to see him in person.

신상 Shin Sang

(shin-sang)

New Product

This is especially detrimental to those with an impulse disorder or someone who wants to earn the title of "early adopter" or "trend leader".

Girlfriend: Hey baby, lets go to the mall and have lunch?
Boyfriend: Lunch? You mean you want to buy that **shin sang** dress, right?
Girlfriend: Just give me your card!

Skinship

Physical Contact

A Konglish for "physical contact", such as holding hands, hugging, etc. "Manner hands (hovering hands)" is the act of trying to avoid any unnecessary "skinship".

My boyfriend likes **skinship** too much! We've only dated once!

슬로건 Slogan

Banner With the Group or a Member's Name

A thin towel, or a banner, with the name of a group or an idol printed on it. They are made and sold by the company the idols belong to, or they are made by fans and distributed for free at concerts to show their "support" during a performance.

At the peak of the concert, all the fans took out their **slogans**.

Small Face

"Face That is Small in Size (a compliment)"

A face that is small in size. It is a compliment as it is believed that smaller faces make facial features look well-defined, and thus photogenic, while giving a youthful look.

Hyoju has such a *small face*! She should audition to become an actor. She'd look great on TV.

(so-ju)
소주 Soju

Traditional Korean Alcoholic Drink

A traditional Korean alcoholic drink made by distilling starchy grains, such as rice, sweet potatoes, potatoes, or tapioca. It is the most popular drink among Koreans and is an indispensable part of Korean life and K-dramas. Most of it is packaged in green bottles (most of the cheaper ones, including the ones that come in green bottles, are made by diluting the spirit made from the traditional distilling method) and it is one of the top-selling liquors in the world.

Hey man, long time no see! Lets go pop a few bottles of *Soju*!

SNS

Social Media

An abbreviation for "Social Networking Service", although it's an English word, it is not widely used outside of Korea (but it's not a Konglish word, though). When used in news articles, it refers to celebrities' Facebook, Twitter, Weibo, Instagram, etc. accounts.

After the scandal broke out, Hunter K shut down all of his *SNS* accounts.

(sok-do wi-ban)
속도 위반
Sokdo Wiban

"Getting Pregnant Before Marriage"

A compound word made up of "속도" *sokdo* ("speed") + "위반" *wi ba*n ("violation"). It refers to a couple that is expecting a baby before officially marrying. This was something to be ashamed of in Korea in the past, but as society became more open, it became something to be congratulated on. In some K-drama settings, couples often decide to use pregnancy as leverage to secure "marriage approval" from their parents (similar to a "shotgun wedding").

Bobby: They just made a wedding announcement!
Windy: Wow, that is a surprise!
Bobby: I'm pretty positive they had a *sokdo wiban* because of her belly.
Windy: That's called a beer belly, dude.

(sol-kka-mal)
솔까말
Sol Kka Mal
TBH ("To Be Honest")

An abbreviation for "솔직히" *sol jik hi* ("honestly") "까놓고" *kka not go* ("openly, publicly") "말해서" *mal hae seo* ("speaking"). It is used more often on the Internet than in real-life conversations.

Mina: **Sol kka mal**, not too many people like *oppa* as much as I do.
Hailey: I don't think so! Don't underestimate my love for *oppa*!

(ssöm-nam/ssöm-nyö)
썸남/썸녀
Some Nam / Some Nyeo
Someone You Are Seeing

Derived from the word "**some**thing", it refers to a male or a female who's got "something (romantic)" going on with another. If you are a male, you would have "*some nyeo* (female)", a girl you have been dating, but you are not officially going out with her yet. Hence, you just have "something (romantic)" going on with her.

No, she is not my girlfriend. She is just one of my many *some nyeos*.

(su-nŭng)
수능 Soo Neung
College Scholastic Ability Test (College Entrance Exam)

Judgment day for all third-year graduating high school students because it is the single most important factor colleges look at when evaluating applicants. Its significance is enormous, to the point where emergency ambulances and police cars are on standby to transport students who are struggling to make it to the test site on time.

Soo neung can mean freedom to many, but it can also mean another year of agony if they don't pass it.

Spazzing
"Freaking Out"

Your body's natural reaction when you are surrounded with extremely strong emotions (joy, excitement, etc.). Fanboys/girls experience this when they see their favorite idol in person. It is often accompanied by screaming and, in extreme cases, passing out.

Henry: Why is she **spazzing**?
Woody: Oh, she just received an invitation to her bias's private fan meeting.

스펙 Spec

Job Qualifications

Originally derived from "**spec**ification", but its meaning has been changed to refer to "work experience" and other "extracurricular activities". Many young job applicants spend a significant amount of time and money on beefing up their "**spec**" (e.g., studying abroad for language training) in order to win the cut-throat competition in the job market.

Martha didn't even bother applying for the job because she thought she didn't have enough *specs* to compete with other applicants.

스포 Spo

Spoiler

Short for "**spo**iler", which is the despicable act of revealing a previously unknown aspect of something, thereby completely ruining someone's opportunity to learn and/or enjoy it.

Don't say a word about the last episode! No one wants you to spo it again!

쌍수 Ssang Soo (ssang-su)

Double-eyelid Surgery

One of the most widely performed plastic surgeries among Koreans who wish to have their eyes appear bigger and more defined. Due to the simplicity of the procedure, many don't even consider it "surgery" but a simple "beauty enhancement".

Ssang soo is considered an "upgrade".

싸가지 Ssa Ga Ji (ssa-ga-ji)

Rude/Selfish Person

Someone whose attitude is extremely inconsiderate towards others to the point that it causes rage.

Jenny: Oh! Free money on the ground!
Eric: Dude! That's my money!
Jenny: Finders keepers!
Eric: You *ssa ga ji*…

싼티 Ssanti

"Looking Tawdry", "Unclassy"

An expression of disparagement, but some idols have incorporated it to make it a part of their unique character.

> OMG, that twerking is so **ssanti**. I wonder if her parents say anything.

썩소 Sseok So

Awkwawrd Smile not Coming From Genuine Pleasure

An abbreviation for "썩은" *sseok eun* ("rotten") "미소" *miso* ("smile"). It is a facial expression occurring from the incongruence between your body and mind, where your mind says "shi*", but your face is trying to smile. It usually ends up as a smile with only one side of the mouth turning upward.

> Mandy: Guessing from your **sseok so**, you are mad at me, right?
> Jillian: Are you kidding me? You just totaled my car!

Stan

Obsessive Fan

A compound word made up of "**st**alker" and "**fan**". It describes an avid and obsessive fan. While the term carries a negative connotation, it is not as bad as *saseng*.

> I hired a private detective and found out my *Oppa*'s address… I am afraid that I am becoming a **stan**.

서브 유닛 Sub-unit

Smaller (project) Group Within a Larger Group

A group formed to serve a different market segment, and while generally comprising existing members, new members are often added just for the project.

> JOA created a **sub-unit** consisting only of rappers.

(sa-hoe-ja/jin-haeng-ja)
사회자/진행자
Sa Hoe Ja/ Jin Haeng Ja

MC (Master of Ceremonies)

The official host of a staged event, ceremony, TV shows, and the like. One of the most important virtues of a 사회자/진행자 in a Korean TV show is the ability to analyze the personality of the guests quickly and listen to them while encouraging those who are shy to speak up. 유재석 (Yu Jae-seok), also known as "국민 (guk min, "very popular") MC" is an example of a good 사회자/진행자.

My friend is so funny and talkative. He would make a great *jin haeng ja*.

(sa-rang-kkun)
사랑꾼
Sa Rang Kkun

Romanticist

"사랑" (*sar ang*, "love") + "꾼" (*kkun*, "master", "expert"). It refers to someone, usually a male, who chooses "love" over everything else and loves his significant other with all his heart.

I'm not a player! I'm just a *sa rang kkun* ;)

(sa-tu-ri)
사투리 Sa Tu Ri

Dialect

In Korea, there are eight provinces that have their own distinct dialect, while the Seoul dialect is the standard language of the nation. The dialects are different in the way they change the sound of the verbs or have totally different sets of words. Because someone who speaks in a dialect could be looked down on as a "hillbilly," people try to fix it before they move to Seoul.

I find girls who talk in *sa tu ri* very attractive, so don't try to fix it!

사연 Sa Yeon

Story

A term you would frequently encounter in TV/Radio shows where a guest is invited to share their stories with the audience/listeners. Some are sad stories that would leave you in tears while others are hilarious stories that would leave you in stitches. Due to the fact that many relatively unknown entertainers rose to instant stardom after sharing a story that went viral, some entertainers, being overly ambitious to become the talk of the town, were accused of fabricating stories, which backfired on them, hurting their reputation.

The super hilarious *sa yeon* the radio show host read to the audience left everyone in stitches.

(sal-in-mi-so)
살인미소
Sal In Mi So

Killer Smile

"**살인**" (*sal in*, "homicide") + "**미소**" (*mi so*, "smile")
= "killer smile" = "amazing smile,"

Nick: Isn't my smile so sexy? Isn't it a *sal in mi so*?
Minju: It sure is because it makes me want to kill you!

스벅
Sbuck

Starbucks

An abbreviation for "**Star**bucks," made by
taking the first and third word, "**스타벅스**."
Used interchangeably with "**별다방**" (*byeol da
bang),* a Korean nickname because "**별**"
(*byeol*) means "Star" and "**다방**" (*dabang*)
means "Coffee Shop" or "Tea House." This is
where people go to drink coffee That's more
expensive than their lunch.

Yeah, let's just meet up at *sbuck* and chat.

(sam-gak-gwan-gye)
삼각관계
Sam Gak Gwan Gye

Love Triangle

A romantic relationship involving three people,
which is a frequently recurring clichéd theme
for K-pop dramas (but we all love it because of
the suspense, especially when the ones involved
do not know they are, in fact, competing for the
same crush!). It's an awful thing to be in a place
where there is no winner - you end up losing
everyone, your best friend and your love.

Sera: I'm afraid of being in a *sam gak gwan gye* with
Jimin and Rap Mon... I wouldn't know who to choose...
Tony: I'm afraid you're delusional.

시즌그리팅
Season Greeting

Fan Merchandise Collection

In a K-pop fandom context - a set of various
types of fan merchants released at the year-end.
Typically, pre-sales begin between the end of
November and the beginning of December, and
some of the popular items include calendars,
posters, photo cards, DVD's, stickers, and
journal notebooks. Most are priced at around
30,000 KRW (~30 USD) but often go above
50,000 KRW (~50 USD).

Yay! Our *oppa's* *season greeting* for 2018 just came out,
and they only have 1,000 of those! Let's go get them!

(sel-gi-kkun)
셀기꾼
Sel Gi Kkun

Someone Who Looks Much Better in Selfies

"셀카" (*sel ca*, "selfie") + "사기꾼" (*sa gi kkun*, "con man/trickster"). Someone who looks like a supermodel in their selfies, mostly achieved with the help of computer programs or applications, such as Photoshop and Photowonder, which is VERY different from how they look in real life.

My Instagram selfies get a ton of likes, but when I meet them, they don't recognize me! Am I a *sel gi kkun*?

(sŏl-lae)
설레
Seol Lae

Heart Fluttering

It's an expression that describes an emotional state where you become nervous, excited, and happy, from the anticipation That'something good will happen, such as meeting your bias.

Why am I so *seol lae*? I have a feeling that something good will happen today...

(sŏb-oe)
섭외 Seop Oe
Casting/Invitation

The act of reaching out to someone with the goal of casting/inviting them to a show, an event, or into a contract. Getting cast/invited in/to a super popular show like Running Man is a huge honor for celebrities, but the opposite is very true as well - show producers casting/inviting a super popular celebrity, like BTS, in/to a show is extremely difficult, but if done, its a guaranteed ratings booster.

How did you *seop oe* such a high-profile celeb?

(sŏn-bi)
선비 Seon Bi

SJW (Social Justice Warrior) / Fun Police / Moralist

Seonbi were virtuous, highly regarded, well-disciplined scholars during the olden days of Korea, who valued lives of study and integrity over wealth and power - simply put, men of justice. Today, in the Internet world, however, its used to refer to someone who's too serious to take a joke and obsessed with an overly strict set of moral ethics with zero flexibility.

Rule #1 : Never invite a *seon bi* to your party unless it's a party of party poopers.

Service

Complimentary / On The House

A Konglish term meaning "complimentary (food, service, item, and the like)," something you'd expect from a place where you are a regular patron.

Patron: What's this? We didn't order this.
Waiter: It's a **service** ;) Please enjoy.

샤프 Sha Peu
(sha-pŭ)

Mechanical Pencil

Like "Sharpie" in English, it refers to "mechanical pencil." It's actually the name of a product named "Sharp," an automatic pencil invented by a Japanese entrepreneur Hayakawa Tokuji.

People call me Mr. Sharp, not because I look sharp, but because I always use a **sha peu**.

시강 Shi Gang
(shi-gang)

Scene Stealer

Short for "시선" (*si seon*, "attention/look") + "강탈" (*gang tal*, "robbery"). It refers to someone/something that draws eyes and attracts public gaze, such as someone with an overwhelming swag, who dwarfs everyone around them, or a surprise appearance such as photobombing.

I wore a full white tuxedo to a funeral, and I made a **shi gang**... in a bad way.

시청률 Shi Cheong Ryul
(shi-chŏng-lyul)

(Viewer) Ratings

The number of people who are watching a specific TV program at a given time. It is of the utmost importance for TV networks because, the higher the rating, the more sponsorship/commercials they can attract, which means more revenue generated. It's a great way to measure a celeb's popularity because, with their special appearance, the show's rating could go up significantly.

Wow! The show's **shi cheong ryul** skyrocketed when CNBLUE made a cameo appearance!

(shi-sul)
시술 Shi Sul

Cosmetic Surgery a.k.a "Beautification"

A term referring to a medical operation intended to improve the appearance of a person. Examples include silicone filler injection, liposuction, and Botox injection. Since its a minor operation comparatively, Korean people consider it to be different from plastic surgery and liken the difference between the two to complete renovation (plastic surgery) vs. partial remodeling of a house (cosmetic surgery).

"Shi sul is a quick and easy way to improve your looks!" says a plastic surgeon in an attempt to lure more clients to his clinic.

(shil-hwa-nya)
실화냐? Shil Hwa Nya

For Real?

"실화" (*shil hwa*, "true story") + ~냐? (*nya*, "is it?" (casual informal). Recently, it has become popular among the younger generation.

Olga: Our *oppas* are coming to Mexico!
Vanessa: Que? Verdad? ***Shil hwa nya?***

(shim-kung-sa)
심쿵사 Shim Kung Sa

To Die of a Heart Attack

"심" (*shim*, 心) means "heart," and "쿵" (*kung*) is the sound of an object hitting the ground/floor, while "사" (*sa*, 死) means "death." Put together, it means "To Die of a Heart Attack," which could happen if you see your favorite idol in the flesh!

I really want to see my *oppas* in person, but at the same time, I'm afraid I'd die from ***shim kung sa***... My heart will explode!

(shin-gi-rok)
신기록 Shin Gi Rok

New Record

"신" (*shin*, 新, "new") + "기록" (*gi rok*, "record"). A newly-set record that exceeds/surpasses previously set records, both good and bad.

Our *oppa's* new album sold more than 5 million copies! That's an all-time ***shin gi rok*** according to The New York Times.

(shin-hon-bu-bu)
신혼부부
Shin Hon Bu Bu
Newelyweds

"신혼" (*shin hon*, "new wedding") + "부부" (*bu bu*, "husband and wife"). A couple who have recently been married, who are probably in the happiest yet most critical moment of their lives because lots of newlyweds break up after a huge argument on their honeymoon trip!

Suga and Jin are really close to each other, like *shin hon bu bu*!

SHINee

SHINee stands for "one who receives the light," and it originally started as a five-member (Onew, Key, Minho, Taemin, Jonghyun) boy group, but lost a member when he decided to take his own life in December 2017, a tragic incident that shocked everyone. They debuted in 2008 with a song titled "Replay" and later that year won the "Newcomer Album of the Year" at the 23rd Golden Disk Awards. They are considered to be one of the best live vocal K-pop groups with highly synchronized choreography and were included in the Forbes list of Korea Power Celebrity in 2014 and 2016, reflecting their popularity all over Asia. Notable songs include "Lucifer," "Sherlock (Clue + Note)," "Everybody," and "1 of 1."

SHINee is the shiniest being in the whole entire universe.

(shin-in)
신인 Shin In
Rookie

"신" (*shin*, 新, "new") + "인" (*in*, 人, "person"). Someone who has just made a debut and is completely new to the industry. It needs to be distinguished from "뉴페" (*new face*), which doesn't necessarily mean someone entirely new, but includes someone who joins a group for the first time, regardless of their experience.

Wow... He's amazing on the stage! Can't believe he's a *shin in*!

SHINee World

As the name suggests, its the name of the fan club for SHINee, often abbreviated as SHAWOL. Fan color is Pearl Aqua.

I believe in life after death, and I'm sure I'll be in *SHINee World* when I die!

Show Me the Money

Korean Rap Competition TV Show

A Korean rap competition TV show broadcast by Mnet, where contestants battle against one another while going through assigned challenges until there is only one winner left. Veterans or more established rappers also appear on the show and act as judges and mentors. The first episode aired in 2012 and has been a popular show ever since, churning out many famed rappers like Cheetah, Loco, Swings, and BewhY.

> My girlfriend can talk trash about her friends for hours, non-stop! She should be on *Show Me The Money*! She's a real gangsta!

SKY

Top 3 Universities in Korea

An abbreviation for "**S**eoul National University," "**K**orea University," and "**Y**onsei University," the top three most prestigious universities in Korea. Getting into one of the **SKY** universities is considered a great achievement, not only academically but socially because many of Korea's influential figures have graduated from one of the **SKY** universities and maintain well-connected alumni associations.

> Tiger Mom: *SKY*'s the limit! You have to get into one of the 3. Okay? Son: I will try ㅠㅠ

싸인
Sign

Autograph

A Konglish term for "autograph," from the word "signature."

> Yay! I got a *sign* from my *oppa*! I can sell it for $500 on eBay...

스밍
Sming

Streaming

Short for "strea**ming**," which is the act of listening to a certain song on a music website, such as Melon and Mnet, because doing so works in favor of the band who sang the song - the number of times a song is played counts towards the chart. Fans do this to help their bias get ranked high on the chart, and it has to meet certain criteria. 1) Sample 1-minute streaming doesn't count, 2) You have to purchase a "listening credit" using real money, and 3) Volume must be turned up.

> We go full-throttle on *sminging* our *oppa's* new song at 4:00PM today!

(so-gae-ting)
소개팅
So Gae Ting

Blind Date

A compound word comprising "**소개**" (*so gae*, "to introduce") + "**팅**" (*ting*, from the word "mee**ting**"). Put together, it means "meeting someone (of the opposite sex) through the introduction (arrangement) of a mutual acquaintance," a popular way of making a new boyfriend/girlfriend.

I came back home from *so gae ting* after 5 minutes because the girl looked nothing like the photo she sent me, and the girl went back home after 3 minutes because I looked nothing like the photo I sent her.

(so-o-rum)
소오름
So O Reum

Chills

A drawn-out way of saying "**소름**" (*so reum*, "chills") to add more dramatic, exaggerated feel to the expression. It has a dual meaning:
1) Horrified (negative) - when seeing a scary movie or 2) Goosebumps (positive) - when watching your favorite bias perform on the stage.

So o reum...! I think I just walked by BTS disguised as a group of soccer players... No one recognized them, but I'm pretty sure it was them!

(so-gam)
소감 So Gam

Thoughts / Feelings / Impression

The feelings you have/get about an incident/situation; a term you hear most at award programs because every recipient is asked to talk about this, but its basically used in any situation - a reporter to an athlete after a sports game or to a criminal after being sentenced in court. Or you can use it to make fun of/provoke your friend after beating him/her at a video game.

Reporter: Hey, you just won the *daesang* award! Give us your *so gam!*

(sok-bo)
속보 Sok Bo

Breaking News

"**속**" (*sok*, "fast") + "**보도**" (*bodo*, "report/coverage") means "breaking news." Something in which you want to see the name of your bias, unless its about their early comeback or topping the Billboard Chart.

Sok bo! I'm hungry. Feed me now before I throw a fit!

(son-pyŏn-ji)

손편지
Son PyeonJi

Hand-Written Letter

"손" (*son*, "hand") + "편지" (*pyeon ji*, "letter"). Unlike those typed-up letters you can easily print, a hand-written letter is a symbol of devotion, sincerity, and love because you put so much effort into it (but not those scary threatening letters by *sasaeng* fans and STANs).

The superstar idol was known for reading each and every *son pyeon ji* his fans sent him.

(su-go)

수고 Su Go

Good Bye

Short for "수고하세요 (*su go ha se yo*)" which literally means "continue taking the trouble to do it" or "keep up the effort," but its more widely accepted as an expression used in place of "goodbye" or "see you." Believed to have originated from workplaces, as its something one would say to other colleagues when clocking off work earlier than them. Important note: use the short form only to your friends, and use the full "수고하세요" form to people older than you/superior or in formal situations.

Su go! I'm outta here!

St.

Style

A Konglish abbreviation for "style," something often encountered in Korean online fashion stores. For example, "idol **st.**" means "idol style," and "teenager **st.**" means "teenager style."

Jake: LOL! What's with the snapback hat? They are so yesterday!
Tim: Nope, see how it's slightly tilted? It's called the new Tim **St**.

SUPER JUNIOR

Super Junior, also known as SJ or SUJU, stands for "best in every field + junior (represents their time as trainees)," and is an eleven-member (Leeteuk, Heechul, Yesung, Kangin, Shindong, Sungmin, Eunhyuk, Siwon, Donghae, Ryeowook, Kyuhyun) boy group formed by S.M. Entertainment. They debuted in 2005 with a song titled "Twins." They rose to international stardom with the smash hit song "Sorry Sorry" in 2009, leading them to win over 13 music awards from MAMA, 16 from the Golden Disc Awards, as well as "International Artist" and "Best Fandom" at the Teen Choice Awards. Notable songs include "Mr. Simple," "Sexy, Free & Single," and "Mamacita."

Does **Super Junior** become Super Senior when they get old?

Super Star K

It's a Korean singing competition TV show series produced by CJ E&M and Signal Entertainment Group (since 2016). It began airing in 2009 and has been churning out new K-pop talents, like Seo In-guk, Busker Busker, John Park, and Ulala Session, with famous stars like Lee Hyori, Yang Hyun-seok, PSY appearing as judges.

It's amazing how many kids rose to stardom because of **Super Star K**.

선배 Sunbae
(sŏn-bae)
Senior in a Certain Field

Someone with more experience or seniority in a certain field, regardless of age. As a *sunbae*, one assumes leadership and provides care to their hoobaes.

Sunbae! We will do anything you say! Just give us an order.

서포트 Support
Large Fan-Events to Support Their Biases

Large events run by K-pop fans and fan clubs to show their love. Examples include buying meal boxes for the idols and staff or helping to promote a drama or a movie in which the idols appear.

Fans created a *support* event where they handed out promotional flyers about their biases' upcoming show.

탈락 Tal Lak
(tal-lak)
Elimination

A term frequently used in competitive games or TV shows (i.e., quiz shows or audition programs) when a participant doesn't make it to the next round.

Ok, the results are in… Jenny, you.... *Tal lak*!

Talent
Drama Actor/Actress

Almost exclusively used to refer to a drama (soap opera) actor/actress. Not used for a movie actor/actress.

Inhye: He looks amazing! Is he a movie star?
Yong: Nah, he is a *talent*. He appeared in the drama 'Forever You'.

(ta-tcha)
타짜
Tajja / Tazza

Card Sharp / Card Shark

Slang for someone who uses skill and/or deception to win at card games, such as gostop and poker. An example of such skills is swapping cards. It's also the name of a K-Movie "Tazza: War of Flowers (2006)."

Dang it... We played poker in Vegas, and Mario won over $1,000 in just 2 hours... I think he's a Tazza!

(tae-mong)
태몽 Tae Mong

Conception Dream

A concept unique to Korean culture in which dreams are believed to foretell the conception of a child. Popular topics of the dreams include fruits, animals, and nature, involving an action that symbolizes conception. For example, one might eat, harvest fruits or crops, embrace animals, or interact with nature. It's also interesting to note that the topic is thought to be related to the gender of the baby. Also important is that such dreams are not necessarily experienced only by the mother, but family members, close relatives, and even close friends sometimes have them.

What was your *tae mong* when your mom had you? I bet it was something cute and pretty!

(tal-dök)
탈덕 Tal Deok

To Quit Being A Fanboy/Fangirl

"탈" (*tal*, "to exit") + "덕" (*deok*, "*otaku*" (geek, mania). The act of quitting being a fanboy/fangirl; the opposite of "입덕" (*ip deok*, "to begin being a fanboy/fangirl).

Can't believe he raped his fans... His fans are going on a *tal deok* rally.

팀킬 Team Kill

Friendly Fire

Originated from FPS (first-person shooter) games, where a player mistakenly shoots and kills a team member. In real-life settings, it refers to someone saying/doing things that cause harm to their own group.

Kong: Juno just spilled the beans on TV. He said one of the group members likes wearing girl's undies.
Chong: That is one hell of a *team kill*.

Teaser Pics

Photos Released by Entertainment Companies Before Official Release

The photos released by entertainment companies before the release of a song/album of an idol/group. They can be either solo shots or group shots incorporating the theme of their upcoming work.

XeeXee's *teaser pics* indicate that being comical will be the concept for their next album.

2030.03.01

Teaser

Sneak Preview

Usually used by entertainment companies before a full release of an album/MV to build a buzz towards the release of the upcoming work.

Sexy Stars just released a 30-second-long *teaser* clip on YouTube before the full album release.

(tŭk-jong)
특종 TeukJong

Exclusive Story, Scoop

Something all reporters and news agencies want every day, but fanboys/girls don't because most of them are related to something negative, such as their bias getting involved in a crime or the groups abrupt disbandment.

Mispatch just released another *teuk jong!* They say MR. & MS. are a married couple!

타이틀 트랙
Title Track

Main Song of an Album

The main promoted track on an album. This is the song that usually has an accompanying music video and is performed on music shows.

The **title track** for their new album is "Magical Moments" because it symbolizes their dramatic return as a group after disbanding last year.

Triple Crown

Winning Three Weeks in a Row on One Music Show

Winning three weeks in a row on one music show (e.g., Music Bank). It is NOT winning on three different shows (e.g., Music Bank, Inki Gayo, M!Countdown) the same week. Once achieved, the song is taken out of the running for #1.

Oppas won the last 2 weeks in a row! If Oppas win again this week, they will achieve the **triple crown**!

Trainee

Aspiring K-pop Idol

Someone who goes through rigorous training with a dream to become a K-pop star one day. The training can last as long as 10+ years before they finally make a debut, but it is not a guarantee. Entertainment companies have the right to release them if they believe their **trainees** don't have what it takes to become a K-pop star.

Before becoming a top star, John T was a **trainee** for 8 years.

(tŭ-ro-tŭ)
트로트 Trot

Old-fashioned Korean Music Genre

Commonly known as "뽕짝" *ppong jjak* due to its distinctive background rhythm, it is the oldest form of Korean pop music. Once considered a genre popular only among old timers, but thanks to the efforts of contemporary musicians (e.g., Jang Yoon Jeong, Dae Sung), it has a considerable fan base among the younger generation as well.

Mira thought only old people like **trot**, but when she heard her bias sing it, she fell in love with it.

(tang-jin-jaem)
탕진잼
TangJinJaem
Small Indulgence

"탕진" (*tang jin*, "squandering/going bankrupt") + "잼" (*jaem*, a slang word for "fun"). A consumption pattern amongst the younger generation in Korea that reflects the current economic recession, represented by an increase in consumption of items that are affordable but give the most satisfaction. Rather than saving up, they find happiness in inexpensive items they like and enjoy. Examples include a doll-picking claw crane, small cosmetics, and collecting fan merchandise.

> BTS merchandise, $9.99
> EXO album, $13.99
> TWICE character socks, $8,99
> I'm broke, but it's fun! *Tang jin jaem*!

(te-re-bi)
테레비 TeReBi
Television

An old-fashioned way of saying 텔레비젼 ("television") due to the fact that 테레비 (*terebi*, テレビ) is how the Japanese people say the word, and during the period of Japanese occupation, many Japanese-style English words were introduced into Korea, and such influence still lingers on.

> Dean: Turn on the *te re bi*!
> Jane: Ha! You sound like my grandpa!

That's No No
"No Way Jose"

An expression (with the minor grammatical error of missing the article "a") that gained popularity after Masta Wu, who served as a judge on Show Me The Money, used it while grilling the participants in the audition.

> Jack: Yo! I'm borrowing your car tonight!
> Tom: *That's no no*!

TEEN TOP

Teen Top stands for "Teenager Emoboy Emotion Next generation Talent Object Praise," a five-member (C.A.P, Chunji, Niel, Ricky, Changjo) boy group formed by TOP Media. They debuted in 2010 with a song titled "Clap." They were chosen as the "Best Male Group" by MTV Music Awards in 2011. Notable songs include "Going Crazy," "Rocking," and "Ah-Ah."

> The band name *TEEN TOP* is one hell of an abbreviation!

티켓파워
Ticket Power

Level of Ability/Popularity To Attract Audience

A Konglish term referring to a celebrity's ability or popularity to attract an audience. Termed so because its generally measured by the number of tickets sold. The greater an audience one can attract, the stronger "ticket power" one is said to have.

*Their last concert attracted more than 20,000 fans in the audience! They have huge **ticket power**!*

Too Much Talker

Chatterbox

Someone who talks too much without ever pausing or giving the listener/audience a chance to escape. It was originally a nickname given exclusively to Chan Ho Park, a former MLB player who is eloquent and loves talking and who made an appearance on a variety TV show to give a short speech about his life, but he just kept going...

*I met this **too much talker** guy who took 2 hours of my time just explaining directions. Turns out that the place was right next door.*

(to-dak-to-dak)
토닥토닥
To Dak To Dak

"Pat Pat"

An onomatopoeia, or a word that imitates the sound of patting someone/an animal, either to show affection or as a gesture of encouragement.

To dak to dak... Don't be too disappointed! You can just take pre-calc again next year.

(tteu-ah)
뜨아 Tteu Ah

Hot Americano

Abbreviation for "뜨거운" (*tteu geo un*, "hot") + "아메리카노" ("Americano"). Originally, it was used widely by teenagers as a chatting/texting abbreviation to save time typing, but its gaining popularity in real-life settings as well.

Tteu ah is how coffee should be enjoyed!

(tti)
띠 Tti
Chinese Zodiac Sign

There are 12 animals in the Chinese zodiac, each animal representing each year in a repeating 12-year cycle. They are rat, ox, tiger, rabbit, dragon, snake, horse, goat, monkey, rooster, dog, and pig. Korean people share this culture and have a belief that one's fortune and destiny are closely tied with another, based on the attributes of the zodiac sign. At the same time, it's a convenient, indirect way of asking how old someone is because you can calculate one's age using the 12-year cycle.

I'm a dog tti, and you are a rooster *tti*. It means I chase you, and that's why I've been stalking you.

(ttong-son)
똥손 Ttong Son
All Thumbs

"똥" (*ttong*, literal meaning "poop," but is idiomatically used to refer to something of "very low quality") + "손" (*son*, "hand"). Describes someone who is uncoordinated or clumsy with their hands.

WTF? You can't even make *ramyeon* noodles? You really have **ttong son**!

튜닝
Tuning
Plastic Surgery

The less-obvious, inconspicuous reference to "plastic surgery" because having one's body altered is something people don't want to talk about openly.

Hm... You look slightly different... Did you have a **tuning** done on your nose?

(tu-pyo)
투표 Tu Pyo
Vote

Became more important recently with the emergence of popular audition/competition programs where viewers are invited to express their opinion through voting, which is done by calling in from your phone, texting from your cell phone, or going to the show's homepage to select the number that corresponds to your favorite contestant.

Did you **tu pyo**? We need to make our oppa win the grand prize this year!

Turn Up

"Lets Go" / "Yeah"

An expression that gained popularity after Dok2 started using it on Show Me The Money. It doesn't have any specific meaning but is used as a continuer/response token in a conversation to add cheerful vibes.

Gary: Where's the party?
Bo: At Adam's! Let's go!
Gary: **Turn-up!**

(twing-gi-gi)
팅기기
Twing Gi Gi

Playing Hard-To-Get

A slang term for "to reject" but used to refer to the act of pretending you're not interested in someone when you really are as a way of making them more interested in you, but if abused, it could backfire, and they will just stop trying.

Stop the *twing gi gi*, girl! Lower your standards and meet someone!

TWICE

Twice stands for "The group will touch people's hearts twice, once through the ears and once again through the eyes," a nine-member (Nayeon, Jeongyeon, Momo, Sana, Jihyo, Mina, Dahyun, Chaeyoung, Tzuyu) girl group formed by JYP Entertainment. They debuted in 2015 with a song titled "Like Ooh-Ah." They rose to stardom with the song "Cheer Up" (2016), which topped the Gaon Digital Chart and won the "Song of the Year" award at the Melon Music Awards and MAMA. They became the first Korean girl group to earn Platinum certification by the Recording Industry Association of Japan. Notable songs include "TT," "Knock Knock," "Likey," and "Heart Shaker."

TWICE is one of the hottest, if not THE hottest, K-pop girl group today.

U-KISS

U-KISS stands for "ubiquitous Korean international idol super star," a five-member (Soohyun, Kiseop, Eli, Hoon, Jun) boy group formed by NH Media. They debuted in 2008 with a song titled "Not Young." With the song "Man Man Ha Ni" (2009), they gained international popularity, especially in Latin America. They won the "Asian Rookie Award" at the Asia Song Festival in 2008 and "Best Male Group Award" at the Korean Culture Entertainment Awards in 2013. Notable songs include "Bingeul Bingeul," "For Kiss Me," and "0330."

U-KISS is the most romantic & cutest band name! Chu~ <3

얼짱 Ulzzang (Uljjang)
(ŏl-tchang)

The Best Looking

Literally meaning "the best face", it is used to describe someone with good looks. Again, it's just the face that matters and nothing else, so even if you are overweight with a huge beer belly, you can still be an *ulzzang* if your face is pretty.

In my selcas, I am an *ulzzang*, but when I take a full body shot, I am an obese *ulzzang*.

엄친아/엄친딸 Umchin A / Umchin Ddal
(ŏm-chi-na/ŏm-chin-ttal)

Golden Boy/Girl

Literally meaning "Mom's friend's son/daughter". It is someone who is better than you in every aspect to a degree that you doubt their existence. Oftentimes, it is an imaginary person your mom makes up to make a comparison with you, hoping to make you try harder.

Bobo graduated high school at 10 and college at 14. She makes tons of money as a businesswoman and can play 5 musical instruments. She is a real *umchina*.

엄마 Umma
(ŏm-ma)

Mom

Also something you say when startled, similar to saying "Oh my god!"

Umma! Dinner! I am hungry!

언니 Unnie
(ŏn-ni)

Older Female Sibling

A term that a female uses to address an older female sibling, but it can be used to address any older female with whom significant emotional intimacy is shared. It can also be used to address a waitress at a restaurant. It can be used in place of someone's name.

Unnie, what should we get for *umma*'s birthday?

(un-pal)
언팔 UnPal

Unfollowing on Instagram

Short for Unfollow. It means ceasing to follow someone's account on Instagram. Note: there is no F sound in Korean.

Ugh! I'm so over with you! I'm going to *un pal* you, pal!

V Live

A smartphone app that lets you follow your favorite celebs, watch your personal broadcasting videos while connecting and interacting with other users by making comments, and give "hearts" to share your thoughts and feelings. They have scheduled shows as well as unannounced guerilla live broadcasts!

Quick! *Oppas* are on the air now on *V Live*!

V.I.P

Big Bang Fan Club

The name of the Big Bang fan club that has been around for more than 10 years and is one of the biggest K-pop fan clubs. They use black/white handkerchiefs and yellow crown lightsticks.

Sarah: I'm a *VIP*!
Bouncer: Yeah. Very Intoxicated Person!
Sarah: Noooo! I'm a member of the Big Bang fan club!
Bouncer: Come right in, then!

Viki

"Video" + "Wiki" = "Viki". Viki.com is the place to go for subtitled drama episodes. Viki puts video content on their channels, which are subtitled in many different languages by community volunteers. Popular shows have their clips subtitled faster (even real-time) than those that are less popular.

Can't find a sub file for Running Man? You might want to check *Viki* first!

V Line

Sleek Jaw Line

The shape of a jawline that resembles the alphabet **V**. It is a compliment because it symbolizes a sleek jawline, which is an attribute associated with "small face".

After losing so much weight, I got my *V Line* back.

Visual

Looks

A reference to one's appearance, usually the face.

Jaeho, the leader of the group Xtars, is also in charge of *visual* because he is the best looking among all.
My *visual* is better than yours! I am so much prettier.

V.I.P

Official Big Bang Fan Club

It is named after a track on their second single. Members usually use yellow crown light sticks or bandanas to show "support". They were nominated as the "Best Fan" by MTV Italy TRL Awards in 2012.

Jenny: I am a *V.I.P*!
Hoang: What makes you so special?
Jenny: I mean I am a member of *V.I.P*! Big Bang's fan club!

비타민 Vitamin

Life of the Party

Also known as "happy virus", it refers to someone who brings good vibes to a group.

Marcus is the most positive person in the world. He is liked by everyone around him. That's why he earned the nickname *vitamin*.

(wan-jŏn-che)
완전체
Wan Jeon Che

Whole Group

"완전" (*wan jeon*, "perfection") + "체" (*che*, "body"). When members of a group work individually, like a solo singer or a TV drama actor, its extremely difficult for them to get together as a whole group as they were when they first debuted, and the more members there are in a group, the more difficult it is. For this reason, many fans long to see the group get together and perform as one group or "완전체."

After many years of solo activities, the members of YKKK decided to come back as a *wan jeon che*.

(wang-ja-byŏng)
왕자병
Wang Ja Byeong

Conceited / Stuck Up / Narcissist Male

"왕자" (*wang ja*) means "prince" and "병" (*byeong*) means "disease/sickness." Put together, it literally means "prince disease/syndrome," a narcissist male who's conceited/stuck up.

I'm the only male student in my Yoga class, and that's when I started having this *wang ja byeong*...

(wan-pan-nyŏ)
완판녀
Wan Pan Nyeo

"The Kate Middleton Effect"

A slang term that literally means "Ms. Sold Out" but is used to refer to a female celeb or an influencer who has the ability to make the item they promote "sold out" because of the fan base they have. It's similar to "The Kate Middleton Effect" in the U.K., where the Duchess of Cambridge causes an instant spike in demand for the fashion items she wears.

The coat Jeon Ji-Hyeon wore in the TV Drama " My Love from the Star" has always been sold out! She's a true *wan pan nyeo*.

(hwa-i-teu)
화이트
White

Wite-Out

A Konglish term referring to "Wite-Out," a correction fluid used on paper to mask errors in text.

Shoot! I just spotted a typo! Give me the *white* right now.

왜? Wae?
(wae)

"Why?"

An expression used to confirm the validity of something. It is also something people say in K-dramas and K-movies after breaking up.

> She dumped me. **Wae**? **Wae**? **Wae**!

완소 Wan So
(wan-so)

"Most Cherished"

An abbreviation for "**완전**" *wan jeon* ("absolutely, completely") + "**소중**" *so joong* ("precious")". It is used in conjunction with other nouns (e.g., 완소 아템 *wan so atem* ("super rare item"), 완소남/녀 *wan so nam/neyo* ("most adorable man/lady")). Simply adding it to another noun brings it to the superlative degree.

> Mariah: I got a new iPhone! This is my new **wan so** item! I will cherish it forever!
> Andrew: Forever? You mean 2 weeks, right?

왕따 Wang Dda
(wang-tta)

Outcast

Someone who has been rejected by society or by a social group, it most frequently occurs in school. It has become a serious social issue, as young victims often choose to end their own lives.

> Before debuting, AJ was a **wang dda** because his parents came from North Korea, but he was finally accepted as a vital part of the group.

화이트 데이 White Day

The Day When Men Reciprocate the Gifts Received on Valentine's Day With Chocolate

March 14 th is observed as a day when men give women chocolate, either as a token of repayment for the gifts received on Valentine's Day or to ask her out.

> I didn't get anything from anyone on Valentine's Day, so I don't have to give anyone anything on **White Day**, either.

(wŏ-ryo-byŏng)
월요병
Wol Yo Byeong
The Monday Blues

월요일 *wol yo il* ("Monday") + 병 *byeong* ("sickness/illness"). The drastic mood swing one experiences after the weekend. Symptoms include lethargy, a sense of hopelessness, and a complete lack of motivation.

Wol yo byeong is the type of disease that you know is inevitable, and it hits you the worst after spending the weekend partying.

(u-gyŏl)
우결 Woo Gyeol
Popular Reality Show by MBC

Short for "우리 결혼했어요" *woori gyeolhon gaet eo yo* ("we got married"). It is a popular reality show where idols/celebs are paired up to experience what life would be like if they were married.

Tim: OMG! Jenna and Min are getting married!
Anna: WTH? No way! For real?
Tim: Nah… just in *Woo Gyeol*
Anna: *Kkam no*l!

(um-tchal)
움짤
Woom Jjal (Um Jjal)
GIF

An abbreviation for "움직이는" *woom jik i neun* ("animated") "짤방" *jjal bang* ("a photo that is attached to a forum thread to avoid automatic deletion by the system after being falsely flagged as an "empty thread"). In the K-pop realm, it is usually an animated short clip of idols making funny faces, bloopers, and dance moves (e.g., wave dance). It is similar to GIFs.

Holly: Why do people post irrelevant photos on their posts in this forum?
Jax: Oh, it's called *woom jjal*. They have to stick it in there so the moderators don't assume there is no content inside.

WINNER

WINNER stands for "aspire to become the best K-pop band," a four-member (Jinwoo, Seunghoon, Minho, Seungyoon) boy group formed by YG Entertainment after winning a reality survival program, WIN: Who is Next, in which they competed against other YG Entertainment trainees. They were the first YG boy group since Big Bang and have won numerous awards at the MAMA, the Melon Music Awards, and the Golden Disc Awards. They debuted in 2014 with "Empty." Notable songs include "Really Really," "Sentimental," and "Color Ring."

There might be many winners in many different fields, but in the field of K-pop, *WINNER* is the only winner to me!

(u-tchu-tchu)
우쯔쯔
Woo Chu Chu
Coochy Coo

An onomatopoeia that phonetically imitates the sound an adult makes to appease/compliment a baby or a little kid. As it is associated with a cute feeling, its often used between a couple as a way of teasing each other, but one should exercise caution when using it as it can give the feeling that one is talking down to/looking down on the listener.

Woo chu chu~! You cute little thing~

(wo-la-bael)
워라밸
Wo La Bael
Work-Life Balance

Reflects Korean society in general, where people are expected (read: forced) to work very hard due to a highly pressured office environment, working overtime every day, including the weekends, and giving up their personal life. Although it has been a social norm, many people recently, especially the younger generation, have started questioning and pondering whats really important in life and coined this term that refers to the "balance between work and personal life."

No work and no play makes Jack a dull boy! You need *wo la bael*!

(u-ri-na-ra)
우리나라
Woo Ri Na Ra
Korea

Literally "our country," but it refers to "Korea," due to the fact that Korean people share the idea known as "단일민족 (*dan il min jok*), or a nation state, a country made up of a single, homogenous race. For this reason, it sometimes creates an awkward moment when used in a conversation with a foreigner, as the term technically doesn't include the listener.

Korean: Welcome to *woo ri na ra*!
Foreigner: Our country? I'm from the Philippines, though.
Korean: Oh, it just means welcome to Korea ;)

(u-yu-nam/u-yu-nyŏ)
우유남/우유녀
Woo Yu Nam / Woo Yu Nyeo

Someone With Superior Genes

Short for "**우월한**" (*woo wol han*, "superior") + "**유전자**" (*yu jeon ja*) + "**남/녀**" (*nam/nyeo*, "man/woman") = someone with superior genes = someone who's tall, fit, handsome/beautiful, smart, and all the good stuff you can think of. It's someone you'd be afraid to stand next to.

No wonder he's a **woo yu nam**! His parents are so good looking and smart as well.

(ut-pŭn)
웃픈
Woot Peun

Tragicomic / Funny Yet Sad

Short for "**웃긴**" (*woot gin*, "funny") + "**슬픈**" (*seul peun*, "sad"). It refers to that awkward moment/situation that manifests both tragic and comic aspects, where its difficult to decide whether you should laugh or cry.

I accidentally farted so loud at my close friend's funeral... It was a **woot peun** moment.

(un-myŏng)
운명
Woon Myeong

Destiny

The force that controls our future, a popular theme of romantic K-dramas, like finding the love of your life in the most random place possible.

I think it was my woon myeong to fall in love with my oppa because my life has changed completely since I knew him.

World Star

Someone Recognized/Popular All Around The Globe

Someone, usually K-pop celebrities and sports figures, who is recognized and popular not just in Korea and Asia, but all around the globe. They have a strong presence on YouTube and international fandom. Some of the examples include BTS, PSY, Lee Byeong-heon (actor), and Yu-Na Kim (figure skater) and Son Heung-min (soccer player/footballer).

Psy became a *world star* with his global mega-hit song, *Gangnam Style*.

엑스맨
X Man

Spy / Double Agent

Originated in a popular variety game show titled "**X-Man**," in which two teams compete against each other playing various games with a huge plot twist: There is one member - you don't know who it is until the end of the show - who's secretly assigned to make his/her team lose the game, and that member was called the "**X-Man**." Ever since then, someone who does more harm than good in a group/team setting is called "**X-Man**.

Daniel scored three own-goals! He must be an *X-man*!

(ya-ja time)
야자타임
Ya Ja Time

To Speak Informally To Each Other / Maknae On Top

"**야자**" (*ya ja*, "to end a sentence in "~**야**", an informal form") + **time**. A fun game where the social hierarchy is completely reversed in a given time duration. It's the only time when maknaes (youngest member) can talk down to older group members (*hyung, oppa, nuna, unnie*), and older group members must talk formally and politely to *maknaes*.

Sunbae: Let's have a *ya ja time*, just for fun ;)
Maknae: Cool! Anyone older than me, kneel before me!
Sunbae 1,2,3: Yes, sir!

YO, MAN!!

YES, SIR!

(ya-sik)
야식 Ya Shik

Late-Night Meal (Snack)

"**야**" (*ya*) means "night" and "**식**" (*sik*) means "food/to eat." Put together, it means late-night meals or snacks, which are the culprit of that extra fat we all struggle to get rid of. It's especially popular in Korea because of the well-developed food delivery system, which is available 24 hours, 7 days a week. Popular menus are fried chicken and *jokbal* (braised pig's trotters).

Ya sik is so irresistible... It's the major culprit of my recent weight gain!

(ye-pan)
예판 Ye Pan

Pre-sale

Short for "**예약**" (*ye yak*, "reservation") + "**판매**" (*pan mae*, "sale"). In a K-pop fandom context, the act of reserving an item before it is released because 1) there is a limited quantity and 2) some fans just want to be the first to get the item. Such items include concert tickets, limited edition fan merchandise, etc.

*Oppa's new album will be having a **ye pan** next week!*

야동 Ya Dong
(ya-dong)

Porn Clips

An abbreviation for "**야한**" *ya han* ("sexy") + "**동영상**" *dong yeong sang* ("movie clip"). They are often stored in a secret folder on a computer with a name that has nothing to do with its content to discourage any unwanted third-party access.

There are two types of men, 1 that watches *ya dong* and 1 that says they don't (liars!).

양다리 Yang Da Ri
(yang-da-ri)

Two Timing Someone

Literally means "two (double) legs" or "two (double) bridges" and is figuratively used to refer to cheating on your boyfriend/girlfriend.

Timmy got caught doing his *yang da ri* and lost both girls.

야! Ya!

"Hey!"

Used to grab someone's attention but shouldn't be used to address someone older.

Jenna: *Ya!* Minho!
Mark: Hi, do I know you?
Jenna: Oh, I thought you were Minho. Sorry!

예능 Ye Neung
(ye-nŭng)

Entertainment

A TV show genre (e.g., talk show, "variety" game show, etc.) that is less formal and fun-oriented than other programs (e.g., documentary, news, etc.). It is a great opportunity for the members of a group because they get a chance to show off their unique talents (e.g., impression, singing, dance moves, etc.) as individuals.

Everybody was surprised to see Mingoo on the *ye neung* TV show last night because he was thought to be a really quiet person.

(ye-het)
예헷 Yehet

"All Right"

The sound, Oh Sehun, a member of EXO makes to express joy and satisfaction.

I finished my homework! *Yehet*!

(yŏ-bo)
여보 Yeobo

"Sweetheart"

A term that a married couple uses to address each other.

I am going to marry Yugyu *Oppa*! He will be my *Yeobo*! *Sa Rang Hae~*!

(yŏ-bo-se-yo)
여보세요
Yeo Bo Se Yo

"Hello (on the phone)"
"Excuse Me (to grab someone's attention)"

Believed to be made up of words "**여기**" *yeogi* ("here") + "**보세요**" *bo se yo* ("please look") = "please look here".

Bubba: *Yeo bo se yo*? Is Mary home?
Wonkyu: Mary? Who's Mary?
Bubba: Oops! Wrong number, sorry!

(yŏl-do)
열도 Yeol Do

Japan

An Internet term mostly used by the younger generation of Korean netizens. Literally means "archipelago", which is the type of landform Japan has, and since there aren't many countries that are archipelagos, netizens simply use it to refer to Japan. It is most frequently used in the form of "**열도의**" *yeol do eui* ~sth = "sth of Japan". For example, "**열도의 발명품**" *yeol do eui bal myeong poom* ("invention")" is "Japan's invention".

Yeol do has their own thing, called J-Pop, and it offers different flavors than K-pop.

여신 Yeo Shin
(yŏ-shin)

Goddess

A title/nickname usually given by the fans of a female celeb to praise her divine beauty.

Frank: Whoa... Amazingly beautiful! She's a *yeo shin*!
Sera: Nope, look at her pre-plastic surgery pictures! She used to be a humble human being just like us.

역대급 Yeok Dae Geup
(yŏk-dae-gŭp)

The Best (Worst) Ever / One For The Ages

"역대" (*yeok dae*, "successive generations, generations over generations") + "급" (*geup*, "level/class") = "The class/level never witnessed until now" = "unprecedented" = "the best (worst) ever" / "one for the ages." Expresses surprise and can be applied to something extremely good or, equally, something extremely bad.

Wow! Our oppa's new music video is super awesome! It's a *yeok dae geup* work.

역주행 Yeok Ju Haeng
(yŏk-ju-haeng)

Climbing The Charts

"역" (*yeok*, "reverse") + "주행" (*ju haeng*, "drive"). A phenomenon in which a song That's been out for a while but hasn't received a lot of attention suddenly gains popularity, thereby climbing the charts in reverse. The biggest example is EXID's "Up & Down," where a fancam of their concert went viral on YouTube, giving a belated boost to their old song. Another example is being featured in a CF (commercial) or a movie/drama series.

WTH? That song is over 10 years old and is ranked #1 on the chart? Why is it making a *yeok ju haeng*?

연애 Yeon Ae
(yŏn-ae)

Dating / (Romantic) Relationship

The most common theme/subject of K-pop songs and K-dramas and probably the most difficult/complex thing in the world that we all struggle so hard to figure out how it works, only to learn that, the more we try, the more complicated it gets.

Things that are on my bucket list :
1. Skydiving
2. Road Trip Across The U.S.
3. *Yeon Ae*

열공 Yeol Gong
(yŏl-gong)

"SMAO (Studying My Ass Off)"

An abbreviation for "**열심히**" *yeol shim hi* ("hard, zealously") + "**공부**" *gong boo* ("study") = "studying really hard".

Kid: Good students' anthem! Enjoy your *bool geum* and *nol to*, and ***yeol gong***!

열정페이 YeolJeong Pay
(yŏl-chŏng-pe-i)

Employers Exploiting Young Labor

Literal meaning is "passion pay". It originated as tongue-in-cheek satire to criticize vicious employers who exploit young employees. Most victims are often interns who feel fortunate to have an opportunity due to the difficult employment conditions in Korea. Knowing this, employers choose to pay very little or nothing for the employee's contribution. They rationalize such an act by arguing that they should work with passion and not for money, as they are learning valuable lessons for free.

Many young Korean job seekers believe ***yeol jeong pay*** should vanish from this world.

열폭 Yeol Pok
(yŏl-pok)

Inferiority Complex

An abbreviation for "**열등감** *yeol deung gam* (feeling inferior) + **폭발** *pok bal* (explosion, rupture) = "jealousy/inferiority explosion". It means acting rude or hostile towards someone out of a sense of inferiority.

Ronda: Ha, did you see Jenny's new dress? I bet she stole it from the store. Look at her hair! I am sure she's wearing a wig.
Darren: Dude… You are just having a ***yeol pok***…

연습 Yeon Seup
(yŏn-sŭp)

Training

Something an aspiring K-pop idol must go through before making an official debut, usually involving singing, dancing, and even acting training, depending on one's talent.

After 7 years of hard ***yeon seup*** as a trainee, Zex finally debuted.

연예인 Yeon Ye In

(yŏn-ye-in)

Entertainer

An "entertainer", it can also be used to refer to someone who is publicly well-known (i.e., a "celeb").

Dang! You have over 100,000 followers? Are you a **yeon ye in** or something?

유혹 Yoo Hok

(yu-hok)

Seduction

The mother of all problems. In K-dramas, when "love lines" become tangled.

Guys who fall for **yoo hok** can lose many things.

용꿈 Yong Ggum

(yong-kkum)

Good Omen

Mainly because the dragon is considered a holy animal in Korean culture. Hence, seeing it in your dream is thought to be a sure sign of good fortune coming your way; many Koreans would head straight to buy a lottery ticket.

Wally bought lottery tickets after seeing G-Dragon, hoping it would count as a **yong ggum**.

(yŏn-sang/yŏn-ha)
연상/연하
Yeon Sang / Yeon Ha

Older (Boy/Girlfriend) / Younger (Boy/Girlfriend)

Literally "age older" / "age younger," generally describes whether one's significant other is older or younger than one's self.

> Chan: My girlfriend is 20 years *yeon ha*!
> Pi: Man, that's a crime! You're robbing the cradle!

(yu-myŏng-in)
유명인
Yu Myeong In

Famous / Well-Known Person

"유명" (*yu myeong*) means "famous/well-known" and "인" (*in*) means "figure/person." Put together, it refers to the state of being famous and well-known, which is the ultimate goal of so many trainees. The easiest method to find out if one is "유명인" is taking the subway and seeing if anyone recognizes them.

> The downside of being a *yu myeong in* is that you have no private life!

(yu-haeng-ŏ)
유행어
Yu Haeng Eo

Fad Phrase / Buzzword

A word or a phrase that has become popular for a period of time. The main difference between 유행어 and 신조어 *shin jo eo* "newly coined term" is that 유행어 doesn't necessarily have to be something new—it can be an existing word.

> *Oppa's* a *yu haeng eo* maker! Anything new, be they expressions, phrases, or words he says on TV, becomes an instant hit and everybody starts using it!

ZE:A

ZE:A, also known as Children of Empire, is a nine-member (Kevin, Hyungsik, Kwanghee, Siwan, Lee Hoo, Taeheon, Heechul, Minwoo, Dongjun) boy group formed by Star Empire Entertainment. They debuted in 2010 with a song titled "Mazeltov." They also broke into subgroups, ZE:A FIVE (Siwan, Hyungsik, Kevin, Minwoo & Dongjun) ZE:A 4U (Kwanghee, Lee Hoo, Taeheon & Heechul) ZE:A J (Kevin, Taeheon, Heechul, Minwoo & Dongjun). There has been a rumor of disbandment recently, but the company has officially denied it. Notable songs include "Aftereffect" and "The Ghost of The Wind."

> *ZE:A* is always in the last section on the list because Z is the last letter of the alphabet, but they are always #1 on my list!

ZE:A Style

The name of the ZE:A fan club (fans call themselves ZE:As). Fan color is pearl gold.

*Gangnam Style? No thanks! I'm **ZE:A Style**!*

(al-mot)
~알못
~Al Mot

Someone Who Has No Knowledge About Something

Short for "**알**지 못하는 (*al ji mot ha neun*, "don't know") 사람 (*sa ram*, "person,' but this part is omitted)," so ~something **알못** means "someone who has no knowledge about something." This is used as a suffix to the first word of another noun, for example, "야구" (*ya gu*) means "baseball," so you take the first word "야" and put "**알못**" after that, making it "야**알못**" (*ya al mot*), to mean "someone who has no knowledge about baseball".

Um... I'm a total newbie and K-pop *al mot*... Who's BTS and what do they do?

(mi-man-jab)
~미만잡
~Mi Man Jab

Anything Under/Below THIS Is JUNK

"미만" (*mi man*) means "below/under" and "잡" (*jab*) comes from the word "잡것" (*jab geot*), which means "junk/useless stuff". It means anything under/below THIS standard is junk/useless, and for this reason, its used as a way to establish a minimum threshold/standard when talking about something. For example, "IQ 140 미만잡" means "anyone below IQ 140 is meaningless/not worth talking about."

Member 1: I've been a K-pop fan for 2 years!
Member 2: 3 years, here!
Member 3: 5 years, right here!
Member 4: 10 years *mi man jab*!
Member 1,2,3: Wow! Big sunbae!

ㄱㄱ

"Hurry", "Lets Go"

An acronym created by taking the initial consonants of the word "고고" (*go go*). It gained popularity as e-sports players started using it when they had to type bursts of short messages to push the game moderator to start the game. The more you type the word, the more powerful the message becomes. It should not be used with someone who is older or who has no sense of closeness with you yet.

(Text from teacher) Ok, guys! Are we ready for a field trip?
(Text from students) ㄱㄱㄱㄱㄱㄱㄱㄱㄱ

ㄴㄴ

"No No"

An acronym created by taking the initial consonants of the word "노노" *no no*. It is used to express disagreement or rejection. It is also synonymous with "안돼 *and wae*. It should not be used with someone who is older or who has no sense of closeness with you yet.

(Text from Jenny) Hey, wanna go hit the movies?
(Text from Mark) ㄴㄴ. Gotta study.

ㄱㅅ

"Thx"

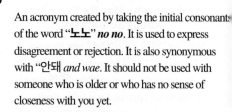

An acronym created by taking the initial consonants of the word "감사" *gamsa* ("appreciation"). Although it is a way of expressing gratitude, the abbreviated form must only be used to address someone very close (i.e., friends), otherwise, it might seem disrespectful.

(Text from mom) Your lunch is in the fridge.
(Text from daugther) ㄱㅅ

ㅂㄷㅂㄷ

"Trembling with Rage"

An acronym created by taking the initial consonants of the word "부들부들" *boo deul boo deul*. Not to be confused with ㅎㄷㄷ ("shivering"), which is your body's reaction to cold or fear.

(Text from Hanna) Yo! I just finished the last hot dog!
(Text from Mitchelle) ㅂㄷㅂㄷ

ㄷㄷ

"Shivering"

An acronym created by taking the initial consonants of the word "덜덜" *deol deol*, an onomatopoeic word describing the act of shivering caused by either cold or fear.

(Text from Suzi) Hey, your boyfriend found out about what you did last night.
(Text from Jane) ㄷㄷ

ㅅㄱ

"Peace Out"

An acronym created by taking the initial consonants of the word "**수고**" *soo go* ("trouble"/"effort"). Aside from its literal meaning, it is used as a way to say goodbye, especially in workplace settings. For example, "**수고** 하세요" *soo go haseyo* can be translated as "keep up the good work". The abbreviated form, "**수고**" and its acronym "**ㅅㄱ**", however, should never be said in formal settings.

(Text from Tim) All right dawg, peace out!
(Text from Ori) ㅅㄱ!

ㅇㅈ

"ACK"

An acronym created by taking the initial consonants of the word "**인정**" *in jeong* ("acknowledgment"). It is used to express agreement or approval. It should not be used with someone who is older or who has no sense of closeness with you yet.

(Text from Brian) Don't you think our gym teacher is too fat to be a good role model?
(Text from Amy) ㅇㅈ

ㅇㅇ

"k"

An acronym created by taking the initial consonants of the word "**응응**" *eung eung* ("yes yes"). It is used to express agreement or acknowledgment in a conversation. It should not be used with someone who is older or who has no sense of closeness with you yet.

(Text from Sera) Did you have lunch?
(Text from Mark) ㅇㅇ

ㅈㅅ

"SRY"

An acronym made up by taking the initial consonants of the word "**죄송**" *joe song* ("sorry, my fault, regrets"). Do not use this abbreviation in a serious situation, as it might seem insincere.

(Text from Wonmi) Hey! Did you spill coffee on my notebook?
(Text from Pam) ㅈㅅ!

ㅊㅋㅊㅋ

"Congrats"

An acronym created by taking the initial consonants of the word "**추카추카**", a colloquial version of "**축하축하**" *chook ha chook ha* ("congrats, congrats"), but it should never be used with someone older, as it is considered rude. You should use the formal version "축하합니다" *chook ha hap ni da*.

George got fired after sending his boss ㅊㅋㅊㅋ for her birthday.

(ship-gu-gŭm)
19금
19 (Ship Gu) Geum

X-Rated

"금" (*geum*) is the first word of "금지" (*geum ji*), which means "prohibition/prohibited," and when used as a suffix, it means "~something is not allowed." Hence, "19금" means "under 19 is not allowed," which is a warning you can see at movie theaters or TV channels before the movie/show program starts.

Oppa's new music video was rated 19 geum due to a violent fighting scene.

2PM

2PM stands for "hottest time of the day," a six-member (Jun. K, Nichkhun, Taecyeon, Junho, Wooyoung, Chansung) boy group formed by JYP Entertainment. They debuted in 2008 with a song titled "10 out of 10." In 2016, they won "Best Album of The Year (Asia)" at the Japan Gold Disc Awards with their album "2PM of 2PM." Jay Park was originally a member of the group but left in 2009 after some comments he wrote about Korea on his social media account in 2005 caused a controversy. Notable songs include "Hands Up" and "My House."

At 2PM, we started singing "10 out of 10".

2NE1

2NE1 stands for "21st century new evolution," a four-member (Bom, Dara, CL, Minzy) girl group formed by YG Entertainment in 2009. They debuted with a song titled "Fire." Another title, "I Don't Care," won the Song of The Year at the Mnet Asian Music Awards (MAMA) in the same year. In 2010, they released their American debut album. They released an English-language single, "Take the World On," which was a collaboration with will.i.am. The song was featured in an Intel Ultrabook commercial. After a long hiatus, they disbanded in 2016. Notable songs include "I Am the Best," "Go Away," and "Come Back Home."

Farewell, 2NE1! You were a good inspiration to anyone who knew you!

(sa-cha-won)
4D/4차원
sa cha won

4-Dimensional

"차원" (*cha won*) means "dimension. We live in a 3-dimensional world, so this term is used to describe someone or something so extraordinary to the point that its beyond control or comprehension. It can be used both as a compliment and as ridicule.

LOL! My nephew is so 4 cha won! He thinks he can find SpongeBob at the bottom of the swimming pool!

(ppal-li-ppal-li)

8282

"GOWI" (Get On With It)

A chat abbreviation for "빨리빨리" (*bbal li bbal li*) because the number "8" is pronounced "*pal*" and "2" is pronounced "*i*," thus 8282 (*pal i pal i*) sounds like "빨리빨리".

(Text Message)
Sister: Come to the bathroom! *8282*! Out of toilet paper! *8282*!